Key Concepts in Marketing

Jonathan Sutherland and Diane Canwell

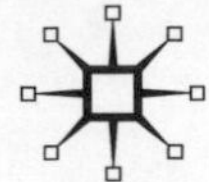

First published 2004 by
PALGRAVE MACMILLAN
Houndmills, Basingstoke, Hampshire RG21 6XS and
175 Fifth Avenue, New York, N.Y. 10010
Companies and representatives throughout the world

PALGRAVE MACMILLAN is the global academic imprint of the Palgrave Macmillan division of St. Martin's Press, LLC and of Palgrave Macmillan Ltd. Macmillan® is a registered trademark in the United States, United Kingdom and other countries. Palgrave is a registered trademark in the European Union and other countries.

ISBN 1–4039–1527–X paperback

This book is printed on paper suitable for recycling and made from fully managed and sustained forest sources.

A catalogue record for this book is available from the British Library.

A catalog record for this book is available from the Library of Congress.

10 9 8 7 6 5 4 3 2 1
13 12 11 10 09 08 07 06 05 04

Printed in China

Contents

Introduction

Marketing has perhaps one of the worst reputations in the field of business as it is perceived to be inherently fraudulent and manipulative, yet in truth it strives to be ethical and is often tainted by those who are not true marketers.

Marketing can be considered as one of the youngest disciplines in the business world, yet it abounds with a bewildering selection of jargon terms and scientific speak that makes the professional very difficult to understand. At its heart, marketing seeks to identify, satisfy and supply customers' expectations, their needs and their wants. Above all, the true professional tries to do this in an honest and fair manner, not seeking to confuse or otherwise deceive the public. However, despite these ideals, marketing professionals have found themselves criticized for what they say, how they say it, and above all, the number of times they say it.

Increasingly, marketing mavericks have fallen foul of legislation aimed at tightening up the profession and closing the loop-holes which allowed the unscrupulous to take advantage. The legislation is complex and by no means perfect, still relying on the professional judgement of marketing specialists and the codes of conduct produced by the various organizations representing the professionals. It is still hoped by these organizations and professionals alike that self-regulation will not be replaced by draconian laws which would inhibit innovation.

It is innovation that drives marketing, and not just in the nature of the advertising campaigns – the ways in which potential customers are targeted – or in the manner in which the profession conducts its business. The business world is continually indebted to developments in the field of marketing, a truly vibrant area full of ideas, true professionals and many with the ability to think and act laterally.

The structure of the book

Every attempt has been made to include all of the key concepts in this discipline, taking into account currently used terminology and jargon common throughout marketing in organizations around the world. There are notable differences in legislation and procedure when we compare marketing, advertising, public relations, sponsorship and the other subdivisions of the discipline in the United Kingdom, Europe, the United States and Japan. Increasingly in Europe, for example, there is a harmonization process in train which is gradually seeking to standardize regulations and procedures.

Each of the key concepts has been placed alphabetically in order to ensure that readers can quickly find the terms or entries that interest them. It is normally the case that a brief description of the term is presented, followed by a more expansive explanation.

The majority of the key concepts have the following in common:

- They may have a reference within the text to another key concept, identified by a word or phrase that is in **bold** type – this should enable the reader to investigate a directly implicated key concept should they require clarification of the definition at that point.
- They may have a series of related key concepts, which are featured at the end of the definition – this allows the reader to continue research and investigate subsidiary or allied key concepts.
- They may feature book or journal references – a vital feature for the reader to undertake follow-up research for more expansive explanations, often written by the originator or a leading writer in that particular field of study.
- They may include website references – it is notoriously difficult to ensure that websites are still running at the time of going to print, let alone several months beyond that time, but in the majority of cases long-established websites have been selected or governmental websites that are unlikely to be closed or have a major address change.

Key concepts – a guide

Whilst the majority of the key concepts have an international flavour, readers are reminded of the necessity of accessing the legislation, in particular, which refers to their native country or to the country in which they are working.

It is also often the case that there are terms which have no currency in a particular country as they may be allied to specific legislation of another country. Readers should check that the description does not include a specific reference to such law and should not assume in these cases that the key concept is a generic one that can be applied universally to marketing.

In all cases, references to other books, journals and websites are based on the latest available information. It was not always possible to ensure that the key text or printed reference is in print, but most well-stocked college or university libraries should have access to the original materials. In the majority of cases, when generic marketing books have been referenced these are, in the view of the writers, the best and most available additional reading texts.

AAU

An AAU (attitude, awareness and usage) study is a type of **tracking study** which monitors changes in consumer attitudes, awareness and usage levels for a product category or specific brand. The major problem with AAU studies is that they inform a business as to what the consumers' views were, not what they might be in the future.

Abandonment

Abandonment is the final stage in a **product's life cycle**, when the profit potential is such that management decides that the best course is to discontinue selling the product. The expense of carrying profitless products often goes beyond what shows up on financial statements. The real costs in managerial time and effort to continue making terminally ill products can be significant, but managers are often reluctant to discard a product because of attachment.

Product abandonment has often serious implications for the business in terms of its impact on the employee levels and their deployment, ongoing relationships with suppliers and distributors, and how the abandonment is viewed by the market itself.

Lambert, Douglas R., *Product Abandonment Decision*. Montvale, NJ: Institute of Management Accountants, 1985.

ABC

ABC, Audit Bureau of Circulation Ltd, is an independent body set up by advertisers and funded by advertisers, media owners and advertising agencies to monitor and officially audit circulation figures. An audit is an independent verification of a circulation, attendance, or electronic media delivery claim. All of the titles in ABC membership are audited at least once a year under the following terms:

- Business press members must use ABC staff auditors.

- Consumer press members may choose either ABC staff or external third-party auditors. If audits are carried out by third-party auditors, ABC staff auditors inspect these titles at random.

ABC audits for titles outside the UK or Republic of Ireland are conducted by ABC staff auditors. Essentially, the ABC inspection by ABC auditors includes a full check on the circulation claim made by the publication.

www.abc.org.uk

Above the line

Any form of advertising for which a commission or fee is payable to a recognized advertising agency operating on behalf of its client(s). The 'line' is an imaginary boundary between those advertising media which pay commission to advertising agencies and those which do not, the latter being **below-the-line** media. Directories, yearbooks and point-of-sale materials are below the line. Typically, 'above the line' is associated with advertising, but in reality the description is a broader term.

Over the past decade or so, the division between above- and below-the-line activities has become increasingly blurred. It is also possible to associate below-the-line activities with **direct marketing** whereas above-the-line activities are more associated with mainstream advertising such as television or radio advertising campaigns.

ACASI

ACASI (audio computer-assisted self-interviewing) has been documented as an effective tool in the US for obtaining a higher prevalence of self-reported behaviours, particularly those associated with HIV transmission. ACASI is an interview method where the person to be interviewed sits in a quiet place on her/his own in front of a laptop with a headset. The questions will be asked by the computer in the appropriate local language via the headset with simple answering instructions where the interviewed person only presses designated buttons.

This means of obtaining information is used by the National Clearinghouse for Alcohol and Drug Information (NCADI), the information service of the Substance Abuse and Mental Health Services Administration's (SAMHSA) Center for Substance Abuse Prevention (CSAP). NCADI is the world's largest resource for current information and materials concerning substance abuse. Large-scale studies using ACASI and allied methods can be viewed at

www.health.org/govstudy/bkd405/appendixa.aspx

Accordion insert

An advertisement inserted in a magazine, folded with an accordion-style fold. In other words, a single sheet of printed matter is folded to fit the overall size and shape of the magazine. This format can be an integral part of the magazine or simply a loose insert.

The principal advantage of an accordion insert is that a mini-brochure can be inserted into the magazine with far more detail and information than could be comfortably fitted onto a normal page or double-page spread.

Account executive

An account executive is an individual who works in an advertising agency or similar organization and is directly responsible for managing the requirements of a client.

Various agencies prefer alternative titles, including account manager, supervisor or director. In some cases, these alternatives imply status and responsibility within the agency itself. Another alternative description, though rarely used, is client-service executive.

Typically, account executives will have an all-round degree of skill based on their coordination abilities, coupled with their negotiation skills. In effect, an account executive translates client requirements into actions, which may involve the creation of advertising copy, the buying of media space and the management of a team of professionals, including freelance specialists to realize the advertising and promotion desire of the client.

ACORN

An acronym for A Classification Of Residential Neighbourhoods. ACORN was developed in the late 1970s by CACI Market Analysis Group, an Anglo-American market research firm, as a basis for sampling and direct mail. It is used as an indicator of the behaviour and attitudes of consumers according to where they live and the home they live in. Given that house purchase is the largest single expense in the household budget, consumers will tend to buy the best they can afford and the ACORN rating is seen as a reflection of their buying habits.

ACORN is taken to show the type of house (age and size) as well as the probable lifestyle and family life cycle. The major advantage of ACORN is that it takes into account several indices or aspects of the consumer including demographics and geographical segmentation.

In the UK there are 39 ACORN classifications which are still extensively used for direct mail shots and telemarketing. Marketing and sales can use ACORN to identify potential consumers for a range of products and services according to the classification. Specific related targeting can be made when offering services on the basis of ownership (such as improvements) or broader criteria for cable and satellite installation packages.

www.caci.co.uk

Acquisition cost

Acquisition cost in the marketing sense is the average investment of money (advertising and loss leading products) for a particular business to acquire a new customer. Businesses will calculate the life-time value of a customer, and then use this figure to calculate what an acceptable level of customer acquisition cost is for them.

Ad hoc survey/research

Ad hoc surveys or research are a form of market research which has been tailored to meet the market research needs, where standardized surveys cannot match the research criteria.

Ad hoc studies are usually fairly large quantitative analyses, which answer questions appearing at various stages of the designing and realization of a marketing campaign. The studies are often conducted on nationwidc representative samples, but the tested group may also consist of persons characterized by a certain feature. A sample usually comprises at least a few hundred people (500–1000). The most important feature of ad hoc surveys is adjusting to the needs of a client, who usually cooperates closely with the researchers at the stage of research designing. Ad hoc surveys are particularly useful in accessing market size, competition, customer attitudes and behaviour and brand awareness. They can also be used in testing reactions to a marketing activity.

Mariampolski, Hy, *Qualitative Market Research: A Comprehensive Guide.* London: Sage Publications, 2001.

Adjacency

Adjacency is the concept that new products and services should bear some relation to the current products and services offered by a business. The degree of similarity (adjacency) and familiarity will have a direct effect on the willingness of existing customers to purchase the new products and services. Likewise, adjacency can be supported by cross-selling techniques, joint promotional campaigns and other allied marketing activities.

In the US, adjacencies are commercial advertising spots purchased from local television stations, generally appearing during the time periods adjacent to networked programmes.

Adoption theory

Adoption theory describes the process by which consumers accept a new product, a new fashion or a new idea. The adoption process has a set of preconditions:

- the awareness stage – when potential customers are made aware of the product or service;
- the interest stage – when the customer's interest must be stimulated;
- the evaluation stage – when the customer considers the product in relation to their needs and desires;
- the trial stage – when the customer is convinced to test the product;
- the adoption stage – when the customer finally makes the decision to continue to buy the product.

The process is shown in the form of a diagram in Figure 1.

Adopter categories are a classification of users or buyers of an innovation according to the time of adoption. Everett Rogers identified five categories within the adoption curve. Rogers' categories are defined in terms of percentage groupings within the normal distribution of the adoption curve as follows: innovators – first 2.5% of all adopters; early adopters – next 13.5% of all adopters. These and the remaining categories are shown in Figure 2.

The adoption curve is a graphic representation of the diffusion of an innovation. The curve illustrates the number of adopters who have purchased a new product in each time period from the launch date. The curve takes the shape of a normal statistical distribution. A small number of people adopt the innovation shortly after it becomes available and this rate of adoption increases until 50 per cent of the potential buyers (or users) have tried it. After this point the number adopting within each time period falls until there are no potential adopters who have not tried the innovation. However this is not always a smooth, steady progression, as shown in Figure 3.

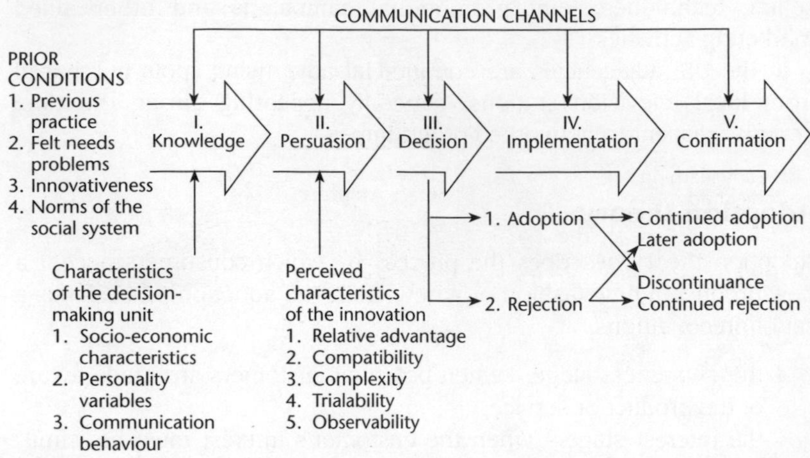

Figure 1 When a person or group first learns of a particular innovation the decision proceeds through forming an opinion about the innovation, to a choice to use or not use it, to implementation of the innovation, to confirmation of the choice. Ultimately the innovation is evaluated and tested to see whether the adoption of it will be lasting. People go through this adoption process at different rates, depending on the innovation.

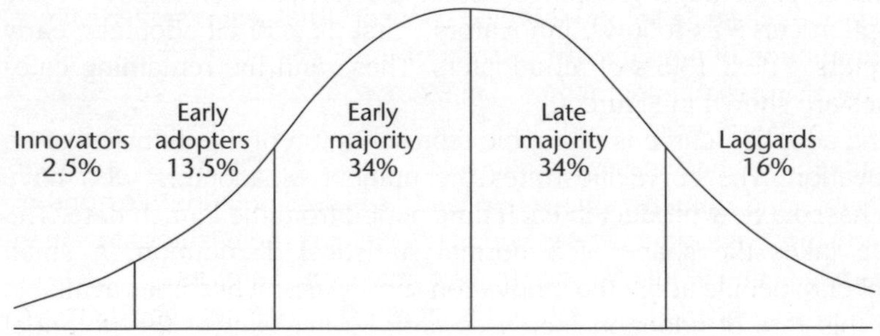

Figure 2 In essence, there are five categories of adopters, with the commensurate percentage of the population noted in each group. The innovators, a very small minority of the population, jump on board almost immediately while the laggards (not intended to be a derogatory term) may never innovate.

Source: Everett M. Rogers, *Diffusion of Innovations* (New York: Free Press, 1962).

A

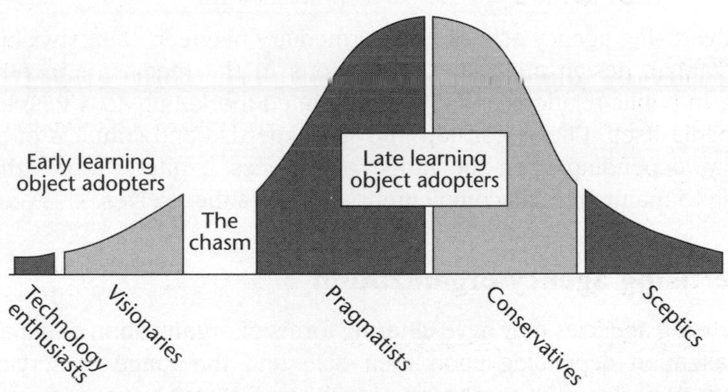

Figure 3 The chasm: the sequence of the adoption of new technologies proposes the theory that from the initial adopters there is a leap across the 'chasm' (in essence a period of acceptance) before the majority of the market begins to accept and adopt the new technology. Note that in the case of new technologies, alternative descriptions have been allocated to the various types of adopters.

Source: Everett M. Rogers, *Diffusion of Innovations* (New York: Free Press, 1962).

Advertising

Advertising is the paid, public and non-personal announcement of a persuasive message by an identified sponsor. In essence, advertising is the promotion of a product to existing or potential customers.

Advertising is an integral part of marketing; it is seen as a key element in the promotion of products and services to customers (either consumers or businesses). Advertising seeks to create a desire to purchase, and influence the needs and wants of potential customers. Advertising, having succeeded in this role, allows the business to satisfy those needs and wants by selling its products and services.

Advertising needs to convince the potential customer that there are benefits to be derived from purchasing the product or the service. False or inflated benefits only result in the customer being dissatisfied with the product or service, and repeat purchases are unlikely. Advertising is strictly controlled in this respect throughout the world and monitored by organizations such as the **Advertising Standards Authority**.

Caples, John and Hahn, Fred E., *Tested Advertising Methods* (5th edn). Englewood Cliffs, NJ: Prentice-Hall Trade, 1998.

A

Advertising agency

An advertising agency acts as an intermediary between clients wishing to organize, design and place promotions in the media (or in other cases, in public relations and other associated marketing activities) and the media itself. Clients can tap into the expertise and contacts of the agency, depending upon the range of services it offers, rather than having to maintain a full complement of experts themselves.

Advertising agency organization

Advertising agencies may have differing forms of organization or departmentalization depending upon their size and the range of services offered. Typically, a full service (offering the widest range of services) will have the departments, sections or functional areas shown in Figure 4.

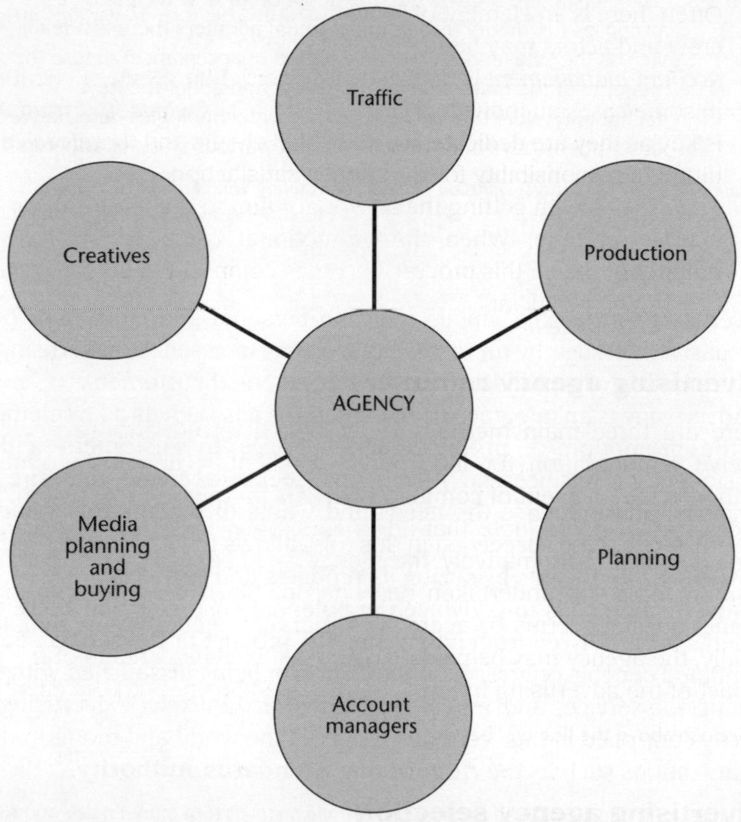

Figure 4 Functions and areas of the advertising agency

- *Planning* is responsible for trying to discover how advertising is received and interpreted and what people find valuable in products and brands. One of the most important elements of the job is to commission, understand and interpret research. Account planning means developing ideas about what leads people to respond to advertising.
- *Creatives* are essentially the 'ideas people' and in basic terms deal with words and pictures, that is to say the copy and the art direction.
- *Media planning and buying* deals with the schedules of marketing messages in the different media (in terms of the duration and scope of the campaign) as well as the purchasing of space or time in the various media through negotiation with contacts at the relevant organization.
- *Production* is actually responsible for making the advertisement. Often there is an element of subcontracting here as studios, camera crew and actors may be required.
- *Account management* is dedicated to a particular group of clients or in some cases an individual client. The role of the account manager is key as they are dedicated to individual clients and therefore carry ultimate responsibility for the client's satisfaction.
- *Traffic* deals with getting the artwork or film to the magazine or TV station on time. When the promotional campaign involves a number of media this process becomes complicated because accurate timing is crucial.

Advertising agency remuneration

There are three main methods by which an advertising agency can receive remuneration for its work from clients. The most common method is the payment of commission based on the costs of advertising placed in the media (note that advertising agencies attract a discount from the media). Alternatively, the agency could be paid on a one-off fee basis for each job undertaken on behalf of the client (payable under normal business terms or aggregated monthly, quarterly or annually). Finally, the agency may be paid on results, a fixed percentage of the net impact of the advertising in terms of increased business to the client.

See also **above the line** *and* **below the line.**

Advertising agency selection

In essence, there are a variety of criteria used by clients to find a perfect match in terms of agency selection. Typically, one or more of those listed in Table 1 would be employed.

Table 1 Criteria for selecting an agency

Selection criteria	Explanation
Understanding	Ability of the agency to appreciate the problems and objectives
Originality	The agency's creative versatility
Management	Degree of the agency's management expertise
Compatibility	Close fit in terms of approach
Presentation skills	Professional and noteworthy pitch
Services offered	Range of internally available services or links with freelance providers
New ideas	Whether the agency has a progressive but still practical approach
Research skills	Availability of research facilities
Media skills	Expertise and contacts in the media
Contact	Approachability
Pragmatism	Sensible and realistic results forecasting
New product development	Experience of dealing with NPD
Point of sale	Experience with creating and dealing with POS materials and campaigns
Global	Multinational or having access to partners in other markets
Culture	Close-matched approach
Existing client base	Avoidance of conflict with similar existing clients
Product or market experience	Previous knowledge or experience in the client's field
Procedures	Good level of internal control and coordination

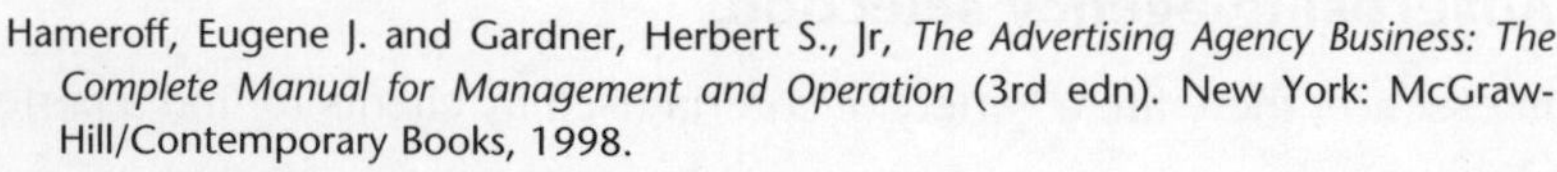
Hameroff, Eugene J. and Gardner, Herbert S., Jr, *The Advertising Agency Business: The Complete Manual for Management and Operation* (3rd edn). New York: McGraw-Hill/Contemporary Books, 1998.

A

Advertising allowance

A payment made, or a price reduction given, to a merchant or other customer as compensation for advertising or promoting products. For example, a business wanting a merchant to emphasize its product may supply standing cardboard displays to be placed near the store's entrance and, as inducement to place them, offer a cash bonus or deep discount on the cost of items to be displayed.

Advertising brief

The statement of the objectives of an advertising campaign (also called the agency brief) agreed between an advertising agency and a client, together with a brief history of the product (idea, organization etc.) to be advertised. It is the starting point for the work of the agency's account management group. The relationship between an agency and its clients is a delicate one. The client should determine the advertising objectives, plan overall advertising strategy and set the advertising budget, while the agency prepares and evaluates advertisements and develops the media plan. The advertising brief is critical because it represents the starting point in the agency–client relationship.

Typically, the agency brief will include:

- situation – current market position, strengths, weaknesses and policies;
- objectives;
- strategy;
- tactics;
- budget;
- product technical specifications;
- customer satisfactions – detailing product benefits and what the user will gain from the product;
- organization profile – background information on the business;
- market analysis;
- pricing of product;
- distribution;
- evaluation criteria – how the marketing communication objectives will be measured;
- timescales and deadlines;
- personnel involved.

Advertising campaign

The advertising campaign involves designing a series of advertisements and placing them in various advertising media to reach a particular target market. Typically, an advertising campaign may be considered as a 'Burst' campaign, which concentrates expenditure into promotional bursts of three or four weeks in length, or a 'Drip' campaign, which allows for a continuous but more prolonged presence in the media.

Advertising campaign objectives

Advertising campaign objectives can be various, dependent upon the overall short-, medium- and long-term objectives of the business. Typically, advertising campaigns are associated with the objectives listed in Table 2; some may be simultaneously associated with several.

Table 2 Advertising objectives

Build strong brand image	Accelerate growth and increase market share	Reach otherwise inaccessible buyers	Influence buying decisions	Support selling through personal contact calls
Promote brand recognition and awareness	Prepare ground for personal selling	Enhance perceived value	Announce new products	Attract new buyers or users
Announce product change	Announce offers/ promotion	Develop corporate image and awareness	Stimulate receptiveness to direct selling	Obtain/expand stock-list
Educate consumers	Expand total market	Change competition – defensive/ offensive	Remind customers of availability	Increase frequency of use
Make announcements to trade	Increase the level of trade confidence	Retrieve lost sales	Stimulate immediate buying action	Keep a product in the public eye

Avery, Jim and Bendinger, Bruce H., *Advertising Campaign Planning* (3rd edn). Copy Workshop. New York: Barnes & Noble, 2000.

A

Advertising elasticity

Advertising elasticity measures the way in which demand has been affected by advertising. The bigger the impact on demand against the investment made in advertising, the more the product or service is considered to be advertising elastic.

Advertising elasticity is measured by using the following formula:

$$\frac{\textit{Percentage change in demand}}{\textit{Percentage change in advertising spending}}$$

> A business increases its advertising by 50% and sees a rise in monthly unit sales from 200,000 to 250,000. The advertising elasticity is 50,000 ÷ 200,000 × 100 = 25%. The change in advertising spending is 50%. Therefore 25(%) ÷ 50(%) = 0.5.

Advertising elasticity is not, however, a vital measure of advertising success or failure as it cannot take into account the time factor. Immediate advertising expenditure does not necessarily mean that sales figures will be affected immediately. The measure does not take into account the fact that advertising spending may have a longer-term effect on sales which cannot be measured in the short term.

Table 3 below gives examples of goods and services that are likely to have each of the levels of elasticity.

Advertising medium

This is a collective term to describe a possible advertising option (or vehicle). Thus television is an advertising medium, but television, newspapers and magazines are advertising media.

Advertising objectives

See **advertising campaign objectives.**

Advertising plan

Closely linked to **advertising campaign objectives**, in which the processes and decisions related to the framing of an advertising campaign are brought together. Fundamental to this is a timetabling of critical events and an identification of responsibilities (including delegation and out-sourcing of expertise), summarized in Figure 5.

Table 3 Levels of elasticity

	Price elasticity of demand	Income elasticity of demand	Advertising elasticity of demand
Inelastic	Necessities, such as water, power, basic foods. Addictive goods, such as cigarettes and alcohol.	Basic goods such as water, toilet paper. Increased income does not imply greater consumption.	Unbranded goods. Goods that are frequently purchased and well known. Goods where the market is saturated.
Unitary	Newspapers, books, every-day items that are not necessities, but are fairly regular purchases.	Electrical goods, restaurant meals. Non-essentials that can be done without.	Those in mature markets, and brands with a high level of customer loyalty.
Elastic	Goods that have a number of alternatives or substitutes (e.g. Coca-Cola – other soft drinks; or the cinema – other forms of entertainment). Luxury goods, products and services that are not necessities and not required as immediate purchases (e.g. designer clothes).	Mainly luxury items such as holidays and new cars.	Branded goods, where the brand name is very important and highly prized. Also goods which are new to the market.

Advertising research

Advertising research studies the effectiveness of either the desired communication or the sales effect, either of which may have been the original advertising objective.

Desired advertising communications objectives fall into the following categories:

- creation of an increased awareness of the product;
- creation or change of attitudes;
- change in the predisposition to buy.

In order to measure the effectiveness of the advertising it is imperative that two surveys are conducted, before and after the advertising

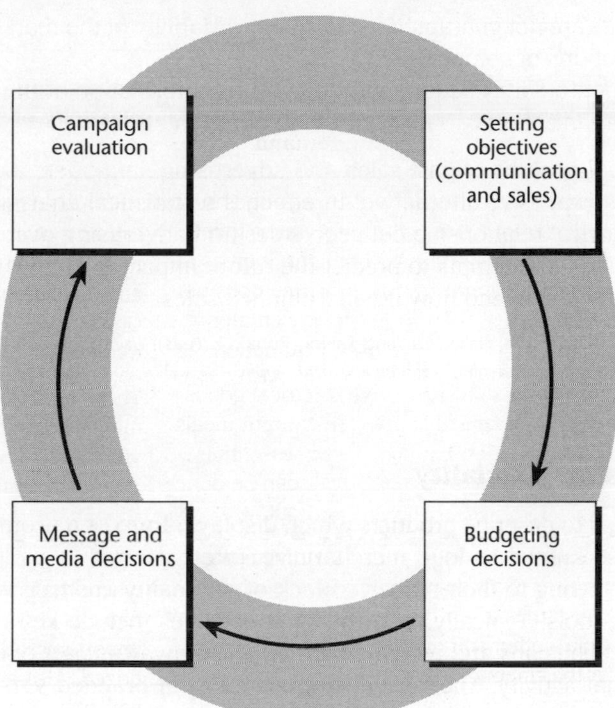

Figure 5 A simple advertising plan

campaign. A continuing series of research studies to measure the effectiveness is known as a **tracking study**. There are two main methods of measuring sales resulting from advertising: field experiments, and statistical analysis of sales and advertising data.

Field experiments involve identifying comparatively self-contained market areas within the whole market and adjusting the level of the advertising within them. Normally the chosen market areas fall into three categories: one group will be exposed to the standard levels of advertising; the second, 25% less than the norm; and the final group, 25% more. The major problems associated with field experiments are as follows:

- It is difficult to maintain the external factors of competition and demand (competitors may run 'spoiling campaigns' such as **sales promotions**).
- Distributors within the low advertising area may run their own promotions during the period to support their own sales.
- Lost sales may be counter-productive in the short term and allow competitors to establish themselves.

- Results are not guaranteed, due to the variability of the markets and the actions of competitors.
- Competitors may acquire vital marketing information at the cost of the organization carrying out the experimentation.

Statistical analysis of past sales and advertising data offers a considerably less expensive alternative. In effect, the statistical analysis looks at the historical relationship between sales and advertising over the life of a product and attempts to predict the future impact of changes in the level of advertising and how it will influence sales.

Morrison, Margaret A., Haley, Eric and Taylor, Ronald E. (eds), *Using Qualitative Research in Advertising: Strategies, Techniques, and Applications*. London: Sage Publications, 2002.

Advertising speciality

A term used to describe products which display a **logo** or a promotional image; also known as logo merchandise, often referred to as 'trinkets and trash' owing to their perceived lack of originality and true value as marketing tools. Typically, advertising specialities include key rings, t-shirts, baseball caps and mouse mats, all given away as part of a larger promotional activity. They are distinguished from branded versions of the same items, which are sold as regular merchandise.

More broadly, 'advertising speciality' can also be used to describe the merchandising opportunities of a football team through selling products (and latterly services such as banking) to fans who wish to display their allegiance to the club by wearing or showing the club's logo. Manchester United, for example, generates in excess of £20m per year from these sales alone.

Advertising Standards Authority (ASA)

UK-based independent organization which was established and is subsequently funded by the advertising industry. Its purpose is to ensure effective self-regulation of advertising in the UK. The ASA is independently chaired and members are appointed to the ASA by the chairman as individuals without affiliations to particular parts or interest groups within the industry. It is a requirement under the ASA rules that some 50 per cent of the members are not associated with the advertising industry.

One of its primary aims is to establish and maintain a strong dialogue with central and local government, consumer groups and trade associations. Through the Code of Advertising Practice, the ASA seeks to control and place sanctions on advertisers who break the self-regulatory guidelines. In effect, however, the ASA lacks teeth and is considered to be very much a part of the advertising industry, upon which it relies for funding. The ASA receives, processes, judges and passes comment on advertising which has received complaints from the general public and other advertisers.

www.asa.org.uk

Advertorial

An advertorial is an advertisement which appears, to all intents and purposes, to be editorial content in print or on the internet. The advertisement is written to appear to be a news story, often with a disclaimer identifying it as such. On television or on the radio, a similar advertorial item is known as an 'infomercial'. Advertorials are often used as a tool of **public relations** when a new product or service is being launched.

Advocacy advertising

Advocacy advertising is usually corporate advertising that seeks to convey the organization's view on a particular issue or to state its position on an issue. It may be typified as a sponsored communication which presents a view on a controversial cause or issue.

See also **advertorial**.

Advocate revenue

Advocate revenue is income derived from a customer who recommends a product or service to another customer. Advocate revenue is a growth area on the internet where present, satisfied customers are encouraged to refer other potential customers to a business in return for a percentage of sales value derived. In essence, the system works rather like an affiliate programme, but rather than being based on sending web traffic to the business via links and endorsements, the relationship rests on the income derived from the customer who has been referred by the advocate.

The term 'advocate' is also closely associated with the **ladder of customer loyalty** (suspect, prospect, customer, client, supporter, advocate and partnership).

Aerial advertising

A form of outdoor advertising where airborne messages are used, including banners pulled by aircraft, skywriting, slogans and logos on airships and balloons, and skydivers.

Affiliate programme

An affiliate programme is a form of advertising on the internet which aims to reward an affiliate (who is a self-selected advertiser) for pushing web traffic to a business.

Affiliate programmes are sophisticated multi-level marketing schemes where existing customers attempt to attract other customers by endorsing the business and carrying banner advertising and links. Some systems allow for multi-tiered affiliation, which rewards affiliates for the traffic generated by affiliates that an affiliate has recruited.

Some larger web-based businesses such as Amazon have their own affiliate programmes, but there are more generic systems such as Beefree, Linkshare or CommissionJunction. Affiliates have the potential to earn significant money by signing up for an affiliate programme to use its excess advertising inventory (unsold banners).

Gray, Daniel, *The Complete Guide to Associate and Affiliate Programs on the Net: Turning Clicks into Cash*. New York: McGraw-Hill, 1999.

Affinity marketing

Affinity marketing is about forming strategic marketing alliances with other organizations, both commercial and not-for-profit, that bring mutual benefits and help both organizations to achieve marketing objectives. Alternatively, affinity marketing can be described as marketing targeted to consumers, based on their previous buying patterns. This is particularly prevalent on the internet where it is typified by email, direct mail or on-site recommendations. A regular purchaser of products or services will be automatically informed of the imminent release of a new product, on the basis of their previous purchases.

After-sales service

After-sales service has become a feature of full product and customer support, often used as a prime discriminator between competing businesses. Typically, after-sales service, which was formerly associated wholly with the carrying out of repairs, maintenance, and advice to customers who had purchased products and services, is now seen as an integral part of the overall marketing strategy.

After-sales service has become a major expectation of customers and is now considered to be an important component of closing a sale. The availability of after-sales service has latterly been associated with the offering of extended warranties beyond the normal guarantee period of the product. These insurance services, sold at a premium, underwrite and compensate for loss leaders offered by the business in order to attract customers. Strictly speaking, these do not fall into the standard understanding of after-sales service as the implication is that customers are being persuaded to purchase after-sales service, rather than the service being seen as an integral part of sales and marketing, customer retention and satisfaction.

Agat line

This is a measure of newspaper advertising space, one column wide and 1¼ inch deep (approx. 3cm).

Agent

An agent is an individual or business that has expressed or implied authority to act on behalf of another business, known as the principal. They are empowered to enter into contractual relationships with a third party on behalf of the principal.

In direct association with marketing, advertising agencies often act as agents in fact and deed when they purchase services and advertising space in the name of their principal (client).

AIDA

Attention, Interest, Desire, Action. This is a traditional model of the purpose and flow of marketing communications and direct sales efforts:

1 create attention;
2 generate interest;
3 develop desire;
4 initiate action.

The term is said to have its foundations in the late nineteenth century as the basic premise of early printed advertisements.

Ambient media

'Ambient media' is a term used to describe advertising opportunities which are often built into the structure of architecture such as bus stations and multi-storey car parks. Ambient media also include advertising spaces which appear on car park barriers, buses, shopping trolleys or cabs. This form of advertising opportunity is called 'ambient media' as it is viewed as being part of the normal environment and, whilst intrusive to some extent, has a more subliminal effect on those who are exposed to its messages.

Ambush marketing

Ambush marketing is the action of another business, often a competitor, seekings association with a sponsored activity without payment to the activity's owner. Ambush marketing typifies the attempt by one business to deflect some of the audience's attention to itself and away from the sponsor.

Ambush marketing was originally a term used to describe the activities of businesses that sought to associate themselves with an event, without paying a fee to the event owner. In this way they 'ambushed' the legitimate sponsor of the event by giving the impression that they were the sponsors themselves. The term is now used in a broader context and describes a generic set of activities that attempt to make associations with an event where there is no legitimate relationship.

Five different areas of ambush marketing are clear:

- *Sponsoring the broadcast of an event* is when a business other than the main sponsor of the event sponsors the broadcasting of the event. It is a legitimate ploy as there is a specific sponsorship opportunity, added to the fact that the ambusher will have a broader audience than the event sponsor provided that the broadcast audience is larger than those present at the event.
- *Sponsoring subcategories within an event* occurs when the ambusher decides to sponsor a defined part of the event and is thus associated with the event as a whole. The ambusher makes full use of its association with the event, at a reduced cost, through aggressive marketing.
- *Purchasing advertising during the broadcast of an event* and its subsequent re-showings not only helps to offset the benefits to the main sponsor, but also guarantees exposure to larger audiences.
- *Non-sponsorship promotions and advertisements* timed to coincide with an event, using broadcast and other media to signal a major presence.
- *Sponsorship suggestion* is also used to imply that a business is in some way associated with an event. Advertisements may be themed around the event itself (such as tennis in the case of

Wimbledon). Other strategies may include the giving away of official merchandise from the event, or tickets to the event, in competitions. Additionally, the ambusher may run advertisements congratulating or stating their support of participants in the event, thus implying that there is a direct link between the ambusher and the event.

See also **guerrilla marketing.**

American Marketing Association code of ethics

The code of ethics supported by the American Marketing Association covers a wide area of issues related to responsibilities and conduct. The code requires members of the AMA to ensure that their 'decisions, recommendations and actions function to identify, serve and satisfy all relevant publics: customers, organizations and society'. In essence it is a professional code with the features listed in Table 4.

Ansoff Matrix

The Ansoff Matrix (Figure 6) is one of a number of classical marketing concepts, which encapsulates the future vision of the business.

H. Igor Ansoff has made major contributions to the concepts surrounding corporate strategy ('A Practical System of Objectives' in *Corporate Strategy*). However, it is for the growth vector matrix that he is best known. The matrix examines the potential strategies available to a business in four areas, cross-referenced as new or existing markets and new or existing products. The matrix suggests the marketing strategies available to the business in each of these areas:

- *Market penetration* – Existing Products into Existing Markets. Management seeks to increase its market share with the current product range. This is considered to be the least-risk strategy of all the options available. Existing customers are encouraged to buy more products and services, those at present buying a competing brand are persuaded to switch, and non-buyers are convinced to begin to make purchases. Any readily recognizable weaknesses in the portfolio of the business need to be addressed and strengthened.
- *Market development* – Existing Products into New Markets. Systematic market research should reveal new potential markets for the existing products. Clearly stated segments are then targeted individually through existing marketing and distribution channels

Table 4 AMA ethics citeria

Ethical criteria	Details
Professional conduct	Members should not knowingly do any harm; adhere to laws and regulations; accurately represent their own training, education and experience; and promote the wider adoption of the code.
Honesty and fairness	Members must deal honestly with all concerned parties, avoid conflicts of interest, establish fair fee schedules and payments.
Rights and duties	Products and services should be safe and fit for their purpose, communications about these items should be honest, good faith should be assumed, and grievances handled in an equitable manner.
Product development and management	Members should disclose risks, identify changes to a product which would affect the purchasing decision, and identify cost added features.
Promotions	Members should avoid misleading advertising, should not use high-pressure sales techniques, and must not use sales promotions which are deceitful or manipulative.
Distribution	There must be no manipulation of supply as a means of exploitation, and no coercion of supply-channel partners, particularly re-sellers, in terms of stocking arrangements.
Pricing	There should be no price fixing or predatory pricing policies, and the full price of a product or service must be disclosed at the time of purchase.
Marketing research	Sales and fundraising must be separated from marketing research, research integrity must be assured, and respondents must be treated fairly.

www.marketingpower.com

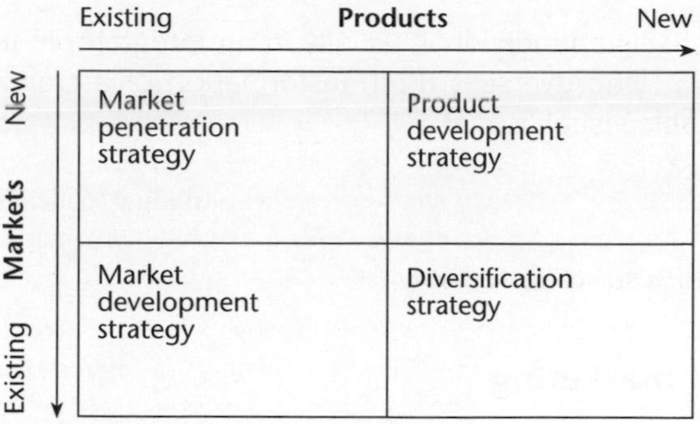

Markets ↓ / Products →	Existing	New
New	Market penetration strategy	Product development strategy
Existing	Market development strategy	Diversification strategy

Figure 6 The growth vector matrix

or new ones are set up to service the new segments. As the business is moving into new markets, it needs to be aware of potential differences in reactions, expectations and other factors.

- *Product development* – New products into Existing Markets.
  Assuming the business has sufficient resources, it can bring new products or developments in the existing products into the market. Provided the business has closely matched the new products with the requirements of their existing markets risks are minimized. The major concern is 'time to market', which means how long it will take to develop the new products and whether the opportunity to quickly defray the development costs is possible.
- *Diversification* – New Products into New Markets.
  This is considered to carry the highest risk of all the strategies. Essentially, there are two options available to the business; the first is synergistic diversification, which relies on the business being able to harness its existing product and market knowledge (production processes, channels of distribution, etc.). The other option is known as conglomerate diversification, which means that the business departs from its existing product and market knowledge. This form of diversification is often achieved by merging with or taking over a business operating in another unrelated area (which in fact converts conglomerate diversification into synergistic diversification).

Ansoff, H. Igor, *Corporate Strategy* (The Library of Management Classics). London: Sidgwick & Jackson, 1986.

Art director

An art director is an individual, usually in an integral role in an advertising agency, who oversees the transformation of a creative concept into a workable visual format.

ASA

See **Advertising Standards Authority.**

Asset-led marketing

A marketing strategy which focuses more on the strengths of the assets (products, services or brands) owned by a business. It is common for an asset to drive the business to extend its brand line by producing products and services which rest on the strength and the reputation of the asset. Extensions to the product line will not necessarily be based on customer needs or market research that has revealed a desire for a new product, but will be a logical extension of the current offering, such as producing ice-cream products from existing and established confectionery ranges.

Assimilation

The term 'assimilation' usually refers to a decision made by a business to incorporate the features of one product into another product. The older product's best-loved features, as far as customers are concerned, are transferred to the new product, making the older product now obsolete. In many respects product assimilation can be likened to **brand cannibalization** in its broadest sense, as one product is sacrificed for the longer-term benefit of a newer product.

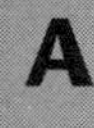

Assimilation is also used to describe the gradual transfer of customers from an existing business which has been merged or has been taken over by another business. The original business's activities, undertaken on a separate basis, are gradually wound down and customers are assimilated into the new business's overall structure and processes.

Assumptive close

This is a sales-related term which describes the situation at the end of a sales encounter with a customer. The salesperson makes the assumption that the decision to buy has already been made by the customer and that all that is required is that a subsidiary or subordinate decision, such as delivery date, actual choice of model or payment method, is needed. The salesperson makes it implicit in a closing statement, such as 'Would you like it now or shall we deliver it?', that the full buying process has reached a conclusion and that only minor points now remain.

Attitudinal scaling

The mindsets or attitudes of consumers are of critical importance in marketing as a means of establishing how consumers can be influenced. Consumer attitude is taken to have three elements:

- the cognitive component, which is the consumer's beliefs or information about the product;
- the affective component, which is the consumer's likes or dislikes regarding the product;
- the behavioural component, which is the consumer's action, tendencies or predispositions towards the product.

Rating scales are often used to assess the attitude of consumers in regard to the product or aspects of the product. Typically, the consumer is asked to place an attribute along a numerically valued continuum called a 'rating scale', an example of which is:

How do you rate the taste of Dr Pepper carbonated drink?

Probably the best   Very good   Neither good or bad   Not good   Probably the worst

1   2   3   4   5   6   7   8   9   10   11

The consumer places a mark along the scale and the researcher assigns a value for each of the marks to aid the analysis of the data. This format of questioning is not generally used as the only means of data collection, because the reasons behind the choice are not given by the consumer.

Using an odd number on the scale allows the consumer to pick a midpoint, and in many cases an even number of options is given to force the respondent to indicate a favourable or unfavourable response. The main criticism of this scaling is that the respondent is not asked to evaluate the product in relation to a specified standard and as a result the respondents may be using different standards and reference points. In order to improve the overall quality of the data collected, the following issues should be addressed:

- When using verbal descriptions such as 'mostly dissatisfied' or 'delighted' make it clear what these statements actually mean.
- Generally use no more than five attitudinal categories unless the respondent is knowledgeable about the subject.

- A balanced scale has the same number of favourable and unfavourable options; however, many researchers use an unbalanced scale with considerably more favourable options as this offers a more useful and measurable form of product evaluation.
- With even numbers of options, respondents are forced to make a decision with regard to the rating. Some questions could include 'non-forced' options such as 'no opinion' or 'no knowledge'.

Attrition rates

Attrition is the opposite of retention – it represents those customers who have stopped buying from an organization and are now buying elsewhere. The attrition rate is the number of customers who have stopped purchasing from an organization over a certain time period, and is often measured as a percentage of the total number of customers.

Audience accumulation

The number of people, households, or organizations exposed to a single media vehicle over a designated period of time.

Audience composition

An analysis of an audience based on characteristics relevant to an advertiser. Typically, these will be the age, gender or lifestyle segments of the audience. A broader description is associated with finding the potential target of marketing communications, by identifying specific audiences for specific messages, again achieved through market segmentation and targeting activities.

Audience duplication

Audience duplication is typified by measures such as 'Opportunities to See' (OTS), which calculates the number of times a unique individual may hear, see or read an advertisement. Audience duplication considers those repeat exposures, calculating the mean number of exposures required to produce an action from the individual. Advertisers will have an ideal audience duplication figure in mind when setting the parameters of a campaign, balancing the fact that over-exposure to certain audiences may be counterproductive when the funds could be used to target other audiences.

Audience profile

Audience profiling aims to identify the key characteristics of readers, viewers or listeners of a given print or broadcast medium. The characteristics, derived from questionnaires and other market research sources, can assist the advertiser in matching the profile of their ideal customer with the profile of the audience, thus making marketing communications all the more effective and targeted.

Audience research

See **media research.**

Audit

An audit is a formal examination of accounts or resources. In the marketing context, however, it is more closely associated with the concept of independent audits which aim to measure the true circulation figures of the print media (i.e. actual sales as opposed to print runs). Prime examples of independent audits are those carried out by the **ABC (Audit Bureau of Circulation)**.

Audit Bureau of Circulation

See **ABC.**

Augmented product

An augmented product is everything that is not to do with the product or the service, but that makes it easier for customers to buy and to make the decision to buy, such as paying in instalments for a holiday or knowing that a product has a guarantee, or even that the business where they made their purchase has a good reputation in dealing with problems.

The concept of an augmented product is part of a broader issue which extends the overall view of the product or the service. A useful way of thinking about the features of a product or a service is to look at it as a broader package. This package includes the product itself, what it is called and how it looks, and additional considerations such as after-sales service. These are known as product levels, which are best understood in the diagram in Figure 7.

- *The core product* – what is the buyer really buying? The core product refers to the use, benefit, or problem-solving service that the

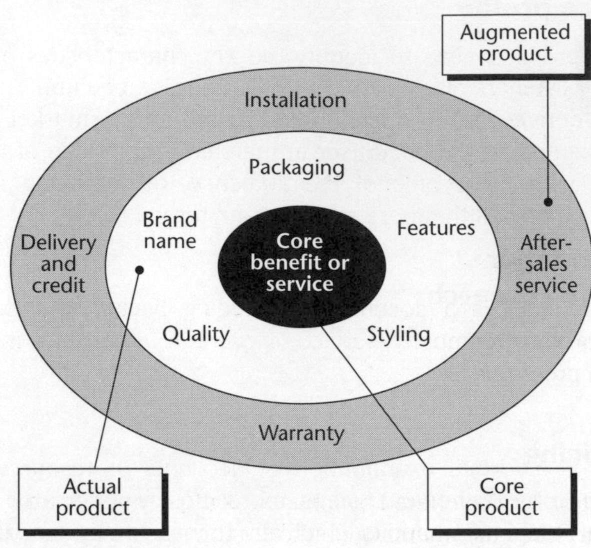

Figure 7 Product levels

consumer is really buying when purchasing the product. In other words the need that is being fulfilled.

- *The actual product* is the tangible product or intangible service that allows the customer to receive the core product benefits.
- *Quality* refers to product performance, e.g. how many attractions are at a theme park, whether the hotel was as described in the brochure or whether the flight left on time.
- *Features* are the product attributes – what it does and what it is for.
- *Styling* refers to the design of the product, how it is made to appeal to the customer.
- *The brand name* helps consumers recognize the product and judge whether it has a good reputation.
- *Packaging* protects tangible products and promotes both products and services by featuring the style and the brand name.
- *The augmented product* consists of things made available to help the customer make an easier choice and convince them that this is the product they should buy, including installation, delivery and credit, warranties, and **after-sales service**.

Backgrounder

A backgrounder is a document containing background information about a product, company, service or event. In essence, it is a stylized form of a press release.

Bait pricing

A product or service offered by a business at an unrealistically low price in order to lure customers. Once the customers have been successfully attracted, the business then attempts to sell higher priced products and services. Bait pricing is considered to be a highly unethical means of promoting a product or service.

The technique is closely associated with bait advertising, which promotes low priced products and services which, in fact, are in low stock or not in stock at all. Customers are offered alternatives to the low priced items, having specifically made the decision to make a purchase. The customers are considered to be more vulnerable to sales pitches under these circumstances. The process of offering lower priced products and services and then attempting to sell higher priced ones is known as bait and switch pricing or selling.

Banded offer/pack

A sales technique where two related products are often literally banded together and sold at a special price during a specific sales promotion. In order for the promotion to be wholly effective, the customer can also see and purchase the two separate items at considerably more than the special offer price, which demonstrates the degree of saving by purchasing the banded pack. Alternatively, single-pack items are removed temporarily from the inventory and are not available for separate purchase.

Bandwidth

Bandwidth is an internet term used to describe the speed at which information can travel, measured in seconds (bits-per-second or bps). A business will seek to establish itself with servers which have a wide bandwidth, allowing quicker access for visitors to its website and for more users to be able to access the site at the same time.

When larger files are concerned, it is imperative that the business has access to considerable bandwidth as these files consume larger amounts of bandwidth in downloading. Perceptually, it is useful to think of bandwidth as a pipe: the wider the pipe, the more information can travel along it.

Banner ad

A banner ad is an advertisement in the form of a banner design inside a graphics frame, usually at the header or footer of a webpage. Visitors to the webpage are encouraged to click on the banner ad to take them directly to an associated or reciprocal link. Many websites have banner ads in order to generate income from the organization placing the banner ad on their website. A fee is usually payable per click on the banner ad. In other cases, a reciprocal banner ad is placed on a website in exchange for a banner ad on another organization's website.

Zeff, Robbin, *Advertising on the Internet* (2nd edn). Chichester: John Wiley & Sons, 1999.

Barksdale and Harris combined portfolio analysis

The Barksdale and Harris model is based on the assumption that products and services have a finite life. In addition, the following assumptions are made:

- that there is a direct relationship between market share, income generated and profit margins;
- that there are economies of scale to be made as product increases and unit costs are driven down.

The stages in the life cycle of a product are explained as follows:

- *Infants* appear during the pioneering stage. They are the highest risk products as they cannot be expected to provide profits. Indeed, these products tend to consume costs as the business needs to promote them to customers.
- *Problem children* have essentially the same description as the Boston Consulting Group matrix (see **Boston Growth Matrix**).

They have a low market share but high growth and are therefore expensive for the business to continue to maintain.

- *Stars* have high market share and a high growth rate, still expensive in terms of promotional and maintenance costs. They are, however, products which need support for future profits and success.
- *Cash cows* have a description similar to that of the Boston Consulting Group matrix as they are good earners with a high market share in what tends to be a low-growth market.
- *Dogs* or 'cash dogs' exist in a low-growth market where they have a small market share. None the less, the products can make a small contribution to the business – these are the products defined as cash dogs. Dogs are products that actually make a loss.
- *War horses* are usually former cash cows which exist in a declining market, but they still retain a high market share. The product itself is sound, but the vagaries of the market have affected its long-term success. A business will try to sustain the product for as long as possible, whilst spending as little as practicable on its promotion. A business will ultimately make the decision that the product should be withdrawn so as to avoid an adverse effect on the image of the business and its other products.
- *Dodos* exist in a declining market where they have a low market share. There is an opportunity for the product to make some contribution as other businesses begin to exit the market, leaving the

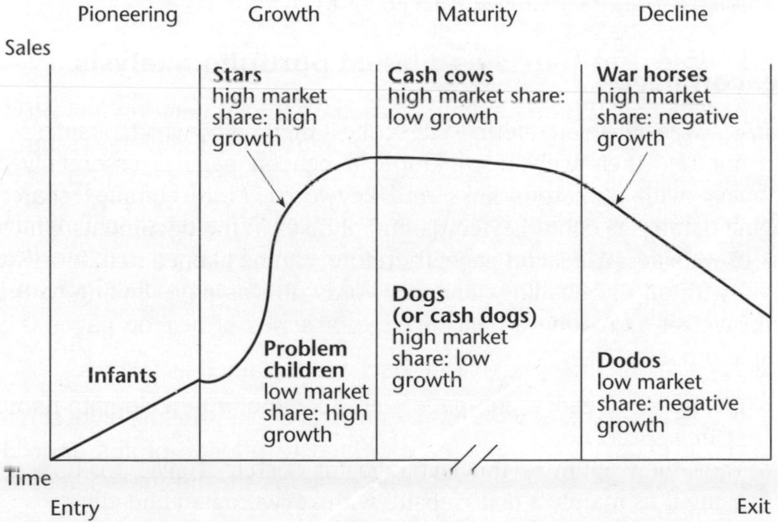

Figure 8 Barksdale and Harris combined portfolio

B

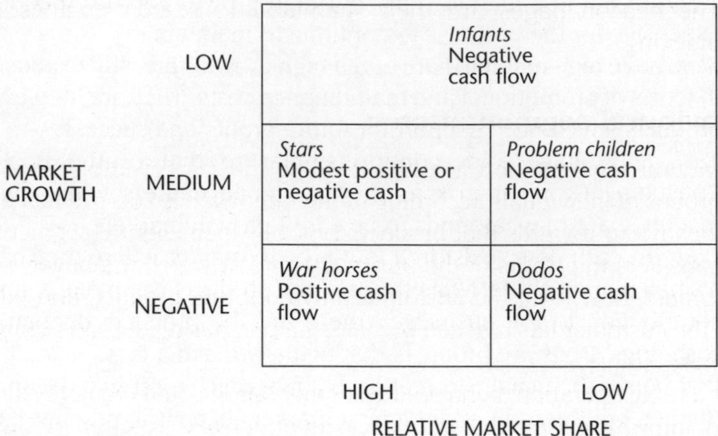

Figure 9 Barksdale and Harris combined portfolio, characteristics of product categories

dodo with a clear field. In these cases, dodos can be converted into war horses. Normally, as the market declines and the market share shrinks, the dodo is rendered obsolete and is withdrawn.

*See also **Boston Growth Matrix**.*

Barksdale, H. C. and Harris, C. E., 'Portfolio Analysis and the Product Life Cycle', *Long-Range Planning*, 15 (December 1982) pp. 74–83.

Beacon pages

B

This is a website-related term to describe a method by which businesses can improve their website rankings. A beacon page is essentially a webpage with numerous links and keywords. More complex search engine databases count keywords and phrases in the documents which link to websites. A beacon page, therefore, can be likened to a doorway page, with all the headings and keywords on this page linking to the main website. Creating a beacon page or series of beacon pages is a simple process:

- Businesses create a one-page website, either a new domain name or free space.
- They then optimize the webpage for search engine positioning, using it as mainly a text website with keywords and headings.
- The page is then linked to the main business's website, possibly to all the subsections or major pages within the main website.

- The beacon pages are then submitted to search engines for indexing.

Behavioural segmentation

Behavioural segmentation involves dividing the market into recognizable groups of individuals according to their knowledge of a product and their behaviour towards that product. Typically, behavioural segmentation considers the status of the buyer, the rate at which the buyer uses the product, how loyal the customer may be to the product, and what stage the customer has reached in making a purchasing decision ('buyer readiness' stage).

For a retail operation, behavioural segmentation could relate to transaction information on the frequency, quantity and type of products purchased. Customers, for example, who buy mainly products in one category, may be likely targets for speciality catalogues or special offers for new products in that category.

Below the line

Below-the-line marketing activities are often confused with sales promotions, but they represent a large area of marketing activities which include direct mail, exhibitions, demonstrations and point of sale materials.

See also **above the line.**

Wilmshurst, John, *Below-the-Line Promotion* (The Marketing series: Professional Development). London: Butterworth-Heinemann, 1993.

Benchmark

A benchmark is a predetermined set of standards against which future performance or activities are measured. Usually, benchmarking involves the discovery of the best practice for an activity, either within or outside the business, in an effort to identify the ideal processes and prosecution of an activity.

The purpose of benchmarking is to ensure that future performance and activities conform with the benchmarked ideal in order to improve overall performance. Increased efficiency is key to the benchmarking process as, in marketing terms, improved efficiency, reliability of data and effectiveness of marketing activities will lead to a more competitive edge and ultimately to greater profitability.

Damelio, Robert, *The Basics of Benchmarking*. Austin, TX: Productivity, 1995.

Benefit segmentation

This market segmentation concept suggests that customers define and seek the direct benefits of a given product or service as the real reasons for their purchases. The goal of using this strategy is to appeal to customers' perceptions through their value systems. Benefits include such consumer attributes as low price, high quality, time savings and convenience. Different customers buy the same or similar products for different reasons. Benefit segmentation attempts to group these customers according to the principal benefit sought by them. Unfortunately, it does seem that there is often no single variable that determines a purchasing decision based on these principal benefits and it is not always clear whether one benefit is distinctive enough to segment the market in this way.

Berry, Leonard L.

Dr Leonard Berry is the director of the Center for Retailing Studies at Texas A&M University. He has been a particularly prolific writer on healthcare services marketing, service marketing, management, quality and retailing.

In his book *Discovering the Soul of Service: The Nine Drivers of Sustainable Business Success*, Berry examined fourteen service businesses to uncover the secrets of their success. He identified nine key drivers of excellence common to the organizations. Above all, he stresses that service-related marketing should be tempered with a humane approach and set of values, as listed in Table 5.

Table 5 Nine key drivers of excellence

• leading with values	• strategic focus	• executional excellence
• control of destiny	• trust-based relationships	• investment in employee success
• acting small	• brand cultivation	• generosity

Berry, Leonard L., *Discovering the Soul of Service: The Nine Drivers of Sustainable Business Success*. New York: Free Press, 1999.

Bias

A term associated with market research which refers to errors in a sample survey. Bias may relate to the use of an unrepresentative sample, upon which a series of assumptions may later be made.

B

Commonly, bias is also associated with the conduct of market researchers in the field, who deliberately or inadvertently impose a bias on the research findings. Typically, bias may creep into a survey when researchers become overzealous in their attempts to collect data which supports their preconceived ideas. It is possible that the respondents pick up on this desire to collect the appropriate responses and as a result provide the responses that they feel the researchers are seeking rather than a true response to the questioning.

Bias can, in most cases, be eliminated or reduced by the introduction of clear and efficient supervision and monitoring of the data collection. Periodic spot checks, observation and cross-checking of results can reveal the degree to which bias has influenced the data that has been collected by the researchers. Some forms of data collection are more prone to bias than others – market research carried out without the benefit of close supervision tends to be more biased than systems set up with integral supervision, such as telephone market research.

Billboards

Billboards are a part of outdoor advertising: typically, established poster sites which can be hired for a period of time by an advertiser. These large poster sites are located in prime positions, notably close to major traffic routes where a large number of potential customers can view the advertisement each day. They are measured in sheet sizes, e.g. 4, 16, 32, 48 or 96 sheets, dependent upon the size of the poster site.

In the US, the term 'billboard' is more generic and includes any poster-based advertisement, such as those in transport hubs, including railroad stations and bus garages. Associated terms include those given in Table 6.

Bingo card

A bingo card is an enquiry card which is usually stitched into a magazine. The bingo card features a series of numbers or codes which correlate with advertisements carried in the magazine. The reader can mark the bingo card and request further information from the advertisers. The bingo cards usually have a prepaid postage mark and the address of a fulfilment agency or the publisher of the magazine. Multiple requests for information from advertisers are encouraged and seen by the publisher and advertisers as a direct response in terms of interest from the reader, which can be measured far more effectively than some other means of measuring the effectiveness of advertising in that medium.

Table 6 Billboard vocabulary

Associated term	Definition
Animation	Moving units, flashing lights, etc., used to gain added attention.
Annual average daily traffic	The annual traffic volume passing the site for the year, divided by 365.
Circulation	Circulation is based on traffic volume (such as cars, pedestrians, buses and trains).
Effective circulation	The number of potential viewers, such as the number of people passing the site who have an opportunity to view the advertisement.
Frequency	Measures the number of times an average family or individual is exposed to an advertising message during a defined period of time. The frequency and reach usually refers to the calendar month (which matches the standard contract and exposure practices).
GRPs (Gross Rating Points)	The total number of impressions delivered by a media schedule, expressed as a percentage of the population. For billboards, GRPs generally refer to daily circulation.

Bingo cards are also known as 'reader inquiry cards', but in both cases the direct response from the reader is seen as a positive measurement of the interest generated by an advertisement as well as of the matching of the readership in terms of the advertisement's relevance to them.

B

Black matter

An advertising term used to describe the dramatic use of blank (usually black) areas of an advertisement. Using black matter to highlight and to attract attention gives a different impression to the reader from that conveyed by a densely packed advertisement with a large amount of information and images. Black matter is used to differentiate the advertisement and is usually employed to create a quality image for a brand, product or service. It is not always the case that the reader is aware of the business being advertised, and black matter is used in these cases to highlight and intrigue the reader, causing interest and a desire to find out more. This is believed to make the reader more receptive to a follow-up advertisement in the same style, but with a greater spread of information.

Bleed

'Bleed' is an advertising, printing-related term which means allowing a picture or advertisement to extend beyond the normal margin of a printed page. The total image extends to the edge of the page.

Blind ad

Blind advertisements are unusual in the sense that they do not reveal the name of the organization placing the advertisement. Stereotypical blind advertisements are usually related to job advertisements or advertisements offering instant solutions to income generation. Post Office box numbers are often used rather than complete addresses, but it is also possible that the reader is encouraged to call a free phone number or premium rate number for further information.

A development of blind advertisements has entered the more conventional field of advertising where businesses run advertisements with only a basic clue from which to make inferences as to who they are. In the latter years of tobacco advertising in the UK, advertisements could not overtly mention business names or products and sought to suggest them instead (e.g. Silk Cut). The use of logos and other devices, such as in the advertisements run by Nike, does not strictly speaking fall into the blind advertisement category as it is clear who the advertiser is, despite the obscurity of the advertising message.

Blind test

A market research and product development term which refers to testing situations where the respondent is not made aware of the brand that is being tested. A common and well-known form of blind test asks respondents to taste different brands of cola drinks and identify which one they normally consume and whether they can identify the other brands.

Blocking chart

A blocking chart is a graphic representation of a planned advertising activity on a calendar. Typically, it would show when advertisements and associated promotions are taking place within a given time-frame as part of an overall advertising and promotions campaign.

Blow-in card

Blow-in cards are cards inserted in magazines, either by hand or by a machine which 'blows' them into the magazines. Magazines may sell these cards to advertisers or use them to advertise their own magazine. Many magazines find bind-in and blow-in cards the most cost-effective method of gaining new subscribers. Publishers may bind in a single card or a page of cards which may be separated along perforated edges. Publishers owning several magazines often advertise related magazines on bind-in cards inserted in magazines whose audiences are similar. Cards may be bound into magazines with saddle-stitch binding or perfect binding.

See also **insertion advertising.**

Blue line proof

This is a printing term that refers to a blue line drawn to indicate where a page should be cut. Multiple-page, one-colour or spot-colour printing of advertisements requires a blue-line proof. A photosensitive coating on both sides of the print turns dark blue when exposed to light, without any processing or special handling.

In the case of multiple-page print jobs, a two-sided blue-line proof is made of the entire form. The blue line is then folded and trimmed as if it were the actual press sheet to check for any problems that would be apparent only after printing and folding.

Blurb

A blurb is a brief advertising description of a product or a service, which may be used as part of an advertisement. It is closely associated with book publishing, which often features blurb on the covers to promote the title. The term 'blurb' does have connotations of bias as the material is specifically written to promote and enhance the product. Blurb will usually not only contain promotional slogans and endorsements, but will tend to stress the positive benefits of the product to the potential customer. It can then be read quickly at the point of sale.

Body copy

Body copy is the main text of an advertisement, with regard to print advertising. Body copy represents the bulk of a printed advertisement excluding the illustrations and headlines.

'Bogoff'

'Bogoff' is a mnemonic which stands for 'buy one, get one free'. Bogoffs are an integral part of sales promotions where the customer is offered a second product free providing that they buy the first product. It is not a standard requirement of a bogoff promotion that the products need to be bundled in any way, neither does the free product necessarily have to be the same as the first purchase. This is a common form of promotion that can be found in supermarkets and other retail outlets.

Boilerplate

An advertising term used to describe a unit of writing which can be re-used on many occasions without any need to change the content. The term is derived from steel manufacturing, where boilerplate is steel rolled into large plates for use in steam boilers. The implication of the term 'boilerplate' is to suggest that the writing has been used on many occasions and is fully tested and effective (strong). As with steel, the writing can be used on many occasions without the prospect of it failing to have the desired effect.

The term can also be used as an adjective, such as a boilerplate paragraph or a boilerplate document. Boilerplates often include mission statements, safety warnings, copyright statements and responsibility disclaimers.

From the 1890s to the 1950s, in the US, boilerplate was actually pre-cast or stamped and distributed to the newspaper industry. This ensured that press releases, advertisements and statements made by a business would be printed as they were supplied.

Boilerplate is still used extensively in **public relations**, notably in the last paragraph of a press release, which is normally a statement regarding the business (such as the number of employees, number of centres, etc.).

Boston Growth Matrix

The Boston Consulting Group (BCG) was founded in 1963 by Bruce D. Henderson as the Management and Consulting Division of the Boston Safe Deposit and Trust Company (The Boston Company).

The theory underlying the Boston Matrix is the **product life cycle** concept (see Figure 10a), which states that business opportunities move through life-cycle phases of introduction, growth, maturity and decline. The Boston classification or BCG Matrix is a classification developed by the Boston Consulting Group to analyse products and businesses by

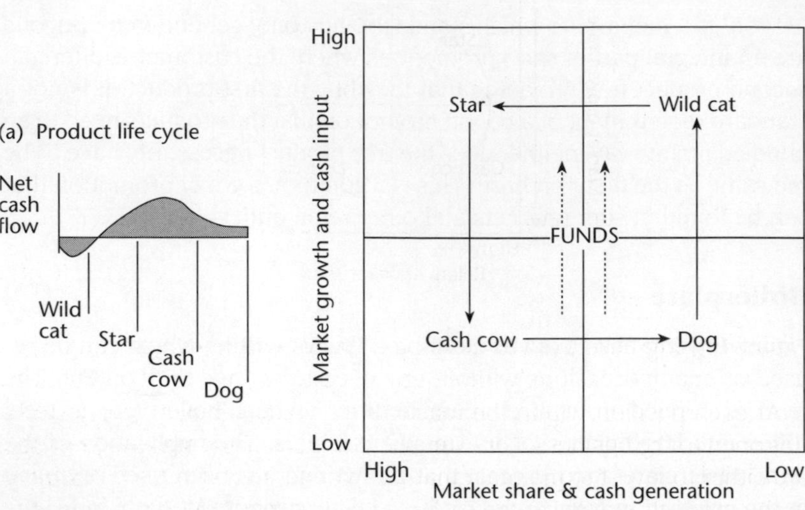

Figure 10 Linkage between the product life cycle and the Boston Matrix

market share and market growth (see Figure 10b). In this, **cash cow** refers to a product or business with high market share and low market growth, **dog** refers to one with a low market share and low growth, **problem child** ('question mark', or 'wild cat') has low market share and high growth and a **star** has high growth and high market share.

These phases are typically represented by an anti-clockwise movement around the Boston Matrix quadrants (see Figure 11) in the following order:

- From a *market entry* position as a question mark product. Products are usually launched into high growth markets, but suffer from a low market share.
- To a *star* position as sales and market share are increased. If the investment necessary to build sales and market share is successfully made, then the product's position will move towards the star position of high growth/high market share.
- To a *cash cow* position as the market growth rate slows and market leadership is achieved. As the impact of the product life cycle takes effect and the market growth rate slows, the product will move from the star position of high growth to the cash cow position of low growth/high share.
- Finally to a *dog* position as investment is minimized as the product ages and loses market share.

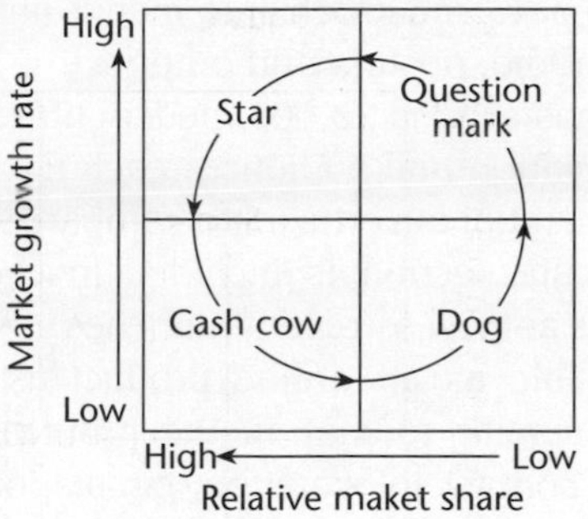

Figure 11 The anti-clockwise movement around the Boston Matrix

At each position within the matrix there are a number of opportunities open to the business. For example, at the cash cow stage the options are either to invest to maintain market share, or to minimize investment in the product, maximize the cash returns and grow market dominance with other products.

www.bcg.com

Bounce-back

A customer reply card, generally used in direct mail pieces or publications to help collect customer data or generate leads.

Boutique agency

A boutique agency is an advertising agency which employs creative specialists who offer design and copy-writing services. A boutique agency is also associated with an advertising agency that simply specializes in one or more types of service, such as creative ideas, designs, advertising copy or media planning. A boutique agency does not offer the full range of advertising agency services but can be used in conjunction with a number of other boutique agencies to provide complementary expertise.

BRAD (British Rate and Data)

BRAD (UK and the Republic of Ireland) is a monthly classified directory of advertising media. The directory categorizes the media into several different areas including: national and regional newspapers, consumer press, business press, new and electronic media (internet sites), television, video, cinema, radio, posters and outdoor.

Collectively, BRAD has around 13,000 media entries which detail the advertising costs, circulation and audience-reach figures. The directory is designed to allow potential advertisers to compare similar titles in the same market. An update section is included in each copy showing recent closures of titles as well as recent launches.

BRAD is also available as an online product as BRADnet, which contains information similar to that in the print version with some 13,000 entries, giving contact information, circulation data and target audience. The BRADnet system is accessed via the internet and enables users to search the BRAD database using multiple search criteria; the lists can then be transferred to Microsoft Excel.

www.intellagencia.com

Brand

A brand is a name, term, symbol or design (or combination of these) which is intended to identify the products or services of one seller or group of sellers. A brand name serves to differentiate a product from those of its sellers' competitors. The Coca-Cola brand encompasses a clearly recognizable logo and the use of red and white on all its related products in order to clearly identify the brand from all other imitators, which in several cases have adopted similar fonts and have used red and white (such as Virgin Cola).

Brand association

Brand associations can be defined as what a brand means to a customer, in terms of what they automatically think about the product or service when asked to recall their views or understanding.

There are a number of ways in which brand association can be achieved:

- from direct experience with the brand (e.g. a past purchase);
- from some form of communication about the brand (e.g. an advertisement);
- from some assumptions or inferences made from other brand-related information (e.g. word of mouth; see also **viral marketing**).

Brand associations provide a critical understanding of diverse consumer-related aspects; this can be used as a measure of the effectiveness of various forms of marketing activities:

- inference making – what the underlying advertising messages may convey to the audience;
- categorization – how the product or service is sorted in terms of its use by the customer,
- product evaluation – what the customer's personal experience of the product is, compared with the claims made;
- persuasion – whether the customer has been convinced to buy the product as a result of its seeming to be a solution to a problem or need;
- brand equity – how the product actually measures up compared with the competition;
- brand perception – the perceived values, features and benefits directly associated with the product or service.

Various studies are routinely carried out in order to ascertain customers' product or brand associations. Marketing research in this area can reveal exactly how effective advertising has been and how it has shaped the perceptions of the customer.

Brand cannibalization

Brand cannibalization is the sacrifice of one product for the benefit of another. Businesses have recognized for many years that brand cannibalization is an effective means by which they can introduce new products or add new products to their portfolio, thus attaining sustained sales and offsetting the competition. Cannibalization does mean increases in the cost of production and distribution as the business is effectively marketing to and providing for smaller target markets.

Cannibalization can protect a business's position, but it is often thought of as being a defensive move. True cannibalization is to be differentiated from own-label development by retailers. In this case, they are cannibalizing the products offered by suppliers which have proved to be steady sellers over a number of years. None the less, the development of own labels offers a defence against competitors, whilst sales are sacrificed in some existing 'manufacturer brands'. Trading sales from manufacturer brands to retailer brands at the point of sale is known as cross-brand cannibalization.

The most enterprising form of own-label cross-brand cannibalization reproduces the appearance (in terms of brand identity) of manufacturer brands with a request on the label for the customer to compare the manufacturer's brand with the own-label product. This form of cross-brand cannibalization represents a very aggressive and proactive merchandising strategy.

The major difference between the two versions of the strategy is the opportunity costs. The manufacturer-brand cannibalization leads to lower margins and profits and is seen as a purely defensive measure. For retailers, however, the conversion of manufacturer brand sales to own-label sales offers an increase in margins. The retailer also has exclusivity of the products and on this basis may be able to establish a successful outlet which only sells own-brand labelled products.

Brand challenger

A brand challenger may be a new product or service in the market, or perhaps an existing product which had been forced by circumstance to be a brand follower in the past. The brand challenger does not accept the dominant position of the brand leader in the market and will seek to undermine and replace that product or service by whatever means at their disposal.

The brand challenger, whilst not having the advantage of being as well established and universally well thought of by the market as the leader, has the opportunity to use its 'upstart' and often uncompromising image to make a definite move to supplant the brand leader. As far as the brand leader product or service is concerned, the brand challenger represents the gravest threat to their position in the market and the leader will seek to off-set and deal with any moves the challenger might make to undermine its position.

See also **brand follower** *and* **brand leader.**

Brand conditioning

Brand conditioning is the use of marketing activities aimed to develop a favourable attitude or impression of a brand. It is designed to improve the customers' belief and trust in the product, perhaps by associating the product with a good cause, or simply to highlight the principal benefits of the product as compared with the competition.

Brand development index (BDI)

A brand development index or BDI is an assessment of the percentage of a brand's sales in a market compared with the percentage of the national population in that same market. A brand development index calculation for the US would look like this:

$$BDI = \frac{\%\text{ of a brand's total US sales in 'Market X'}}{\%\text{ of the total US population in 'Market X'}} \times 100$$

Brand development strategy cycle

The brand development strategy cycle is a series of steps and processes aimed to describe the progressive building of a brand. The steps are considered to be a continuous cycle of events. The steps are:

1 invest in new brand;
2 use consumer communication strategies to build awareness of the product and its attributes;
3 develop a sales incentive programme, trade promotions, merchandising and point of sale to support the brand;
4 influence consumer choice through brand recognition, which builds customer demand for the brand;
5 encourage retailers to routinely stock the brand;
6 build up a wider distribution network;
7 strengthen ties with distributors and retailers;
8 as brand sales increase, encourage retailers to become more comprehensive in their stocking of the brand;
9 increased sales, cost efficiencies, volume building, and improved profits should free up funds to invest in a new brand, in which case return to step 1.

Hart, Susannah and Murphy, John (eds), *Brands: The New Wealth Creators*. New York: New York University Press, 1998.

Brand differentiation

Brand differentiation is also known as product differentiation. Brand differentiation involves the identification of tangible and intangible benefits or features that can be used to differentiate the brand from competing products or services.

Tangible features or benefits tend to be conscious and rational benefits such as the precise function of the brand and what it achieves or provides to the customer. The intangible benefits tend to be emotional or subconscious features that the business wishes to attach to the brand, such as providing warmth or nourishing food to the family, safety or other physiological needs. Differentiation strategies include featuring low prices, larger selections, convenient, efficient and rapid service, the latest or most trendy product, prestige or best value overall and reliability.

Brand equity

Brand equity includes discussion of creating measurable value for a brand name, often referred to as a super-brand or power brand; it also includes the measures of such value, which include rankings of the most valuable brands, return on investment (ROI) for advertising spending, or brand awareness. David A. Aaker identifies the measures of brand equity:

- Loyalty measures
- Price premium
- Satisfaction
- Perceived quality
- Leadership measures

- Differential measures
- Popularity
- Perceived value
- Organizational associations
- Brand personality

- Awareness measures
- Brand awareness
- Market measures
- Market share
- Market price

Aaker clearly identifies the fact that some of the most important assets of a business are intangible (company name, brand, symbols, slogans, associations, perceived quality, name awareness, customer base, patents, trademarks and supply channel relationships). These are the assets that make up the brand equity of the business and are seen as being a primary source to ensure competitive advantage and the future prosperity of the business.

Recently, many businesses have damaged their brand equity by undertaking marketing activities which have devalued the brand name (such as short-term price reductions or extending the brand range in an inappropriate manner).

Businesses such as Canada Dry and Colgate-Palmolive have created an equity management position to safeguard their brand names. Other businesses, such as Datsun who transformed themselves into Nissan, added to their brand equity by such a move. Others have been less successful, such as Schlitz beer.

Aaker, David A. and Biel, Alexander L. (eds), *Brand Equity and Advertising: Advertising's Role in Building Strong Brands* (Advertising and Consumer Psychology Series). Hillsdale, NJ: Lawrence Erlbaum Associates, 1993.

Brand essence

Brand essence, in many respects, is barely distinguishable from brand identity. Brand essence focuses upon what the brand actually does and how it looks. It is possible to visualize brand essence in terms of two key dimensions:

- the brand's core competencies/qualities;
- the brand's personality or style (including a brand's heritage and values).

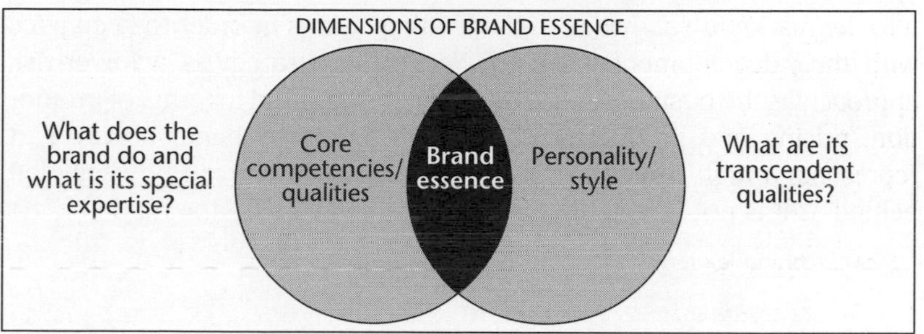

Figure 12 Brand essence

Brand extension

Brand extension is usually taken to mean the introduction of a new product, in a different product category, using the same name as is being used for an existing product.

Brand extension involves using existing customer loyalty to extend the range of product offerings (such as Mars ice creams or white chocolate Kit-Kat). The higher the level of customer loyalty, the more likelihood there is of success for the new product, thus making brand extension a low-risk expansion strategy. Brand extension is distinguished from multi-branding, which uses different brand names for similar products serving similar customer needs in the same market (e.g. Procter & Gamble and Unilever who offer a large number of different brands which essentially do the same job).

The key aspects of brand extension strategy are:

- extending a strong attribute or performance characteristic;
- extending a strong benefit association;
- extending an association with a consumer attitude or belief;
- extending the brand on the basis of brand essence (as distinct from its personality or benefits).

Brand follower

A brand-follower strategy may be adopted initially by a new business or perhaps a business that has established products and services that have little to offer in terms of added value. In essence, a brand follower copies or mimics the more successful products and services in the market.

A brand-follower strategy may involve the duplication of features and benefits similar to those of the leading brands, or perhaps setting the price within the same parameters. The strategy tends to be a reactive approach to marketing as it requires a close and constant investigation into the marketing activities of the leading brands in order to keep pace with their developments. On one level, this strategy is a lower-risk approach as the business is not breaking new ground in terms of promotion, pricing and product attributes. On the other hand, however, it represents a high risk strategy as the brand follower can be easily left behind as it is not innovating or at the leading edge of the market.

See also **brand leader**.

Brand identity

Brand identity is the range of visual features of a product which aim to assist recognition. Typically, a brand identity will include the name, image, typography, colour, package design and slogans developed and associated with the product.

Krumroy, Robert, *Identity Branding*. Greensboro, NC: Identity Branding, 2000.

Brand image

B

Brand image is a measurement of the totality of consumer perceptions about a brand, or how they really perceive it. This image may not always coincide with the brand identity. An organization will work tirelessly to ensure that the consumer's experience of the product or the service matches how the business would wish the consumer to perceive it.

Schmitt, Bernd H. and Simonson, Alex, *Marketing Aesthetics: The Strategic Management of Brands, Identity and Image*. New York: Simon & Schuster, 1997.

Brand leader

A brand leader is a brand which has the largest share or most dominant position in a market. A brand leader is the **benchmark** against which all other brands are compared; equally, those other brands attempt to emulate the brand leader and are known as **brand followers**. Clearly, many businesses attempt to become the brand leader in a given market, but it is not unusual for this position to be held, on a near equal footing, by several different brands. If brand leadership is measured simply in terms of market share, then there is often a clear leader. However, alternative measures of brand leadership revolve around the notion that the most influential and ground-breaking brand in a market is considered to be something of a brand leader. In this case, other 'copy-cat' brands (brand followers) may seek to emulate the brand's features, benefits and image in order to gain a more dominant position in that marketplace.

Although there is no clearcut blueprint in acquiring brand leadership, many of the more successful brands who claim to be brand leaders have followed a series of strategies which can be summarized as three steps (see Table 7).

Table 7 Three-step approach to brand leadership

Three steps of brand leadership		
1	Visioning	The business quantifies and assesses the relationship it wishes to have with its customers
2	Alignment	The business and its products and services are aligned to serve the desired relationships, both creatively and meaningfully
3	Anticipation	The business attempts to generate a degree of momentum which keeps it ahead of the customers' expectations in order to continue to engage them.

Aaker, David A. and Joachimsthaler, Erich, *Brand Leadership: The Next Level of the Brand Revolution*. New York: Free Press, 2000.

B

Brand loyalty

Brand loyalty is a consumer's preference to buy a particular brand in a product category; it is also the ultimate goal a business sets for a branded product.

Customers tend to become brand loyal when they perceive that the brand offers them the right mix of product features and images. Of equal importance is an appropriate level of quality at the right price. Having established this link, customers are then more likely to use this as the foundation of their buying habits.

Typically, a customer would make a trial purchase of the brand, and assuming that they are fully satisfied, they will continue to buy the brand on the basis of the knowledge that this is a safe and reliable purchase. Loyal brand purchasers will be prepared to pay higher prices and they will actively recommend the brand to other purchasers.

Brand loyalty is an important concept and a reality for businesses for the following reasons:

- It has been estimated that in the US, for example, an average business loses 50 per cent of its customers every five years (around 13 per cent annually). In any attempt to make a modest increase in growth of 1 or 2 per cent, the business has to add the annual loss to the equation. The reduction of customer losses can dramatically affect business growth and brand loyalty is seen as a major tool in achieving this goal.
- As brand loyalty increases, customers become less sensitive to price increases making it possible for the business to charge premium prices for its products and services. Brand loyalists recognize that the brand offers them some unique values that they could not enjoy from a competing brand. Brand loyalists may be encouraged to buy more by the introduction of promotions, but money-off deals only tend to subsidize purchases that were already being planned by the loyal customers.
- Brand loyalists are willing to search for their favourite brand and are less sensitive to promotions offered by competitors. The business offering thc products or services which enjoy brand loyalty also reap the benefits of lower costs in advertising, marketing and distribution.

Given the fact that it has been estimated that it costs some six times as much to attract a new customer as it does to retain an existing one, businesses constantly seek means by which they can foster brand loyalty. Typical approaches include those described in Table 8.

Freeland, John G. (ed.),. *The Ultimate CRM Handbook: Strategies and Concepts for Building Enduring Customer Loyalty and Profitability*. New York: McGraw-Hill, 2002.

Brand manager

'Brand manager' is a job title often used in the FMCG (fast moving consumer goods) area. Each product or service in this area of business is promoted via a specific brand and brand image.

The role of a brand manager is somewhat similar to that of an industrial product manager, although the role entails a more hands-on

Table 8 Means of achieving brand loyalty

Consumers must like a product in order to develop loyalty to it, therefore positive brand attitudes are important	To convert occasional purchasers into brand loyalists, habits must be reinforced.	Consumers must be reminded of the value of their purchase and encouraged to continue purchasing the product in the future.
To encourage repeat purchases, advertisements before and after the sale are critical	The business needs to become a customer-service champion.	Advertising shapes and reinforces consumer attitudes; these attitudes mature into beliefs, which need to be reinforced until they develop into loyalty.
The business needs to make sure that customers get what they want from the product.	To give customers an incentive to repeat-purchase, offer them the chance to win a prize, gift (with proofs of purchase) or in-pack discounts.	Tie up the distribution so that it is easier for the customers to buy the brand than competing brands.

responsibility for marketing activities and perhaps a less thorough technical knowledge of the product or service itself. The scope of the role differs from business to business and indeed from product area to product area, but brand managers may be responsible for a single territory only or for the global marketing of products and services. Equally, a brand manager may be responsible for a new range of products and services within the brand category.

Proctor & Gamble can be seen as one of the pioneers of brand management, a structural tactic which they have employed since the 1930s. A history of their brand management and its effect on the business can be found at www.pg.com

B

Brand mark

A brand mark is a recognized symbol, design, image, colouring or lettering that has become associated with a product or service. Brand marking is an integral part of establishing the overall identity and image of the brand. Unlike the **brand name**, the brand mark cannot be spoken as such.

See also **logo**.

Brand name

The brand name of a product or a service, which includes spoken letters, words or groups of words, used to help establish a **brand identity** and **brand image**.

Brand personification

Brand personification entails the projection of an image onto the brand. In other words, the brand is given a personality; typically the question asked is 'If the brand were a person, what sort of person would it be?'

This approach is known as projection, and enables the business to assign characteristics to the product or service and its associated advertising and marketing activities. The process usually begins with qualitative brand research to establish the essence of the brand make-up.

Establishing what the brand personality is can be an inexact science as there are often alternative personalities that could be adopted. One particularly successful technique is to establish a personality that closely matches the target audience. Some personalities focus on the aspirations of the target audience (such as designer goods), others may imply such notions as coolness or luxury, and others may simply rest on solutions to problems and be portrayed as a friend upon which a customer can rely.

An alternative approach is to develop a storyline behind the product or service, in which case the question that would be asked is 'Can you give me a story or scene that captures the essence of ——?' In these instances, a scenario is created which allows potential customers to envision themselves in the scene or story, a situation that could be applied to their own lives. This is a more personal application of the brand personality, as each member of the target audience will have an individual interpretation and placement in the story.

B

Brand placement

Brand placement has been a feature of movies and television programmes for a number of years, although it has only been recognized as such in the last decade. Brand placement can be described as being a paid product message within a programme, that aims to influence the audience. The appearance of a recognized brand is often unobtrusive, but planned by the programme makers.

The prospect of a movie star entering a bar and asking for a beer by its brand name, rather than simply requesting a beer, is too tempting an opportunity to ignore. Not only does the product or brand placement more closely reflect the reality of asking for a brand by name, but it also allows the inference that the star positively endorses the brand itself. The concept of brand placement has been somewhat extended in recent years and now covers the gamut of paid inclusion of branded products or brand identifiers through the broader range of media programming. There have been increases in brand placement in a wide variety of TV shows (particularly quiz shows where the name of the provider of the prize is identified). Brand placement now appears in novels and short stories, lyrics, music videos and even computer games.

Brand placement offers considerable advantages over traditional advertising in three major areas: conceptual, mechanical and behavioural (see Table 9).

Table 9 The advantages of brand placement

Advantage	Description
Conceptual	Brand placement is cost-effective compared with paying for a full advertising campaign. It can reach markets that are otherwise difficult to reach as well as portraying the brand in its natural environment (actually being used).
Mechanical	Consumers have developed ways to actively avoid overt advertising messages (zipping, zapping, and channel grazing). Brand placement cannot be subjected to these tendencies and practices. The hidden advertising messages within the programme or film is almost subliminal and is therefore not avoided by audiences. Traditional advertising is constantly facing increased avoidance tendencies, which are overcome using brand placement techniques.
Behavioural	Placing the brand in its context overrides the problem of habituation faced by traditional advertising. There is a tendency for the audience to ignore overt advertising once they have been subjected to the message a number of times. The context-based brand placement reinforces the learning process in a more subtle and effective manner.

Carrh, James A., 'Brand Placement: a Review', *Journal of Current Issues and Research in Advertising*, 20 (November 1998), pp. 31–49.

D'Astous, Alain and Chartier, Francis, 'A Study of Factors Affecting Consumer Evaluations and Memory of Product Placement in Movies', *Journal of Current Issues and Research in Advertising*, 22 (November 2000), pp. 31–40.

B

Brand positioning

See **product positioning.**

Brand pyramid

The concept of a brand can be thought of as a pyramid consisting of different layers of meaning and involvement. Typically, the pyramid is used to identity the gradual tiers of establishing the meaning of the brand and the attempts a business makes to increase the customer's degree of involvement, perception and interest in the brand (see Figure 13 and Table 10).

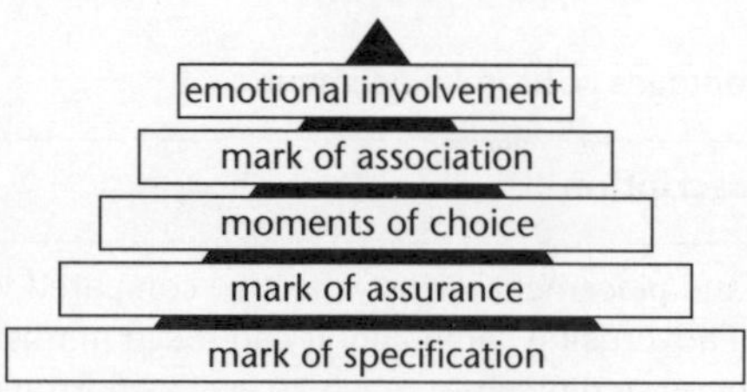

Figure 13 Brand meaning – the brand pyramid

Brand segmentation

Brand segmentation is closely allied as a term and concept to **market segmentation**. Market segmentation helps to identify the key target markets or audiences for a particular product or service, whereas brand segmentation takes this process a stage further by tailoring the brand to exactly suit the needs of those target markets.

Having identified the target markets, the business then adapts the look, feel and perhaps the brand image and name itself to each of the markets. An example of the process could take the following form:

1. The business identifies the price or quality segment that they wish to address (e.g. mass market, mid-market, up-market or luxury).
2. The business identifies the most appropriate distribution channels to serve that market (e.g. discount stores, mass merchant outlets, department stores or speciality retailers).
3. The business then identifies the key geographical locations appropriate to the price or quality segment identified as well as the chosen distribution channel(s), (e.g. urban, rural, high street or mail order).

Table 10 The levels of the brand pyramid

Brand pyramid level	Description and example
Mark of specification	At the simplest level this is an identifying mark to distinguish the product from alternatives. There is an implicit statement of specification, such as the amount of fat in a brand or the size of the brand.
Mark of assurance	The statement of a minimum standard of quality, implicit in the customers' notions of the business. Customers may view Ford cars as being reliable or McDonald's as having specific service and quality standards.
Moments of choice	This is the part of the process that requires the brand to be automatically associated with the fulfilment of a need. Customers may associate Coca-Cola with the need to quench their thirst or eat Mars confectionery for a boost in their energy levels. Ultimately, some brands have transcended this process and have become directly associated with a situation and a solution, e.g. 'Hoover the floor' or 'needing a Kleenex'.
Mark of association	This part of the process refers to the establishment of a close association between the brand and the customer. The customer is encouraged to make a close connection with the brand, perhaps on an emotional level, but more commonly associated with their self-image, such as Apple Mac users (who have been persuaded to consider themselves to be an elite), or an individual who is seen to be reading (and understanding) the *Financial Times*.
Emotional involvement	Full emotional involvement and connection is made between the customer and the brand. The brand becomes part of a suite of brands which identify the customer and his or her nature. An individual may be described as Gucci wearing, Porsche driving and Pimms drinking, all of which serve to identify and categorize the individual by virtue of the brands preferred and consumed.

B

Having followed this process, the business specifically addresses the key characteristics of the target markets in terms of age, education, income or marital status. The brand is then applied to each of these groups, taking into account the price/quality, distribution and geographical determinants and it is then decided whether to adapt or amend the brand offering as appropriate (such as offering budget versions of the same brand, larger sizes, changes in image, etc.).

Bedbury, Scott and Fenichell, Stephen, *A New Brand World: Ten Principles for Achieving Brand Leadership in the Twenty-First Century*. New York: Viking Penguin, 2002.

Brand strength

Guilding and Moorehouse identified seven factors which contribute to the strength of a **brand**:

1 market share and leadership (domination in the brand's market);
2 market (current and expected growth characteristics);
3 stability (brand loyalty);
4 trend (sustainability of the brand over time);
5 support (marketing expenditure and quality);
6 protection (patent, copyright, etc.);
7 internationality (brand spread and availability in different markets).

Brand switching

Brand switching refers to the buying habits of customers, who may well switch their allegiance to another brand for a temporary period. A consumer may have a brand preference, such as for Coca-Cola, but be faced with the need for a cola soft drink when the only option is Pepsi or another proprietary brand. In order to satisfy their need, they brand switch because of the unavailability of the preferred brand. In this case, the brand switch may be a one-off and when faced with the need on another occasion, the customer usually switches back to their preferred brand. In other instances, the brand switch may encourage the customer to remain with the new brand, finding it more appropriate to their tastes than they expected.

It is possible to research consumers' buying and switching habits in a marketplace to determine their attitude to brands and the likelihood of their switching from a brand. If a consumer's propensity to switch is known, then the market can be modelled to help predict future market share. This modelling process is valuable as it can reveal the relative positioning of competing brands in the market.

Businesses will commission brand-switching research to reveal the likelihood of competing brands stealing their customers. This can help focus attention on defensive measures to protect the market share and reduce the possibility of customers being tempted away (such as improvements to the distribution channels, which would remedy the problem as in the example given).

Brand valuation

In the early 1980s, Interbrand conducted what was probably the first ever brand valuation for Rank Hovis McDougal. The essence of the process was to be able to place a monetary value on the business's brands for the balance sheet. At the time, the Rank Hovis McDougal management needed this information in order to contest a hostile takeover bid. They could then use this information, with solid valuation figures, to request additional funding whilst demonstrating that the hostile bid was an undervaluation of the business.

Heavily branded products and services have a premium price or valuation attached to them which reflects the worth of the brand in both current and future-potential terms. As waves of acquisitions have come and gone in various industries, it has become common practice to undertake brand valuations with the purpose of attaching price tags to brand names. Equally, as in the Rank Hovis McDougal case, these valuations assist the business in successfully applying for additional funding from investors on the basis of the valuations.

In effect, the brand valuation encompasses the goodwill which would be acquired as a result of acquisition. Clearly, the goodwill is a complex mix of tangible and intangible assets attached to each brand name. It is commonplace for the valuation to be considerably higher than the actual tangible assets of the business as it will include intangible assets such as copyrights, patents, customer loyalty, distribution contracts, staff knowledge and experience.

In the 1980s, tangible assets accounted for over 80 per cent of brand valuations. Over the succeeding years this has gradually dropped to around 50 per cent of the brand valuations, underlining the point that the prices paid during acquisitions are more closely linked to the intangible assets.

Brand valuations are not simply carried out as a precursor to acquisitions, but are also of great value to brand management and strategy. Businesses recognize the importance of brand valuation as a true indication of the relative importance of brands in their portfolio of products and services (see Table 11).

Table 11 Applications of brand valuation

Brand management and development	Improving management communications	Benchmarking of competitors
Monitoring value year on year	Creating a brand-centric culture	Internal licensing, brand control and tax planning
Mergers and acquisitions	Joint-venture negotiations	Evaluating the economic damage of trade mark infringements
Financing and insolvency	Identifying the value of intangible assets	Balance sheets

Lindemann, Jan, *Brand Valuation*. Basingstoke: Palgrave Macmillan, 2003.

Brand valuation methodology

Brand valuations are similar in their methodology to valuing a business. Typically, a business would discount the profit or cash flows it produces to a net present value. Similarly, this is applied to brand valuations where profits produced by the brand are discounted to their net present value using a discount rate. The discount rate serves to reflect the risk associated with the income streams, in other words, the strength of the brand which drives the profit streams.

Central to brand valuation methodologies is an assessment of the economic use of the brand. In other words, how much value has been added to the business by owning the brand? It then follows that the relative security and growth prospects of the brand are a key indicator of the earnings potential of that brand. Brand valuation methodologies based on this premise look at four major aspects:

- *Financial analysis*, which looks at the earnings of the business and the earning specifically of the intangible assets;
- *Brand analysis*, which looks at the way in which the brand creates demand in particular markets and how much of this demand can be attributed to the intangible dimensions of the brand;
- *Market analysis*, which assesses the strengths and weaknesses of the brand (in order to assess the future earnings of the brand);
- *Legal analysis*, which establishes the fact that the brand is a legally owned asset and that there are no other claims of ownership outstanding or disputed.

Brand values

A concept closely connected with brand personality and **brand personification**. Brands are taken to be associated with a certain range of values; in effect the brand encapsulates a set of values, such as functional benefits or style.

These brand values which are associated with the product or service are then communicated through the brand to the consumer. Consumers have had a growing tendency to seek products and services which go further than simply providing for their needs and wants. Brand values, therefore, tend to rest on concepts such as trust and familiarity. Establishing clear and unequivocal brand values assists the business in building strong customer relationships and associations, which in turn lead to **brand loyalty**. This does mean that the business can place a greater long-term reliance on the brand in order to produce a steady income stream.

Goodchild, John and Callow, Clive (eds), *Brands: Visions and Values*. Chichester: John Wiley, 2001.

Branding

Branding is the adoption of values, image, awareness, recognition, quality, features, benefits and name, for a product. Branding, in effect, encompasses the intangible values created by a badge of reassurance, which simultaneously differentiates the product from the competition.

Businesses will brand their products primarily for differentiation, but branding is a hook upon which to hang the advertising and promotion of the product. Coupled with this, branding also encourages customers to accept and recognize the product, helping them with their buying decisions. Above all, branding reduces the need for the business to compete with other businesses purely on the basis of price.

There are several different types of brand or branding solutions:

- individual brand (e.g. Kit-Kat, Clio);
- blanket family brand name for all products (e.g. Dyson, Heinz);
- separate family names for different product divisions (e.g. Nescafé and Rowntree);
- company trade name combined with an individual product name (e.g. Ford Focus, Microsoft Age of Empires).

Branding is relevant only for those products: (i) that can achieve mass sales, because of the high cost of branding and the subsequent advertising; (ii) whose attributes can be evaluated by consumers. The advantages of branding include those listed in Table 12.

Table 12 Advantages of branding

• It facilitates memory recall, which encourages self selection and customer loyalty.	• It is a means of obtaining legal protection for product features.	• It assists with market segmentation.	• It builds a strong and positive image (particularly if the brand name is the business name).
• It makes it easier to link advertising to other marketing communications.	• Display space and point-of-sale promotions are more easily obtained.	• Associated products can be added, launched under the brand name.	• Personal selling is no longer a key requirement to obtain sales.

Guilding and Moorehouse developed the concept that there were five factors which contributed to brand valuation:

1 authorization, which involves justifying marketing expenditures;
2 forecasting and planning, which requires the setting of budgets and objectives;
3 communication and coordination, which stresses the internal marketing benefits;
4 motivation on the part of the business to see the benefits;
5 performance evaluation, which recognizes the lessons to be learned from the processes.

Keller, Kevin Lane, *Strategic Brand Management: Building, Measuring, and Managing Brand Equity* (1st edn). Englewood Cliffs, NJ: Prentice-Hall, 1997.

BRC (business reply card)

B

An advertising or direct marketing term used to describe a card distributed with an advertising piece. The card is pre-printed with the address of the advertiser or a fulfilment house engaged by the advertiser to deal with the responses. Normally, the return postage is prepaid by the advertiser. The recipient is offered the opportunity to respond to an offer, usually for further information.

Bricks and clicks

'Bricks' refers to a physical presence of a business, also known as mortar, whereas the 'clicks' are the virtual aspects of the business (its web presence).

See **clicks and mortar**.

British Code of Advertising, Sales Promotion and Direct Marketing

Advertising and marketing have been largely self-regulating since the 1880s. The first advertising code of practice was published in 1925 (Association of Publicity Clubs). The Advertising Association was set up in the following year with a department specifically charged with the task to 'investigate abuses in advertising and to take remedial action'.

The first international code of advertising practice was launched by the International Chamber of Commerce in 1937, which provided, amongst other things, a framework upon which many of the national self-regulation systems have been based.

In 1961, the Code of Advertising Practice Committee (later the Committee of Advertising Practice) came into existence, establishing the first British Code of Advertising Practice. This format has been developed over the years and the current codes can trace their lineage directly back to this original.

In 1962, the **Advertising Standards Authority** was established as an independent organization to administer the code. In order to do this, the Advertising Standards Board of Finance levies 0.1% on all display advertising. In 1974, the first Code of Sales Promotion Practice was established. The ASA remains a self-regulating organization working under the terms of the European Directive on Misleading Advertising (1984), with statutory reinforcement through the Office of Fair Trading.

On 3 March 2003, the eleventh edition of the CAP Code was published and advertisements, sales promotions and direct marketing produced after this date must comply with the CAP Code.

The Code applies to:

- advertisements in newspapers, magazines, brochures, leaflets, circulars, mailings, emails, text transmissions, fax transmissions, catalogues, follow-up literature and other electronic and printed material;
- posters and other promotional media in public places, including moving images;
- cinema and video commercials;
- advertisements in non-broadcast electronic media, including online advertisements in paid-for space (e.g. banner and pop-up advertisements);
- viewdata services;
- marketing databases containing consumers' personal information;
- sales promotions;
- advertisement promotions.

At its heart, the code seeks to ensure that the advertising is decent, legal, honest and truthful.

See also **American Marketing Association code of ethics; ethics/social responsibility.**

www.cap.org.uk

British Rate and Data

See **BRAD.**

Broadsheet

'Broadsheet' is a printing term which applies to a newspaper size normally over 50 cm deep and 10 columns wide.

Broadside

'Broadside' is an advertising, print-related term which is used to describe a single folded sheet of paper with printing on one or both sides. The sheet can be opened out to reveal a large advertisement.

Bulk mailing

Bulk mailing involves the mailing of large numbers of identical marketing communications at a reduced rate via the postal services. Each postal provider will have a set minimum quantity and can usually offer a sliding scale of charges per item dependent upon the weight of each item and the total number of items in the bulk mailing activity. The rates for bulk mailing differ from country to country.

Bundling

'Bundling' or 'product bundling' refers to a sales situation when two or more products or services are offered together, which enhances the overall offer to customers. The practice relies on the customer recognizing the relative value of the bundle compared with the opportunity of purchasing the products or services individually. The key considerations to businesses of bundling are:

- that it can increase unit sales volume;
- that it may reduce margins on the products or services;
- that new channels of distribution may be opened and new customers found;

- that the business runs the risk of cannibalizing sales of other brands, thus reducing unit contributions.

Bundling does give a business the opportunity to dispose of overstocks or items which are reaching the end of their **product life cycle** (by which time they will have little or no value).

Fuerderer, R., Herrmann, A. (Editor), Wuebker, G. and Hennig-Schmidt, H., *Optimal Bundling: Marketing Strategies for Improving Economic Performance*. Hamburg: Springer Verlag, 1999.

Buried ad

A term associated with newspaper or magazine advertising which is used to describe an advertisement surrounded by other advertisements. Alternatively, a buried ad can also be described as being an advertisement in the bottom corner of the page, with other advertisements surrounding the remaining two sides. In both cases, the ad is placed amidst other advertisements.

Buried offer

A sales and advertising term used to describe an offer contained in the body copy of an advertisement. The offer is made without the specific inclusion of a coupon or indeed the highlighting of the offer within the advertisement. The purpose of the buried offer is to reward customers who have actually read the full advertisement. Usually, the buried offer will be of greater value than the standard offer featured in the advertisement.

Business reply card

see BRC.

Buyer behaviour

Buyer behaviour seeks to explain the processes related to a customer choosing a product and following it through to purchase.

A stylized example of buyer behaviour can be found in Howard and Sheth's Buyer Behaviour Theory, a model to show how customers settle on a brand choice:

- There are many brands which customers are unaware of. Howard and Sheth suggest that this *unawareness set* means that these brands are not taken into consideration in the buying process.

- The customer makes a purchasing decision by choosing from his or her *awareness set*, which is made up of the brands of which he or she is aware.
- Within the awareness set, there will be a group of brands which automatically spring to mind and become, in effect, the short list; Howard and Sheth call this the *evoked set.*
- There are also brands which the customer is completely indifferent about and which are thus not considered. These are called the *inert set* of brands.
- Worse still, the customer may also be aware of the fact that several brands are not acceptable for a number of reasons, perhaps due to a negative experience with them. These are also not included in the short list of brands for consideration and are called the *inept set* of brands

Howard, John A. and Sheth, Jagdish N., *Theory of Buyer Behaviour*. Chichester: John Wiley, 1969.

Buying intent

This is a scale used to measure the likelihood of a customer or a respondent actually making a purchase of a product, service or brand. Typically, aggregated figures will be assessed recording the propensity of the customer to make a purchase, within which grades would be assigned such as 'will definitely buy' or 'undecided as yet'.

Buying service

An advertising agency and media-related term used to describe a service offered to advertisers. Normally, an advertising agency would act as the media buyer or service for the advertiser, ordering and placing advertising space in relation to an advertising campaign agreed with the client.

Some agencies are specialist media-buying services, which charge the client around a 5% surcharge on the advertising space cost (list price). Given that these media-buying agencies are accredited agencies with the media and usually attract a discount of 15% from the industry, this represents a marginally better deal for the client than paying up to 15% as a surcharge for purchasing advertising space, which can be expected from a full-service advertising agency.

Buying signal

'Buying signal' is a sales-related term used to describe the often coded message from a customer who wishes to be brought towards a sale close. Experienced sales personnel are adept at recognizing the signal from the customer and only need to prompt and suggest a close in order to achieve a sale.

The accepted methodology and response a sales person is expected to deliver upon hearing a buying signal is to follow up with a closing statement or closing question. For example, a customer may say, 'This fax machine is ideal for me, it is very popular isn't it? I suppose you haven't got any have you?' If the sales person were to reply by saying, 'Yes it is very popular, we won't have any in until next week', the customer would leave and buy elsewhere. Instead the sales person replies, 'They are great aren't they. I could have one delivered to you no problem next week if you'd like to pay now!'

Call centres

A sales, customer-service and direct marketing term used to describe a location or facility designed to take and make inbound and outbound telephone communications. Call centres are widely used for **telemarketing** by businesses aiming at direct sales contact with prospects.

Increasingly, call centres are located in areas remote from the regions they directly serve, largely because of the enormous cost differentials enjoyed by businesses prepared to relocate their call centres in less developed nations. Costs, in terms of both pay and premises, are considerably lower in countries such as India. Other notable call-centre-orientated countries include the Republic of Ireland, where pay rates and the fact that English is the primary language, as well as active canvassing, have caused a considerable exodus of businesses to that country.

Another major trend in call centres is that many businesses have taken the step to outsource to dedicated call-centre facilities, which are able to man the centre continuously. In addition, using the differentials in time zones, call-centre outsourcing allows a business to have a total 365-day coverage in normal business hours, again reducing costs by not employing staff during unsocial hours.

Call to action

A call to action is a sales, advertising and marketing term for what is often considered to be the final desired objective of many marketing communications. A call to action, in essence, is to convince the consumer to make a purchasing decision or a purchasing enquiry. A business may consider a call to action as being a simple case of persuading the potential customer to contact the business. For example, in the case of email marketing, the call to action would be for the potential customer to click on a link in the email to send them to a website.

CAPI (computer-aided personal interviewing)

Computer-aided personal interviewing is a sophisticated marketing research aid that utilizes a smart program which can filter out null or invalid responses. The respondent in the personal interview keys responses directly onto a computer (often a laptop) and the whole process is managed by a specifically designed program.

The program checks for invalid responses and is designed not to accept responses outside prescribed limits. By the responses being keyed in directly, the data is captured and can later be edited and downloaded to a remote location for analysis.

CAPI has been seen to be very effective in eliciting truthful and personal details about the respondent, who does not feel inhibited in answering questions. It has been very useful in the collection of data related to health matters and buyer behaviour.

Card rate (rate card)

'Card rate' or 'rate card' is an advertising and publishing term which relates to the published prices for advertisements. Traditionally, the card rate would have been related to newspapers and magazines, and represents the undiscounted costs of insertions. The term equally applies to broadcast media and internet advertising. The card rate can be likened to the recommended price and is often subject to discounts and negotiation. The prices quoted can be seen as the opening price for advertisement insertions.

Cartoon tests

Cartoon tests are used in market research, specifically in the field of qualitative research. The respondent is presented with a series of cartoons and prompted to suggest the dialogue or interaction of the characters featured in the illustrations. Usually, blank speech bubbles are featured to assist the respondent in suggesting conversations and interactions.

Cartoon tests are designed to access the hidden feelings and thoughts and perhaps also the subconscious thoughts and desires of the respondent, via visual imagery.

Cash cow

Cash cows are part of the **Boston Growth Matrix** and represent well-established products or services which are likely to be in the mature phase of their **product life cycle**. Cash cows are well entrenched, with sales that have grown to a stable level.

Cash cows are considered profitable products or services which are making positive contributions to a business's cash-flow. A business that has the advantage of having a cash cow or a number of cash cows as part of its portfolio is often encouraged by the income to consider the launch of product variants on the same theme. This often ends in failure as it only serves to fragment the market and undermine the general sales and profitability of the cash cow. Instead, many businesses use the cash generated by the cash cow to develop and launch new products and services. They will inevitably target growth markets, whilst they continue to support the cash cow and its hard-won market share.

Some businesses also attempt to strengthen the position of their cash cows but this is often a costly and unsuccessful strategy. This leads to businesses recognizing that they need to set an upper limit on the support, providing it maintains the market position.

Cash cows are vulnerable to cheaper substitute products which offer better or equal benefits. Equally, cash cows, being older than more modern substitutes, may have less technically developed means of production, making the unit costs higher and the cash cow less attractive than the newcomers. If a new competing product is successful, the cash cow's product life cycle will be shortened, reducing its financial return.

CASIE (Coalition for Advertising Supported Information and Entertainment)

CASIE was founded in May 1994 by the Association of National Advertisers (ANA) and the American Association of Advertising Agencies (AAAA) to guide the development of interactive advertising and marketing on the internet.

Category Development Index

See **CDI**.

CATI (computer-aided telephone interviewing)

CATI is a market research method that involves using an interviewer-administered telephone survey. The system utilizes a computer-based questionnaire.

Causation

Causation in the field of marketing refers to changes on one variable that observably trigger a change in another variable. For example, an increase in the base interest rate could be seen as having a causational impact on high-street spending and buyer confidence.

Cause-related marketing (CRM)

Cause-related marketing (CRM) is a commercial association between a business and a charity. Normally, this partnership involves the marketing of an image, a product or a service for mutual benefit. On the one hand, the business gains the commercial advantage of its relationship with the charity, whilst the financial and marketing expertise of the business is brought to bear for the benefit of the charity's goals and objectives.

Studies have shown that CRM is an effective tool in marketing and can enhance the overall reputation of a business. This is underlined by the generally accepted view that over 75 per cent of businesses actively involve themselves in some form of CRM and that nearly 90 per cent of consumers feel that CRM gives them a more positive view of a business.

Pringle, Hamish and Thompson, Marjorie, *Brand Spirit: How Cause-Related Marketing Builds Brands*. Chichester: John Wiley, 2001.

CDI

The Category Development Index (CDI) relates the percentage of a category's sales in a market to the percentage of the population in that same market. A CDI calculation for the US markets would be structured in the following manner:

$$CDI = \frac{\text{\% of a category's total US sales in 'Market X'}}{\text{\% of the total US population in 'Market X'}} \times 100$$

Census areas (US)

A US market research term used to describe the areas as defined by the US Census Bureau. The areas are categorized into either nine **census divisions** or four census areas. The census itself is a systematic measurement of the population and its whereabouts on a given day, when the census takes place.

Census divisions (US)

A means by which the US Census Bureau categorizes the areas of the US. The nine census divisions or groups of states are shown in Table 13.

Table 13 The US census divisions

Census division number	Census division name	States included in the division
1	Pacific	Alaska, California, Hawaii, Oregon, Washington
2	Mountain	Arizona, Colorado, Idaho, Montana, Nevada, New Mexico, Utah, Wyoming
3	West North Central	Iowa, Kansas, Minnesota, Missouri, Nebraska, North Dakota, South Dakota
4	East North Central	Illinois, Indiana, Michigan, Ohio, Wisconsin
5	West South Central	Arkansas, Louisiana, Oklahoma, Texas
6	East South Central	Alabama, Kentucky, Mississippi, Tennessee
7	South Atlantic	West Virginia, Delaware, Florida, Georgia, Maryland, North Carolina, South Carolina, Virginia, Washington DC
8	Middle Atlantic	New Jersey, New York, Pennsylvania, Rhode Island
9	New England	Connecticut, Maine, Massachusetts, New Hampshire, Vermont

Census regions (US)

A means by which the US Census Bureau categorizes the areas of the US. The four census regions (groupings of states) are shown in Table 14.

Census tract (US)

A US market research term which describes an area within a zip code group. The census tract denotes households with uniform social and economic characteristics. The tracts tend to have between 2,500 and 8,000 residents.

Table 14 The US census regions

Census regional area number	Census region name	States included in the region
1	West	Washington, Oregon, California, Idaho, Montana, Wyoming, Colorado, New Mexico, Arizona, Utah, and Nevada
2	Midwest	North Dakota, South Dakota, Nebraska, Kansas, Missouri, Iowa, Minnesota, Wisconsin, Illinois, Indiana, Ohio, and Michigan
3	South	Texas, Oklahoma, Arkansas, Louisiana, Mississippi, Alabama, Florida, Georgia, South Carolina, North Carolina, Virginia, Washington DC, Maryland, West Virginia, Kentucky, Delaware, and Tennessee
4	Northeast	Pennsylvania, New Jersey, New York, Connecticut, Rhode Island, Massachusetts, Vermont, New Hampshire, and Maine.

Channel captain

A distribution term which describes a powerful member of a distribution channel, in most cases the channel captain will be the manufacturer of the product. Manufacturers are not always the channel captain, as it very much depends on the structure of the market as well as the relative strength of the manufacturer, wholesaler or retailer.

In the case of most food products, the channel captains tend to be the supermarket retail chains, whose sheer buying power makes them the channel captains. Channel captains can determine exactly how the distribution system functions, making demands on manufacturers and wholesalers in terms of price, delivery mechanisms and even product specifications.

C

Channel management

Channel management involves the selection and motivation of distribution channel members and the periodic performance evaluation of their efforts and commitment.

A manufacturer, for example, may wish to agree performance targets (in terms of quotas, delivery times, procedures for dealing with lost or damaged goods, promotion and marketing agreements, training and overall service to customers). The manufacturer will periodically review these arrangements and be prepared to take remedial action when there are deviations from the agreed performance standards. In most cases, the producer or ultimate supplier controls or significantly influences the channel members, who are dependent upon and therefore subordinate to the producer.

Forsyth, Patrick, *Channel Management*. Chichester: John Wiley, 2001.

Cheshire

'Cheshire' is a direct mail and postal marketing and sales term which describe a brand of labelling machine. The machine can print continuous address labels, which it then cuts and fixes to envelopes or packaging (such as those used by Amazon). Cheshire labels are printed in a continuous form, generally 4 labels across and 11 down.

Churning

'Churn' or 'churning' is the percentage of customers who have been won and lost over a period of time. A business may have attracted 20% new customers, but at the same time lost 15% of its existing customers. In this way, a business may have an ever-changing customer base.

Much time and effort is expended on reducing the churn rate, which is often described as being the time that elapses from when a customer ceases purchasing from a business to the time at which they start re-buying the product or service. The concept is very much related to **customer retention**.

Circulation/audit

Circulation is a print-media and advertising term which describes the total number of copies of a publication that have been sold or distributed. Advertisers will pay advertising rates based on these figures: generally, the higher the circulation (in some cases the more targeted), the higher the costs.

Most reputable newspapers and magazines are independently audited (*see* **ABC**), because there is often a tendency to misunderstand the subtle differences between print runs, distributed copies, sales and returns policies. For most print publications, circulation does refer either to an audited figure or to the average number of distributed copies.

The term is also applicable to outdoor advertising where it is used to measure the total number of people who have an opportunity to see a billboard or poster site. Equally, circulation is used as an alternative to audience when describing the number of people watching or listening to broadcast media.

Classified Advertising

Classified advertisements are normally associated with local newspapers, although many national newspapers and magazines offer classified advertisement space. In most cases, the advertiser pays per work or column inch, the exact dimensions of which will differ from publication to publication. Typically, classified advertising focuses on individuals buying and selling electrical goods, cars, houses and services. Classified advertising may also include a number of **blind ads** from anonymous businesses.

Clicks and mortar

'Clicks and mortar' describes a business which has both an on-line and an off-line (physical) presence, as opposed to being a virtual business which only exists on the internet. Typically, the business may have an on-line presence in addition to its more tradition high street stores (such as Body Shop).

Clickstream

'Clickstream' is an internet advertising term used to describe the analysis of the ways in which visitors to a website travel through the pages of the site.

The clickstream data is used by web analysts to identify the optimum path through a site. Careful analysis will reveal the most satisfying website structure as far as the user is concerned (clear access and direction to popular pages in the site), as well as helping to maximize the cross-selling opportunity of the website.

Click-through rate

This is a web-related term used by advertisers to measure response to a

banner advertisement. A click-through occurs when a user clicks on the advertisement and is sent to the advertiser's webpage.

Client publics

'Client publics' is a term usually associated with non-profit organizations. The description is used more widely as an alternative description of the direct consumers of a product, as opposed to 'general publics' which refers to the population at large, usually with no ongoing association with the business or its products and services.

Closed questions

A closed question is most closely associated with questionnaires in market research studies. A closed question is typified by 'yes or no' or multiple-choice type questions. This structure forces respondents to place their answers in pre-determined boxes which facilitate statistical analysis. It is a considerably easier task to automatically process the results of questionnaires if questions are closed, because the limited number of specified answers can be sorted, correlated and summarized using a computer program.

The main disadvantages of closed questions revolve around the use of badly formed or non-tested questions which have not anticipated the likely answers, or do not allow sufficient breadth for the respondent to give an answer which most closely matches their honest response.

Closing

'Closing' is a sales-related term which is applied to the final stage (excluding after-sales service) in the sales process. Closing involves attempting to persuade the customer to make a commitment to buy. Typically, this comes when the salesperson has ended dispelling any buying hurdles or objections.

Cluster

'Cluster' is a term related to market research and is a category assigned to a neighbourhood. 'Clustering' is based on the assumption that the households share particular demographic, social and economic characteristics. The assumption goes on to suggest that these clusters can be measured and dealt with as having sufficiently similar characteristics for the individuals to have broadly similar buying habits, attitudes, needs and wants, and other responses.

See also **cluster analysis.**

Cluster analysis

Cluster analysis occurs in market research after the preliminary identification of a **cluster** or series of clusters. Cluster analysis involves multivariate statistical classification techniques aimed at discovering whether individuals fall into different groups. Quantitative comparisons of multiple characteristics are assessed with the guiding notion that the differences within any group should be considerably smaller than the similarities.

Everitt, Brian, Landau, Sabine, Leese, Morven, Ash, Carol and Schober, Jane (eds), *Cluster Analysis*. London: Edward Arnold, 2001.

Cluster sampling

'Cluster sampling' is a term related to both **clusters** and **cluster analysis** and is therefore a market research technique. Cluster sampling consists of selecting clusters of units in a population, often based either on a desired feature or on **random sampling**.

The advantages of using cluster sampling are related to the ease of data collection. Having identified a suitable cluster or set of clusters, the researcher can then more easily access the individuals as they are geographically close, which reduces research time and associated costs as well as enabling swifter follow up research and checking procedures.

Clutter

'Clutter' is a term related to advertising effectiveness and describes the bewildering array of advertising messages aimed at audiences. Each additional advertisement reduces the effectiveness of all other advertisements. The concept implies that customers are only able to take account of a defined number of messages; the role of advertising in this respect is to make the individual advertisements stand out in the customers' minds, and to offset the detrimental impact of the clutter.

'Clutter' is also used as a term to describe a printed advertisement or indeed a broadcast advertisement that is literally surrounded or hidden by other advertisements. All advertisements are competing for the attention of the reader, viewer or listener.

Coated stock

A print-media and direct marketing term which refers to paper with a slick, shiny and smooth finish, often selected for its quality appearance.

Cognitive dissonance

Cognitive dissonance is a term associated with psychological approaches to the study of buying behaviour. Dissonance takes place after a major purchase when the customer wrestles with the fact that they have made a decision about which they may now be unsure. Typically, customers begin to recognize aspects of the purchase which have dissatisfied them, or they are informed by others of the alternatives they could have chosen, after the event. Customers will attempt to rationalize their buying decision in order to eliminate this discomfort and degree of uncertainty (dissonance). Customers will seek the positives and ignore the negatives to justify their decision-making processes.

Festinger, Leon, *Theory of Cognitive Dissonance*. Stanford, CA: Stanford University Press, 1970.

Cold call

'Cold call' is a sales-related term which describes the process of sales personnel making a first contact with potential customers, either face to face or via the telephone. The potential customer, not having ever expressed an interest in the product or the service offered, is 'cold' to the sales pitch.

A cold call is often made to specific targeted customer segments which have been matched in some way as being potentially interested in the offering. Cold calling often involves a high percentage of rejection.

Schiffman, Stephan, *Cold Calling Techniques*. Avon, MA: Adams Media Corporation, 1999.

Collateral materials

Collateral materials are sales brochures, catalogues and other materials which are delivered to consumers (or dealers) by a salesperson, rather than by mass media. The delivery of collateral materials often offers the salesperson an opportunity to open or extend a dialogue with the potential customer.

Combination rate

'Combination rate' is an advertising and media-buying term which is used to describe a special media-pricing arrangement. Commonly, different types of media are owned by the same business and they may offer advertisers and agencies a special package deal which is a combination of print and broadcast advertising space.

Commercialization

Commercialization is the process of bringing a product or service idea to the marketplace. 'Commercialization' refers to putting into place the necessary manufacturing, distribution and marketing infrastructure required to deliver the product or the service to the end user.

Comparative advertising

Comparative advertising involves a specific reference, in an advertisement, to other products and services being offered by a competitor. Typically, the advertisement will explicitly compare the brand with one or more other competitive brands on the basis of attributes and benefits of the product or the service being advertised.

In the UK, in common law, comparative advertising using a competitor's trade mark is lawful unless the advertising includes false statements about another's goods, services or business which are made maliciously, causing damage, and thus amounting to trade libel. It is also unlawful for the advertising to contain a misrepresentation which is likely to mislead the public into buying the defendant's goods and thus harming the plaintiff, which amounts to 'passing off'. There are other restrictions on advertising – involving price comparison, in the Consumer Protection Act 1987; on credit, in the Consumer Credit (Advertisements) Regulations 1989; and more generally in the Control of Misleading Advertisements Regulations 1988 and the Trade Descriptions Act 1968.

See also **competitive advertising**.

Competitive advantage

The term 'competitive advantage' refers to a situation where a business has a commercial advantage over the competition by being able to offer consumers better value, quality or service. Normally, a competitive advantage would be measured in terms of lower prices, or in the case of more benefits and greater quality, higher prices are possible as a result of the competitive advantage enjoyed.

Porter, Michael E., *Competitive Advantage: Creating and Sustaining Superior Performance*. New York: Simon & Schuster, 1988.

Competitive advertising

Competitive advertising is, in many respects, similar to **comparative advertising**. If anything, competitive advertising is all the more explicit in terms of its comparisons and focus on the use of the brand, its features and advantages. A narrow line needs to be drawn in competitive advertising so as to avoid unfair and unfounded comparisons and claims as well as criticizing competing brands without foundation in fact.

Payne, Adrian, Christopher, Martin, Peck, Helen and Clark, Moira, *Relationship Marketing for Competitive Advantage: Winning and Keeping Customers* (The Chartered Institute of Marketing: Professional series). London: Butterworth-Heinemann, 1998.

Competitive analysis

'Competitive analysis' or 'competitor analysis' is a term associated with the detailed recognition of competitors in a given market or brand segment. Ideally, the business would investigate the strengths and weaknesses of its competitors and their products or services, encompassing their strategies, objectives, reaction times and patterns as well as consumer and market attitudes towards them. The analysis is aimed at assisting the business to identify key targets in terms of threats and opportunities. This technique can be seen as a key component of **SWOT analysis**.

Fleisher, Craig S. and Bensoussan, Babette, *Strategic and Competitive Analysis: Methods and Techniques for Analyzing Business*. Englewood Cliffs, NJ: Prentice-Hall, 2002.

C

Competitive information system (CIS)

A marketing data-capture system which aims to collect, collate and assess intelligence regarding the operations of competitors. Ideally, a CIS needs to encompass the following criteria:

- A clear decision regarding the information that needs to be collected.
- The design of appropriate data-capture methods.
- A system by which the data can be analysed and evaluated in a

timely manner (note that aged data may be of little value or at worst may suggest strategies that are no longer appropriate).

- A communications system which allows the dissemination of the information.
- The incorporation of the data into the decision-making process, coupled with an ability to assess the quality of the data collected so that systems can be refined.

Competitive intelligence

Competitive intelligence (CI) is increasingly seen as a distinct business-management discipline, which provides an input into a whole range of decision-making processes.

There are four stages in monitoring competitors, known as the Four Cs:

1 *Collecting* the information.
2 *Converting* information into intelligence (CIA: Collate and catalogue it, Interpret it and Analyse it).
3 *Communicating* the intelligence.
4 *Countering* any adverse competitor actions.

Competitive orientation

Competitive orientation is often seen as a measure of an organization's ability to recognize, consider and respond to the activities of competing businesses. A business which looks closely at the activities of the competition may be more inclined to make short-term adjustments to its own activities in order to offset any adverse effects on its operations.

Competitive orientation is another important factor in creating superior value for buyers. In order to create value for buyers which is superior to that of the competitors, a business must understand the short-term strengths and weaknesses as well as the long-term capabilities and strategies of both the main current competitors and the key potential competitors.

Slater, Stanley F. and Narver, John C., 'Does Competitive Environment Moderate the Market Orientation–Performance Relationship', *Journal of Marketing*, 58 (1994), pp. 46–55.

Competitive pricing

'Competitive pricing' policy relates to a pricing strategy that takes into account periodic or permanent movements in the prices charged by competitors for similar products and services offered in the market.

C

A business will systematically monitor the pricing structures of the competition and, if necessary, bring its prices into line with the major competitors. The 'competitive pricing strategy' approach is often closely allied to the overall **competitive strategy** of the business, linked to the stage that the product or service has reached in the **product life cycle**.

Campbell, Robert, *Competitive Cost-based Pricing Systems for Modern Manufacturing.* Westport, CT: Greenwood Press, 1992.

Competitive strategy

A potentially complex area of study, this includes all of the activities of a business aimed at maintaining a competitive edge in the market. The overall options of competitive strategy can be summarized as shown in Table 15.

Table 15 Competitive strategy options

Characteristics	Introduction	Growth	Maturity	Decline
Sales	Low	Rapidly rising	Peak	Declining
Costs	High per customer	Average per customer	Low per customer	Low per customer
Profitability	Negative	Rising profits	High profits	Declining profits
Customers	Innovators	Early adopters	Middle majority	Laggards
Competitors	Few	Growing number	Stable, but beginning to decline	Declining numbers
Marketing objectives	Create product awareness and trials	Increase market share	Maximize profits and defend market share	Milk brands and reduce costs
Competitive strategies				
Product	Basic product	Product extensions	Diversification	Eliminate weaker products
Price	Cost plus	Penetration	Competitive or matching the competition	Price reductions

⇒

Table 15 Competitive strategy options (*continued*)

Characteristics	Introduction	Growth	Maturity	Decline
Place	Selective	Intensive	More intensive	Eliminate unprofitable areas of the distribution
Advertising	Build product awareness among early adopters and dealers	Build product awareness and interest in the mass market	Focus on brand differences and benefits	Reduce to level needed to retain loyal customers
Sales Promotion	Heavy use to encourage trials	Reduce as mass market begins to make purchases	Increase to encourage and discourage brand switching	Reduce to minimum

Doyle, Peter, 'The Realities of the Product Life Cycle', *Quarterly Review of Marketing* (Summer 1976).

Wasson, Chester R., *Dynamic Competitive Strategy and Product Life Cycles*. Austin, TX: Austin Press, 1978.

Weber, John A., 'Planning Corporate Growth with Inverted Product Life Cycle', *Long Range Planning* (October 1976), pp. 12–29.

Competitor profile analysis

Competitor profile analysis is a market research methodology which seeks to quantify the key success factors in a given industry or market, incorporating the same criteria for major competitors. By assigning a score to the importance or closest match for both the industry and the competitor, an aggregate score is derived (see Table 16). These scores indicate the key determinants of success and show how well suited, or perhaps vulnerable, a given competitor may be. Obviously an extension of this profiling analysis would be to carry out a similar exercise with your own business.

Compiled lists

Lists are compiled from a variety of sources including telephone directories, public records, the US Census Bureau, US Postal Service information, surveys, birth records, door-to-door canvassing, and warranty cards

C

Table 16 Competitor profile analysis: Key success factors

Success factor	To industry (A)	To competitor (B)	Score (C)
Product quality	1 2 3	1 2 3	1 2 3 4 5 6 7 8 9
Product mix	1 2 3	1 2 3	1 2 3 4 5 6 7 8 9
Price	1 2 3	1 2 3	1 2 3 4 5 6 7 8 9
Distribution dealers	1 2 3	1 2 3	1 2 3 4 5 6 7 8 9
Promotion ability	1 2 3	1 2 3	1 2 3 4 5 6 7 8 9
Manufacturing operations	1 2 3	1 2 3	1 2 3 4 5 6 7 8 9
Overall cost situation	1 2 3	1 2 3	1 2 3 4 5 6 7 8 9
Financial strength	1 2 3	1 2 3	1 2 3 4 5 6 7 8 9
Organization structure	1 2 3	1 2 3	1 2 3 4 5 6 7 8 9
General management ability	1 2 3	1 2 3	1 2 3 4 5 6 7 8 9
Human resource quality	1 2 3	1 2 3	1 2 3 4 5 6 7 8 9

Total Weighted Score

A The scale of importance is 3 = high, 2 = moderate, and 1 = low.

B The scale for the rating is 3 = strong, 2 = moderate, and 1 = weak.

C a × b.

Completion rate

'Completion rate' is a term associated both with market research and with the sales process. In terms of market research, 'completion rate' refers to the number of respondents who successfully finish a questionnaire, normally postal or internet-based.

In sales terms the phrase is used to describe those customers who complete the sales process from initial inquiry to final purchase.

Complex segmentation

'Complex segmentation' is a market research term and describes a segmentation process or methodology which incorporates a variety of segmentation variables that would normally be sufficient to categorize the target markets individually. Complex segmentation is used to more clearly define specific target markets and to identify key and related aspects of their profile which may be useful triggers when framing marketing plans and activities.

Compulsive consumption

Consumer behaviour researchers have recently drawn attention to compulsive behaviour such as compulsive buying. Compulsive buying is related to low self-esteem or poor impulse control and is more common and occurs more frequently in women, who tend to buy clothing and jewellery. One likely context in which to study compulsive buying is internet shopping since it is an environment that may 'enable' compulsive buying. Recently internet addiction has become an important issue that has drawn attention in society. Compulsive buying and internet addiction behaviours have a number of similarities. Both are viewed as highly addictive and may lead to impulse control disorders and compulsive behaviours, which are higher in prevalence than other psychiatric problems. Because there is little research connecting compulsive buying to internet addiction, this study is valuable for examining the possibility that there might be a link between internet addiction and compulsive consumption among internet shoppers.

Faber, R. and O'Guinn, T., 'A Clinical Screener for Compulsive Buying', *Journal of Consumer Research*, 19 (1992), pp. 459–69.

Concentrated marketing

Concentrated marketing is a marketing strategy that sees a business focusing primarily on obtaining a brand leadership or market domi-

C

nance in a single market or a small number of markets. All marketing activities will be concentrated on having the maximum impact on these markets and the business will be less active in other markets as a result.

Concept testing

Concept testing is usually undertaken at a relatively early stage in product or service development. Concept testing attempts to discover whether attributes and other features of the prototype product or service have appeal to a carefully selected group of individuals who are representative of the proposed market as a whole. These individuals are exposed to preconceived ideas about the new product at an early stage in order to ensure that when the product is launched it exhibits many of the features or desired attributes identified.

Conjoint analysis

After being developed in the 1970s, conjoint analysis has become an important marketing research method. It is used to help define a new product or to suggest improvements to an existing one. Prior to the use of conjoint analysis, customers were not often able to assign specific degrees of importance to product attributes. The tendency had been for them to state that all of the attributes were of equal importance, but this was only the beginning of the problems. Other issues had emerged:

- Individual product attributes in isolation tend to be perceived differently than in the combinations found in a product.
- It is difficult for a survey respondent to take a list of attributes and mentally construct preferred combinations of them.
- If the respondent is presented with combinations of attributes that can be visualized as different product offerings, then the process is somewhat easier.
- Research in this area becomes impractical when there are several attributes that result in a very large number of possible combinations.

Conjoint analysis allows a subset of the combinations of product features to be used to determine the relative importance of each feature. The analysis is also based on the assumption that the relative values of attributes considered jointly can better be measured than when considered in isolation.

During the study, a respondent could be asked to arrange a list of product attributes in decreasing order of importance. The rankings can then be manipulated by a computer program to find the utilities of differ-

Table 17 Steps in a conjoint analysis programme

Step	Detail in the process
1	Product attributes are chosen, such as appearance, size, shape etc.
2	Values and options are chosen for each attribute.
3	The number of options is reviewed in light of the fact that the more options, the more onerous the task for the respondent.
4	Products are defined as combinations of attribute options and these options are then refined to produce a definitive set for the respondent to consider.
5	The form in which the combinations will be presented to the respondent is chosen, including verbal presentation, paragraph description, or pictorial presentation.
6	A decision is now made as to how the responses will be aggregated. Essentially, one of two options is chosen: either use the individual responses, or pool all respondents who have similar preferences
7	A decision is now made as to how the data will be analysed. Various complex mathematical models are applicable, including vector (linear) models and ideal-point (quadratic) models.
8	The data can also be processed by using statistical software written specifically for conjoint analysis.

ent values. The utilities can be determined using a subset of possible attribute combinations and the results can assist in the prediction of combinations that were not actually tested.

Setting up a conjoint analysis research programme is somewhat complex, but the steps shown in Table 17 are fairly standard.

C

Consumer expenditure survey (CEX) (US)

Data gathered in an ongoing survey by the Bureau of Labor Statistics, on the expenditures of consumers.

Consumer market

'Consumer market' is a blanket term used to describe all of the households or individual customers who buy products and services for personal consumption as opposed to making purchases on behalf of a business.

Consumer orientation

Consumer or customer orientation is a marketing principle that aims to describe a business which views its entire operations in terms of the end user, all product development, production, distribution and marketing being aimed at fulfilling consumer needs and wants. This is a marketing concept that is diametrically opposed to a product or production orientation, which seeks to find markets and persuade consumers to buy existing products and services that have not been designed initially to match their needs and wants.

Consumer panels

Larger **FMCG** and **market research** agencies often retain a group of consumers in specific sectors. They are used as respondents to answer specific research questions relating to product testing, taste testing, and advertisement testing amongst a host of other pre-market tests.

The consumer panels are ideal for immediate short surveys where a specialist rather than another form of sample is required. Data gathered from the consumer panels may be in the form of open discussions, observation, or complex questionnaires.

Sudman, S. and Wansink, B., *Consumer Panels* (2nd edn). London: Butterworth-Heinemann, 2002.

Consumer price index (CPI) (US)

The CPI measures the current cost of purchasing a fixed set of goods and services and compares it with the cost of the same set at a specific base year. In effect, this is a very similar technique, with an identical purpose, to the retail price index (RPI) as used in the UK. The measurement is a broad indication of the degree of inflation on basic goods. A standard 'basket' of essentials is usually chosen to reflect the real changing costs to the average customer.

C

Consumer profiles

A consumer profile aims to identify and quantify the habits and characteristics of the ideal or most common customer. As a primary market research and market segmentation methodology, it allows a business to more clearly match its products and services with the market, thus improving and influencing the buying habits of the customers.

Reliable data is required to create a consumer profile and this will tend to be derived from sources that can provide information on demographics which include variables such as age, gender and income level. Additional and more complex consumer profiling can also investigate and quantify such aspects as lifestyle and buying habits, but these measures need to be precise and match the basic criteria.

Consumerism

In the 1970s, 'consumerism' was taken to mean marketing and advertising specifically designed to create customers, in other words to make the product or service offerings as approachable and pertinent to the customer as possible. It is probable that consumerism can actually be traced back to the early 1960s when President Kennedy proposed that consumers should be accorded their rights in law.

Since that time, the term has taken on a radically different meaning in that it is more closely associated with the rights of consumers. Consumerism can be defined as illustrating to businesses in general that the customer is no longer to be considered as an individual who can be manipulated by marketing, and that their responses to advertising and other marketing activities are no longer as predictable as they may once have appeared. Consumers now flex their muscles and demand products and services that more closely match the claims made in marketing communications; they are supported by many non-governmental organizations or consumer groups coupled with local and national government bodies responsible for the advancement of consumer protection.

The two alternative definitions can be seen as being almost opposite in their meaning and it is the latter definition that tends to be applied to the term.

Aaker, David A. (ed.), *Consumerism: Search for the Consumer Interest*. New York: Free Press, 1982.

Continuity programme

A continuity programme aims to ensure that a particular marketing activity has a degree of control and coordination as well as longevity. Over extended periods of time, advertising and promotion needs to be consistent and non-contradictory as well as always being present as far as the target markets are concerned. In this respect, a continuity programme seeks to address continuous marketing communications of a consistent nature over a given period of time, which often extends beyond and links different advertising or marketing campaigns.

See also **continuous advertising**.

Continuous advertising

Continuous advertising involves the scheduling of advertisements to appear on a regular basis. This means that a business will tend to run advertisements even when it is known that there is a seasonal or periodic (but predicted and regular) dip in the demand for the product or the service.

The key point of continuous advertising is to constantly remind the consumer that the product or service is still available and to subconsciously reassure them that when they need the product once more, it will be available.

Stowell, Daniel M., *Sales, Marketing, and Continuous Improvement: Six Best Practices to Achieve Revenue Growth and Increase Customer Loyalty*. Indianapolis, IN: Jossey Bass Wiley, 1997.

Continuous data

'Continuous data' is a market research term which relates to the ongoing collection, collation and analysis of market information. Continuous data collection is now far more common than in the past as businesses recognize the fact that up-to-date and precise market data is essential for decision making.

Periodic or sudden shifts in the market can be instantly picked up and actioned if continuous data collection is underway. Typically, the analysis of data derived from **EPOS** or other sale-recording methods can be used for internal data gathering as can an analysis of the fluctuations in the share price of competitors.

Contra

A sales and advertising term which relates to a partnership agreement between two parties in which funds do not change hands. Typically, a supplier of products or services would offer their goods in exchange for advertising space in the media. The media owners would then be able to sell or offer the products or services direct to their readers, listeners or viewers and the supplier would receive 'free' space in return.

Alternatively, different media may chose to enter into a contra deal in order to trade advertising space at an agreed rate of exchange based on the rate card prices. Again, no funds would change hands and both sets of media would enjoy the benefits of exposure in alternative media vehicles.

Control group

The use of a control group in market research enables a researcher to assess the precise impact of a marketing activity. Notionally, the control group will not be exposed to the same stimulus as another set of groups, allowing the researcher to compare the reactions before and after the stimulus. The control group should remain largely undisturbed as their views and attitudes are pre-stimulus.

Controlled circulation

'Controlled circulation' is a print-media term, but now increasingly associated with web publishing. A controlled-circulation publication is only offered to a limited and often specialist audience. Controlled-circulation publications are increasingly common in the business-to-business market.

Revenue for controlled-circulation publications can come from one of two sources. First, the controlled nature of the publication is an implied statement as to the value of the material in the publication. It is therefore common to find that subscription prices are high and single subscription sales are the norm. As far as advertisers are concerned, the controlled publication offers a much more focused target audience and therefore these publications tend to charge premium prices for advertising space. This is based on the supposition that the readership is likely to be more receptive to targeted advertising messages than a more general audience.

Convenience products

This is a sales and merchandising term used to describe products which customers buy on a frequent basis. It is generally accepted that in these cases, the customer requires the goods immediately and makes little effort to make purchasing comparisons.

Conversion

'Conversion' is both a general marketing and a sales-related term which refers to the percentage of potential customers who are positively converted into actual buying customers. A salesperson will use the term to describe the number of actual enquiries that have been converted into sales. On the internet, the term is often used to describe the relative figures of visitors to the site and those who made a purchase from the site.

A **brand manager** will use the term 'conversion' to quantify the number of brand-using customers who have been persuaded to **brand switch** as a result of the marketing and advertising associated with the brand that is being managed.

Conversion rate

The conversion rate refers to the number of users that complete a **call to action** such as making an online purchase or completing an online form. The conversion rate is often measured as a percentage.

Cookie

A cookie is a computer code contained within a text file and is used to identify customers and analyse their online behaviour and website trends.

Cooperative advertising

This is an advertising arrangement in cases where a manufacturer agrees to pay a certain percentage of a retailer's or dealer's media costs for advertising the manufacturer's own products. This is seen as being an integral part of the management of a distribution channel where the various parts of the channel support one another's efforts.

Young, Robert F. and Greyser, Stephen A., *Managing Cooperative Advertising: A Strategic Approach*. New York: Free Press, 1983.

Copy

'Copy' is an advertising term which encompasses all spoken words or written text in an advertisement. The creation and wording of the promotional message is usually undertaken by an experienced **copy writer**.

C

Copy testing

'Copy testing' is an advertising research term which involves the investigation into an advertisement's potential effectiveness prior to the release of the advertisement into the media, specifically in relation to the **copy** content.

Alternatively, copy testing can also be associated with the measurement of consumer responses to an advertisement. In these cases, several different versions of the copy will be used in different media and an assessment can then be made of the most effective combination of copy.

Copy writer

A copy writer is usually either an advertising agency employee or a free-lancer employed to create advertising **copy**.

Core product

'Core product' refers to the stripped down version of a product, which simply identifies the main benefits, features and functions of the product or service. The product core is often well disguised beneath the totality of the product offering, which includes all of the associated features and benefits together with such aspects as **packaging** and **branding**.

See also **augmented product.**

Corporate branding

Corporate branding is a key marketing strategy that aims to establish a business's name as the primary **brand identity** across the range of products and services offered. Corporate branding seeks to make full use of a strong company name in order to support its various products and services, making it straightforward for the customer to be able to purchase with a degree of contentment and assurance that new products are not only closely aligned to the accepted brand name but also share the brand's characteristic quality and service.

Schmitt, Bernd H. and Simonson, Alex, *Marketing Aesthetics: The Strategic Management of Branding, Identity, and Image*. New York: Simon & Schuster, 1998.

Corporate hospitality

Corporate hospitality has a number of different goals, but is essentially concerned with the entertainment of individuals who are not the employees of the business.

The focus of corporate hospitality is to motivate and engage stakeholders, essentially those who are external to the business but who may influence its future commercial success. In this respect the strategy can focus on distributors or possible or actual customers. Targets can also include legislators or politicians. Most successful corporate-hospitality efforts tend to be associated with specific events that have some linkage to the business or interests of those being entertained.

Corporate identity

Corporate identity relates to the identifying marks of a business. This typically includes logos and brand names, which are then transposed onto all written communications, product markings, brochures, advertisements, websites, uniforms and vehicles etc.

Corporate identity is, in effect, a **branding** technique applied to a business rather than a product or a service. This is an extensive part of the marketing industry as it also involves the creation of both visual and audio symbols, colours and strap-lines.

Corporate image

Corporate image is concerned with the associations made by customers, the general public or other stakeholders when they are asked to state their impressions of a business. The responses may be positive or negative and in some cases there may be no impression at all. Public relations activities are designed to either heighten or amend the corporate image of a business.

In itself, a corporate image can be an intangible asset or a liability. A positive and strong corporate image can add immeasurably to the value of a business and in many respects is the embodiment of goodwill. In a more practical and day-to-day purpose, a corporate image can have an impact on a customer's likelihood to purchase products or services, or can attract investors or employees.

See **corporate marketing**.

Fombrun, Charles, *Reputation: Realizing Value from the Corporate Image*. Cambridge, MA: Harvard Business School Press, 1996.

C

Corporate marketing

Corporate marketing or advertising can be seen as an integral part in supporting the **corporate image**. Typically, a business will advertise itself rather than a specific product or service, with the sole intention of improving the long-term customer recall of the business.

Corporate sponsorship

Corporate sponsorship refers to situations where a business chooses to become involved, financially or otherwise, in supporting cultural or entertainment activities, in some cases charitable causes.

Corporate sponsorship allows a business to have a presence associated with a popular or prestige event, effectively underwriting the event itself financially in exchange for the association and the attendant benefits of free advertising and marketing activities at the event.

There is often a close association with **corporate hospitality** as it is often the case that the event is used for this purpose, to impress and entertain business stakeholders. In recent years, corporate sponsorship has come under attack from **ambush marketing** tactics, when other businesses have sought by various means to undermine the association between the core sponsor and the event.

Corporate strategy

Corporate strategy can be seen as the overarching strategy put in place by a business, which encompasses the deployment of their resources. Corporate strategy is used to move a business towards its goals in the various areas of its activities, including production, finance, research and development, personnel and marketing.

Lynch, Richard, *Corporate Strategy*. Englewood Cliffs, NJ: Prentice-Hall, 2002.

Corporate VMS

Corporate VMS (**vertical marketing system**) is a production, distribution and marketing system which brings all of the processes involved in bringing a product or a service to the market under the control of a single business (or series of related businesses).

Channel management is clearer and more tightly controlled, as all aspects of the channels of distribution are owned and managed by the same business or associated businesses within a group under common ownership.

Cost comparison indicator

An advertising term associated with the comparative measurement of the costs of different advertising media. Comparing unlike forms of media requires a careful approach which looks at the overall target-market audience figures for each of the media (in addition to this, the quality of that audience may be measured). Against these gross figures, the price of advertising in the different forms of media is calculated, and by dividing the cost by the estimated audience, comparative cost figures can be generated. These are usually quoted in terms of CPT or **cost per thousand**.

Cost leadership

'Cost leadership' refers to a situation where a business has achieved a lower cost of bringing a product or service to the market than its competitors. Under most circumstances, this cost-leadership factor is sufficient to make the business a market leader or, at the very least, for it to have a substantial market share. The term also suggests that the business has a greater capacity to spend on marketing activities because of the lower unit costs, assuming of course that the business is not pursuing a policy of low pricing to capture a greater share of the market.

Schiff, Jonathan B., *Winning in Cost Leadership: Best Practices in Activity-based Management*. Chichester: John Wiley.

Cost per acquisition (CPA)

CPA is a direct-marketing term which refers to the actual average costs incurred by an organization to secure a customer. For example, a direct mail shot with a total cost of £100,000 nets some 5,000 new customers, therefore the CPA is 100,000/5,000 = £20.

Cost per lead (CPL)

Cost per lead is the amount an advertiser will pay once a visitor has provided enough information for the advertiser to be able to start a relationship.

Cost per order (CPO)

An internet marketing-based term which describes the amount an advertiser will pay once a visitor has clicked through an advertisement or sponsored link and made the desired purchase.

C

Cost per rating point/cost per percentage point (CPP)

An advertising and media-buying term which refers to the cost for each 1 per cent of a specified audience related to the advertising space. In other words, an advertisement with a price tag of £20,000 in a magazine with a circulation of 200,000 would have a cost per rating point of £0.10.

Cost per sale (CPS)

Cost per sale is a measurement of how much advertising spend it takes to generate one sale. For example, if an advertiser spends £5,000 on online advertising which generates 50 sales, the cost per sale would be £100.

Cost per thousand (CPT)/(CPM)

Cost per thousand is a calculation used in advertising and media buying in order to assess the comparative cost of advertisement space in different media. By dividing the total cost of the advertising space with the number of readers, viewers or listeners, reasonable comparisons can be made between disparate forms of advertising media. Cost per thousand is often, confusingly, referred to as CPM.

Cost-plus pricing

Cost-plus pricing methodology is one of the most common forms of pricing policy; it is also one of the more straightforward forms. The pricing methodology simply involves adding a predetermined percentage or gross figure to the costs of production or purchase, thereby creating a price point for the product or the service.

This basic form of pricing does not individually take into account current market conditions and is in many cases considered to be too prescriptive in its structure for standard use. Despite this, many base prices are calculated in this cost-plus assumption.

Counter advertising

Counter advertising is a tactical advertising ploy which seeks to deliver a contrary marketing-communications message to an advertisement which may have preceded it. The advertisement may be used to adopt a controversial position on an issue or simply to counter the effect of the advertising it is trying to undermine. Typically, wildly different claims and positions will be in evidence between the two opposing advertisements.

Coupon

A coupon is a sales-promotion tool which is used to temporarily reduce the purchase price of a product or service in order to stimulate immediate demand. It is often used to promote new or improved products with the intention of creating a greater volume of sales, increasing repeat purchases, or to support the launch of different packaging, sizes and features.

CPA (cost per action)

Cost per action is the amount an advertiser will pay once a visitor has clicked through an advertisement or sponsored link and completed the desired **call to action**, such as making an online purchase or completing an online questionnaire.

CPC (cost-per-click)

Cost-per-click is an internet marketing formula used to price advertising banners. Advertisers will pay internet publishers (website owners) according to the number of clicks a specific advertisement banner attracts. Current costs are in the range of $0.10 to $0.20 per click.

CPM/CPT

See **cost per thousand.**

CPTM

CPTM is a variation on the cost per thousand and therefore related to advertising and media buying. CPTM means 'cost per one thousand targeted ad [advertisement] impressions'.

Creative(s)

A creative is part of an advertising agency team who is responsible for the artwork and the copywriting associated with the creation of advertisements. Creative individuals will tend to be working under the job titles of 'art director' or 'copywriter'.

Creative director

A creative director is usually a key player in an advertising agency and is responsible for the management and coordination of the **creative** team.

CRM

See **cause-related marketing** *and* **customer relationship management.**

Cross elasticity

Cross elasticity suggests that the quantity demanded of a particular product or service is related to, and varies as a result of, the price of other products and services. In other words, it is a measurement of the responsiveness of the demand for one product compared with the price of another.

The formula for measuring cross elasticity of demand for good X is:

$$\frac{\textit{\% change in quantity demanded of good X}}{\textit{\% change in price of another good Y}}$$

Cross elasticity can show that two like products are substitutes for one another, in which case it will have a positive influence. Therefore, an increase in the price of one will increase the demand for the other. In cases where products are complementary to one another, an increase in the price of one will have a negative cross-elasticity effect on the other. An increase in the price of console games will make the demand for consoles drop. Where there is no relationship between two products, the cross elasticity is 0, indicating that a change in the price of one of them will not affect the demand for the other.

Cross-selling

Cross-selling is both a general marketing term and a sales-specific term. In marketing, 'cross-selling' refers to situations where products can be seen as clear substitutes for one another and can, in fact, perform the same function. In these cases, customers may automatically **brand switch** if they see no perceivable advantage in buying one rather than the other. Clearly, marketing seeks to differentiate between products and services which are essentially the same in order to combat this tendency.

In sales, the term is more appropriate to the notion that, having been sold a product or a service, customers are more inclined to purchase associated products and services particularly if these are endorsed overtly by the purchased item or the seller.

Harding, Ford, *Cross-selling Success*. Avon, MA: Adams Media Corporation, 2002.

Cumes

'Cumes' is a media buying and advertising term used by A. C. Nielsen, which is an abbreviation for 'net cumulative audience'. Cumes measures the number of unduplicated individuals or households in a broadcast programme's audience within a specified time.

The scope of the term has been expanded to refer to any unduplicated audience of a print media or a medium schedule.

C

Customer acquisition cost

Customer acquisition cost is the total cost it takes for an organization to acquire a new customer. The most common method of calculating the acquisition cost is to divide the total amount spent on marketing (usually a specific campaign or promotion) by the number of new customers attracted by the campaign.

Customer loyalty

Customer loyalty seeks to define the degree to which customers will remain unpersuaded by other advertisers or other businesses' products and services and continue purchasing from the same business. Given the high costs of attracting new customers to a brand, businesses are prepared to invest heavily in customer loyalty programmes aimed at ensuring that customers do not **brand switch**.

Clearly, customer loyalty is very much related to the overall position of the brands and the business in the market and can be the foundation of an ability to generate profits. Low customer loyalty is generally accepted to be a measure of a brand's inability to sustain, nurture and satisfy customers.

Hill, Nigel and Alexander, Jim, *Handbook of Customer Satisfaction and Loyalty Measurement*. Aldershot: Gower Publishing, 2000.

Customer relationship management (CRM)

Customer relationship management is based on the assumption that there is a relationship between the business or the brand and the customer. This is a relationship that needs to be managed both through the individual buying stages and in the longer term.

CRM is very much related to fostering **customer loyalty** and, in the longer term, **customer retention**.

CRM can be used in call-centre support and direct marketing operations; software systems assist in the support of customer service representatives and give customers alternative means by which they can communicate with the business (such as mail, email, telephone etc.). Some sophisticated CRM software programs have email response systems which process incoming emails and determine whether they warrant a personal response or an automated response. Recent figures indicate that systems such as this can handle around 50 per cent of the requests from customers (typically requests for additional information, passwords, and responses to email marketing; see **e-marketing**).

Other CRM software systems incorporate the facility for customer representatives to take part in live chat rooms or co-browsing, offering the business a less formal environment in which to make contact with customers. CRM software can also queue customers on the basis of their profiles, by requesting that the customer logs in to the website. It is then possible to pass the customer on to individuals in the customer service team, who may be better suited to dealing with customers who share similar profiles. CRM software also provides the facility to maintain and update a database of information about each customer (in other words a case history).

Customer retention

'Customer' retention is a marketing term used to describe activities designed to ensure that customers remain customers and are not lost to the competition. Customer retention can measure the degree to which a business loses its customers and suggest reasons why they have been lost. Remedial activities are then put in place to stem this trend and in the longer term activities and policies are created in order to prevent similar losses. Data is collected regarding lapsed customers through customer retention-focused market research, which seeks to identify reasons why customers are no longer purchasing from the business.

Murphy, John, *The Lifebelt: The Definitive Guide to Managing Customer Retention*. Chichester: John Wiley, 2001.

Customization

Customization is a trend that has been slowly developing over recent years and aims to create bespoke products and services which closely match the exact needs and wants of customers.

Traditionally, customization and low costs were mutually exclusive: the period of mass production meant that unit costs could be driven down at the expense of providing specifically for customer needs. Uniformity was the key word; in order to purchase bespoke products and services, a premium price was charged by specialists or small suppliers.

Interactive technologies, such as the internet, now allow customers to purchase products and services produced to their own specifications by automated systems. This means that customers can be encouraged to specify their exact requirements, for which an additional, but not crippling, extra charge is levied. This allows marketing activities to revolve around this aspect of a business's offering, focusing on the personalized nature of the product or service. The process has also become known as mass customization as, in point of fact, the specifications are often prescriptive and the variations from the norm not as wide as one would expect to be the case.

Kelly, Sean, *Data Warehousing: The Route to Mass Customisation*. Chichester: John Wiley, 1996.

DAGMAR

DAGMAR is an acronym for Defining Advertising Goals for Measured Advertising Response, which is an advertising-effectiveness approach. The concept suggests that rather than measure the effectiveness of advertising in the conventional sense by noting shifts in the sales figures, a more holist approach should be adopted – that of achieving communications objectives.

See also **hierarchy of effects.**

Data marts

A data mart is taken to mean a repository of data (usually having been gathered from operational information and other sources) which is designed to serve the needs of groups of employees or departments in an organization.

The data mart or **data warehouse** needs to store the information in such a way that it is familiar in terms of content, presentation, and ease of use. The creation of a data mart begins with an analysis of the needs of the groups which will be using the facility, whereas a data warehouse tends to begin with the data and then tries to format this information so that it can be of use to various users.

Data marts would hold vital market and operational data of great value to marketing professionals in a business, access being ensured through either local or wide area networks.

Hackney, Douglas, *Understanding and Implementing Successful Data Marts*. Reading, MA: Addison-Wesley, 1997.

Data mining

Data mining is a database activity used by direct marketing and other areas in marketing to examine patterns and relationships within data sets, which can assist the business in predicting future results.

Data mining uses a combination of machine learning, statistical analysis, modelling techniques and database technology. The typical applications include **market segmentation**, customer profiling, evaluation of retail promotions, and credit risk analysis. Data is loaded into a database, where software then searches for similarities, differences and patterns that can aid the creation of market initiatives and product launches.

Ehling, Dagmar, *Data Warehousing for Dummies* ('For Dummies' series). Chichester: John Wiley, 1997.

Data protection

A term related to the storing of information, particularly customer details, on databases. Data protection, which differs in scope from country to country, seeks to protect individuals from the misuse of data which has been captured and stored by businesses or specialist data centres. In most cases, those with data files relating to them have the right to request sight of the material and to insist on amendments to it if it is inaccurate or misleading.

More broadly, data protection seeks to control the indiscriminate sale or sharing of data held on customers by businesses for the purpose of direct marketing and other marketing activities.

Carey, Peter, *Blackstone's Guide to the Data Protection Act 1998* (Blackstone's Guides). London: Blackstone Press, 1998.

Data Protection Act 1998 (UK)

The Data Protection Act 1998 received Royal Assent in July 1998 and came into force on 1 March 2000. It gives effect in UK law to the 1995 EC Data Protection Directive (95/46/EC). The Act applies to computerized personal data (as did the original 1984 Act), but now covers personal data held in structured manual files.

This clearly has implications for marketing in terms of the scope and uses of information collected, collated and used by an organization to target customers and track their buying and consumption habits.

The Act applies to the processing of personal data, including its collection, use, disclosure, destruction and holding. Organizations (called controllers) which process personal data are required to comply with the data protection principles. These require data to be:

- fairly and lawfully processed;
- processed for limited purposes;
- adequate, relevant and not excessive;
- accurate;

- not kept longer than necessary;
- processed in accordance with individuals' rights;
- kept secure;
- not transferred to non-EEA countries without adequate protection.

www.lcd.gov.uk/foi/datprot.htm

Data warehousing

Businesses tend to have a number of different databases with collections of information on various aspects of their business. A data warehouse combines this data and standardizes formats so that each of the separate databases can be interrogated as a whole. A data warehouse is a central aggregation of data (which can be distributed physically); a data mart is a data repository that may derive from a data warehouse or not, and that emphasizes ease of access and usability for a particular designed purpose. In general, a data warehouse tends to be a strategic but somewhat unfinished concept; a data mart tends to be tactical and aimed at meeting an immediate need.

Database marketing

Database marketing is the process of using a database to collect and analyse information on previous marketing activities for the purpose of using this information to help the development of future marketing activities.

See also **data mining** *and* **data warehousing**.

Dealer loaders

Dealer loaders are gifts or incentives given to retailers or dealers who agree to purchase a specified quantity of products.

Decision-making unit (DMU)

A decision-making unit is a group of people, usually taken to mean a business or perhaps a department, which makes collective decisions with regard to purchasing. A DMU can, of course, be a household although the term is usually more closely associated with business-to-business marketing and sales.

Stereotypically, a DMU would have individuals who fulfil the following roles: a specifier, an influencer, an authorizer, a gatekeeper, a purchaser and a user.

Decline

This is the final stage of the standard **product life cycle**. As sales decline, the business has several options:

- maintain the product, possibly by adding new features and finding new uses;
- try to reduce costs and continue to offer the product, possibly to a loyal segment;
- discontinue the product, selling off any remaining stock (if it is a product) or selling it to another business that is willing to continue the product.

An alternative to accepting the inevitable end of a product's life cycle is to consider re-launching the product, perhaps with a new image or identity. Many businesses will, however, consider terminating the product entirely and perhaps take the option of **dumping** the product (often continuing production) in another country.

See also **abandonment.**

Decoy

A term applied to marketing and advertising when a business promotes a product or a service or simply itself in order to generate interest. The advertisement is a cover for the promotion of something different, perhaps a higher-premium product or service. Once interest has been generated, the prospects can be approached to sell them the main purpose of the advertising and marketing campaign.

De-dupe

De-duping is an activity associated with direct mail campaigns which seek to identify and eliminate duplicate names and addresses on a database prior to sending mail out.

Delphi technique

The Delphi technique is a market research method which involves defining a problem by interviewing a panel of experts. The process requires **depth interviews** aimed at ascertaining the views of individuals such as managers, sales personnel and other participants and then aggregating the views in order to achieve a forecast.

Demographic segmentation

Demographic segmentation is a key market-segmentation process which involves segmenting the market into various subdivisions according to factors such as age, gender, income and social class. The divisions and their use are listed in Table 18.

Table 18 Market segmentation

Criterion	Use and description
Age	This is a segmentation variable which is used for clothes and other products and services where fashion, for example, is a key determinant of buying habits.
Education	A segmentation criterion which makes the assumption that higher education leads to a better standard of living. There is a linkage made between media habits and education and, accordingly, the media seek to tailor their content along educational and social-class lines. This assists advertisers in targeting their advertising.
Family	Family size has an impact on the size and frequency of purchases.
Gender	An important segmentation variable as many products and services are targeted towards males or females.
Income	A segmentation variable very much linked to education and age. Independently, income is a direct measure of possible purchasing power, but it needs to be considered in relation to other variables, such as age and size of family.
Nationality	There is increased interest in this segmentation variable, which looks at nationality or ethnic background. Businesses have recognized that there are clearly definable target segments for what would have been, in the past, speciality items, including food, clothing and hair products.
Politics	This segmentation variable is notoriously difficult to quantify as it is unlikely that many individuals are openly prepared to state their political affiliations. None the less, significant inferences can be made from the types of media which individuals read, as most (notably newspapers) have a distinct political leaning.
Social class	Social class is considered to be one of the most important segmentation variables, as it seeks to incorporate jobs and job status, as well as income, and is a multi-variant segment in its own right.

Demographics

Demographics is a market research term which involves the study of human populations. Demographics measures the size, density, location, age, gender, race and occupation, as well as other variables related to population statistics.

Dependent variable

'Dependent variable' is a market research term that applies to situations where a researcher identifies the key, or independent, variable upon which the demand relies. For example, a market research company may look at the demand for branded sports goods, recognizing that their demand is variable according to what is happening in the sports environment. If a football World Cup is currently being played, then the demand for branded national team kits is a dependent variable.

Depth interview

A depth interview is a market research interview technique and involves a face-to-face unstructured interview with a respondent. Depth interviews are used to collect meaningful and complete information from a respondent.

A depth interview is useful because the information gathered can be clear, in terms of interpretation and subsequent analysis. Respondents are also more willing to provide personal information. Depth interviews are, however, rather time-consuming and unless a standardized reporting system has been established, they are also complex to analyse. Amongst many of the different face-to-face market research techniques, the costs for this system are relatively high, given the fact that this is a one-to-one situation.

Descriptive research

Descriptive research is a branch of market research which aims to describe in great detail problems and situations arising in a market. The results are often used to determine the potential demand for a product or the attitudes of consumers in a given market.

Desk research

Desk research is the collection of **secondary data** in **marketing research**.

Developmental relationship marketing (DRM)

Developmental relationship marketing is a relatively new branch of marketing and aims to use product-segmentation techniques to identify key product images and related advertising messages. DRM looks at the behavioural patterns of consumers in an attempt to uncover their unconscious drives, which can then be addressed in the product message.

DRM is derived from behavioural marketing and seeks to understand what motivates consumers and encourages them to make a purchasing decision. In this respect, DRM deals with customers' needs, wants, aspirations, personality and attitudes. It then seeks to identify what triggers those motivators, as well as addressing issues such as **customer retention**.

Diary panel

A diary panel is a nationwide panel of households which is maintained by a market research agency. Each of the households is encouraged to keep a record of their purchases, consumption and usage of products and services. They then post the diary back to the agency on a monthly basis.

Diary panels not only provide the basic data on purchases, consumption and usage, but also give vital clues as to the respondents' reactions to promotions in the preceding month. A business would use the information to help calculate total market and brand share and identify brand switchers, or those who make repeat purchases. The system is also useful as it positively identifies which member of the family has used the product, how often, when and where, and for what purpose.

Many businesses believe that these diary panels provide a unique opportunity to understand what influences users and their purchasing patterns.

Dichotomous question

A dichotomous question can be found on a questionnaire and is usually a simple 'yes or no' question. Dichotomous questions are often used at the beginning of each section of a questionnaire in order to screen out those to whom the succeeding questions do not apply. Not all dichotomous questions are necessarily simple 'yes or no' questions, however. Provided there are clear choices for the respondent, who is then directed to the appropriate sub-section of questions, the exact makeup of a dichotomous question can vary.

Differential pricing

Differential pricing is a pricing policy which sets different pricing levels and structures to different markets or customer groups for the same products and services. An example of this would be to offer a different scale of charges for products and services to full-time students or the unemployed compared with standard pricing for other customers.

Differentiated marketing

Differentiated marketing is a partner strategy to differential pricing, as it provides the means by which different markets or customer groups, who are offered the same product at different prices, learn about the product. Differentiated marketing is also a broader issue as it addresses a business's need to target several markets simultaneously and create versions of the same product or service for each of those market segments.

Diffusion

The term 'diffusion' relates to the pre-launch stage of a product or a service. Diffusion is the process by which a new product or service gradually becomes known to its eventual users. In this respect, the diffusion process looks very similar to a **product life cycle**. There are several determinant factors which affect the diffusion process, notably the scale of investment, the structure of the market, the characteristics of the new product and its potential range of use.

See also **adoption**.

Direct channel

A direct channel is essentially a direct distribution system in which products and services are delivered straight to the end user, without the use of an intermediary. Notable direct channels include direct sales and, in some cases, standard mail order.

Direct mail

Direct mail is a direct marketing activity and involves, essentially, the sending of advertisements through the post. The direct mail usually includes advertisements or offers for products and services. An individual example of direct mail is a 'direct mail-shot', which is typified as being a solitary campaign, as opposed to a longer campaign that entails the mailing of several prompts to the same potential target market. Longer campaigns also use a rolling system of identifying their target markets and sending out batches of mail over a period of time, in order to increase the response rate and spread out the effect of receiving orders.

Direct marketing

According to the Institute of Direct Marketing, direct marketing is: 'The planned recording, analysis and tracking of individual customers' responses and transactions for the purpose of developing and prolonging mutually profitable customer relationships.' Direct marketing seeks to be a very targeted method of approaching customers. Having analysed and tracked customers' previous buying patterns, direct marketing activities aim to profit from more directly applicable offers.

Tapp, Alan, *Principles of Direct and Database Marketing*. Englewood Cliffs, NJ: Prentice-Hall, 1998.

Discretionary income

Discretionary income is the amount of an individual's income available for spending after the essentials, such as housing, food and clothing, have been paid for. Discretionary household income is *disposable income* after deductions to pay for basic necessities. Many businesses depend on this discretionary spending for their sales and profits. Discretionary income has continued to rise over the past few years as the result of the 'baby-boom generation' having reached their peak earning potential.

Discretionary market

A discretionary market is a segment of consumers which is not usually the main target of a business. A discretionary market can be considered as a subsidiary source of income and may be targeted periodically through marketing activities. The discretionary market does not match the main criteria associated with the product or the service and as such the sales are unpredictable.

Disguised/undisguised question

Disguised and undisguised questions are used in market research. A disguised question will be posed seeking to reveal information that is not readily apparent to the respondent. An undisguised question, on the other hand, asks for the information clearly and the respondent realizes the implications of the answer.

Display advertising

An advertising and media-buying term which is used to describe all advertising other than simply set-text-based classified advertising. Display advertising covers a wide range of complex features, requiring an element of design in terms of the mix of text and images.

Disposable income

This is the amount of income left to an individual after taxes have been paid; the remainder being available for spending and saving. In effect, disposable income should also take into account necessary deductions prior to the individual receiving their wage or salary. So, in this respect, the calculation of disposable income should also include pension contributions and insurance. In other words, disposable income can be likened to net pay.

Distribution

Distribution is the physical movement of products and services from the producer to the end user and often involves the transfer of ownership through intermediaries between the producer and the end user. A distribution channel ends when an individual or a business buys a product or service without the intention of immediate resale.

Part of the distribution channel involves organizations such as storage and transport companies and banks. They are integral parts of the distribution process, but they are outside of it in the sense that they never take ownership of the product or service; they merely aid the channel.

A business faces several different options when setting up the distribution system for its products and services. The key features of how this distribution channel is organized usually depend on the following:

- a determination of the role of distribution and how it will help achieve the marketing objectives;
- the selection of the type of channel and whether intermediaries are required;
- an assessment of the intensity of the distribution, which allows the business to assess how many intermediaries will be needed at each level and in each area;

- the choosing of specific channel members which most closely match criteria set by the business.

Distribution, direct

See **direct channel.**

Distribution, indirect

Indirect distribution involves the inclusion of at least one intermediary between the producer and the end user. The exact nature of the distribution channel in indirect distribution very much depends upon the type of product or service being delivered and, more especially, on the type of market to which it is being supplied. In effect, there are three different models of indirect distribution: consumer goods, business to business goods, and services. The key indirect channel choices can be seen in Table 19.

Table 19 Indirect distribution

Consumer goods	Business to business	Services
Producer to consumer, or door-to-door	Producer to user	Producer to consumer
Producer to retailer to consumer	Producer to industrial distributor to user	Producer to agent to consumer
Producer to wholesaler to retailer to consumer	Producer to industrial distributor to reseller to user	
Producer to agent to retailer to consumer	Producer to agent to user	
	Producer to agent to industrial distributor to user	

Distribution, multiple

Multiple distribution channels are used by businesses either to avoid dependence on a single channel, or when they wish to reach two or more target markets which could not be served by a single distribution channel. Multiple distribution channels tend to be used when a business

D

is essentially selling the same product to other businesses or direct to consumers. Multiple distribution channels are also widely used by multinational businesses and specifically those which have a broad portfolio of different products and services. In these cases it would be inappropriate to use the same distribution channel to supply products and services. Other businesses use multiple distribution channels to reach different segments within a single market, such as an airline selling directly to larger businesses whilst using travel agents to supply smaller businesses and consumers.

One of the most common reasons for the use of multiple distribution is when products are being sold into a market which has a wide geographical spread. It is necessary to use a wide variety of different intermediaries in order to service this market.

Distribution research

Distribution research is concerned with the investigation of data related to the distribution process. Different businesses adopt differing policies on the depth to which their distribution research is undertaken. Amongst the data being analysed are:

- the number of calls made in a given time;
- the number of sales compared with the number of calls;
- the average sales revenue per call;
- the average profit per call;
- the sales revenue per customer;
- the profit per customer;
- the average order value;
- the sales expenses compared with sales revenue;
- the sales expenses compared with profit per customer;
- the number of new accounts as a percentage of the total number of accounts;
- the actual performance compared with the forecasted figures.

Zipkin, Paul (Foreword), Song, Jing-Sheng and Yao, David D. (eds), *Supply Chain Structures: Coordination, Information and Optimization* (International Series in Operations Research and Management Science). Amsterdam: Kluwer Academic Publishers, 2001.

Dog

'Dogs' are one of the four parts of the **Boston Growth Matrix**. Products sold into segments in which the business is not one of the leaders, and in which the market is not growing, are classified as 'dog' products.

These products are likely to be in the mature phase of their **product life cycle**. Their markets exhibit slow, static or even negative growth. There will be little new business to compete for and any strategic moves to increase market share are likely to provoke a vigorous competitive reaction.

Dogs may be linked to low profits, and the prognosis for investment is generally low. Unless some new competitive advantage can be introduced, it is likely that these products or businesses will not be able to compete and will not attract the resources necessary to improve the product's position within the market. If future market demand is considered likely to last for some years, then the commercial risk of building market share may be worthwhile. Generally however, alternative more attractive investment opportunities could probably be found elsewhere. Therefore dogs should remain within the portfolio only so long as they contribute something to the business. Dog producers should provide:

- positive cashflow;
- contribution to overhead expense;
- strategic need.

If (as is often the case with dog products) the opportunity is moribund, decisive action should be taken such as:

- focusing attention and resources on other segments that will provide a better return;
- focusing attention and resources on other segments which can be ring-fenced;
- maximizing cash-flow from the product by reducing to a minimum all production and marketing costs;
- disposing of the product, selling the rights to the product or the business;
- dropping the product from the portfolio.

Dot-com Pure Play

A Dot-com Pure Play organization is a web-only or virtual business that only exists on the internet. Its sole point of contact with customers is through a website, although this may be supported by dedicated call lines. In its purest form, it is not a fulfilment house, in the sense that it holds no stock and relies on suppliers or manufacturers of the original product or service to carry out this function on its behalf.

The primary focus of the organization is to establish a marketable web presence and serve as a conduit for orders for a variety of suppliers and partners dedicated or otherwise.

Double permission marketing

Double permission marketing requires the potential customer to respond twice to confirm that they are willing to receive marketing communications from a business. Usually, this means that after an initial contact with the business (often initiated by the customer in response to a mailer), the business contacts the customer to confirm that they are still interested in receiving information and periodic marketing messages.

The primary focus of this method is to ensure that marketing and sales can concentrate on better prospects rather than those with a vague interest in the products and services. In the majority of cases, the second confirmation request is sent by the business by automated technologies such as email replies or bulk mailer systems.

See also **permission marketing.**

Double-truck/centre spread

'Double-truck' (US) and 'centre spread' (UK) describe two side-by-side pages in a magazine or a newspaper. This flexible advertising space offers a business the opportunity to produce a memorable advertisement, dominating the entire attention of the reader without the prospect of there being any other opposing interest on view. Normally a magazine or newspaper will charge a premium price for a double-page spread, which is another way of describing this term.

Drive times

A term applied to radio advertising which refers to the periods in the day during which the majority of listeners may be driving to and from work.

Drucker, Peter

Drucker was born in 1909 in Vienna and educated in Austria and the United Kingdom. After working as a newspaper reporter and an economist for an international bank, he moved to the United States in 1937. He taught politics and philosophy at Bennington College, then became Professor of Management at the Graduate Business School of New York University. Since 1971 he has been Clarke Professor of Social Sciences at Claremont Graduate University (the graduate management school there was named after him in 1984). Drucker has received several honorary doctorates and is the Honorary Chairman of the Peter F. Drucker Foundation for Non-profit Management.

In the words of Peter Drucker, 'marketing is the entirety of the business from the perspective of the customer'. He also wrote 'Marketing is so basic that it cannot be considered a separate function. . . . It is the whole business seen from the point of view of its final result, that is from a customer point of view.'

Drucker's main point is that marketing should be effective enough to make the process of selling superfluous.

Drucker, Peter, *The Essential Drucker*. London: Butterworth-Heinemann, 2001.

Dual branding

Dual branding or co-branding is a relatively new marketing concept, but has, in fact, been in operation for many years. Dual branding is particularly prevalent in the fast-food market where customers are offered quick takeaway services alongside traditional seated restaurants. The purpose of dual or co-branding is to offer a wider variety of products and services in one location. The brands are designed to complement one another.

There has been a considerable amount of experimentation, notably by Pepsico, who own the brands KFC and Pizza Hut. Outlets offer both products under one roof in a co-branding situation.

It is believed that co-branding can generate up to 20–30 per cent more sales, collectively, as against a standard restaurant, since co-branding appeals to a wider market.

Dual branding is distinct from offering competing or complementary businesses the opportunity to sell their products and services under the same roof. In many respects this system is very similar to dual branding as it performs the same function of attracting a wider range of customers to a single outlet.

Dummy

A dummy is a simplified version of a product or an advertised item, often used at pre-launch stage. A dummy is presented to interested parties and used in market research to elicit reactions prior to the product's being put into production or placed in the media.

Dumping

'Dumping' is a sales-related term which has considerably negative connotations. Dumping is the practice of selling obsolete products and services into an overseas market at a lower price (often) than had been charged in the home market. Normally products and services which have reached the decline stage of their **product life cycle** are identified as being ideal candidates for dumping procedures. Dumping is not entirely restricted to obsolete products as the practice can be seen as a means by which a business can achieve a significant influx of income by reducing its margins on a product or service overseas, whilst retaining the margins at home. Typical examples of products which have been dumped in this way are those in the consumer electronics industry, notably from Japan and South Korea. The US and the European Union have begun to set up protectionist measures to prevent this practice.

A rather more sinister form of dumping involves the selling of products which have not met with safety standards or other criteria in the home market. Overseas markets are chosen which have less protection for their consumers, notably in the pharmaceuticals market, where potentially dangerous drugs are sold openly overseas, though they have been either banned or restricted in use in the home market.

Economies of scale

Strictly speaking, 'economies of scale' is an economics-related issue. However, it has considerable implications in terms of marketing options. The basic concept revolves around the fact that a business needs to build up a critical mass. In other words, it must be large enough or powerful enough relative to the market to be able to influence it, if it is to enjoy any degree of success. It is notoriously expensive to establish a presence in any but the smallest markets. The concept suggests that small businesses are simply too small to register any impact on larger markets. Businesses need to be able to assign a certain percentage of their turnover towards product development and marketing activities. However, in the case of small businesses, this percentage, in real terms, will inevitably be minuscule. Once a business has reached a point where it is a larger trading entity, it can enjoy many of the benefits associated with larger-scale production or distribution. In other words, as the size and scope of the business increases, the generally held view is that the unit costs are driven down. The corollary is that when a business has achieved economies of scale, a greater amount of funds are available to further improve its market position.

Electronic point of sale

See **EPOS**.

Electronic trading exchange

An electronic trading exchange, in marketing terms, refers to a system which has been designed to link a business with its suppliers and distributors. The link is made via the internet and manages agreements with regard to suppliers, tenders, delivery, warehousing, and payment transfer. The system also allows the management of purchase agreements, and internal purchase processes (such as purchase authorizations, budgets, and stock management).

The system is designed to allow all of the partners in the distribution

Table 20 Email versus internet research

Email research strengths	Email research weaknesses
Visual images may be used to make the questionnaire more interesting.	It is not possible to know who actually completed the questionnaire.
Cost is very low	If the answer is not clear, there is no chance to follow up with another question to make it clearer.
Very little time is required to set it up.	Only those interested are likely to reply.
It is easy to see how many questionnaires are coming back; more can be sent if needed.	It cannot reach everyone; only those with email access.
The respondent can complete the questionnaire on their own.	Email filters (which stop unwanted emails) may prevent the email getting through.
If the questionnaire can be filled in without stating name, the respondent may be willing to answer personal questions.	The research relies on being able to get the email addresses in the first place.

⇒

and marketing process to have access to updated information, reduce costs in terms of the purchasing of goods, assist in tracking the progress of orders, instantly report on the receipt of goods, and facilitate payment.

E-mall

An E-mall is a form of internet shopping which seeks to replicate a traditional shopping mall, in effect bringing several traders under the same 'roof'.

E-malls allow the user to browse and purchase items from a variety of different store sites and use a single shopping basket to collect those items and then pay with a single transaction at the end of the shopping trip. The software used then sorts and forwards the orders to each of the retailers in the mall, who then ship the products direct to the buyer.

In marketing terms, to enhance the shopping experience, each of the stores has a distinctive look and feel, but the same methods of navigation and product selection are used. The E-malls tend to be enhanced with Online Order Tracking and Secure Credit Card Payment Processing.

E

Table 20 Email versus internet research (*continued*)

Internet research strengths	Internet research weaknesses
Audio and visual aids may be used.	You need to find out where the respondent lives to see whether what they are saying is useful.
The respondents can complete the questionnaire on their own.	If the answer is not clear, there is no chance to follow up with another question to make it clearer.
If the questionnaire can be filled in without stating name, the respondent may be willing to answer personal questions.	Only those who are interested are likely to answer the questionnaire.
It is a fast way of obtaining data.	It cannot reach everyone; only those with internet access.
It can be used for anyone who visits a website or just for those that have registered with the website.	It is not possible to know who actually completed the questionnaire.
Respondents do answer personal questions.	Only those who have found the website will take time to fill in the questionnaire.
Respondents can be asked whether they would help with further research.	There may be a long period before enough respondents have completed the questionnaire.

Belch, George E. and Belch, Michael A., *Advertising and Promotion: An Integrated Marketing Communications Perspective* (5th edn). New York: McGraw-Hill Higher Education, 2000.

E

E-marketing (internet marketing)

E-marketing involves the utilization of electronic communications technology in order to achieve specific marketing objectives. This is often referred to as 'email marketing'.

Using the internet as a way of collecting market research information offers two different methods, email research and internet (or website) research. Email research is just like a more modern method of a postal survey. A questionnaire is emailed (posted) to the respondents and they email it back. Internet research involves putting the questionnaire on a website and hoping that people will spend the time to fill it in. The relative merits of the two methods are summarized in Table 20.

E-metrics

E-metrics are the measurements or statistics which are used to judge whether a website or an e-business is effective.

End matter

'End matter' is an advertising, publishing and public-relations term used to describe material, outside the main body of a document, that may provide useful information for the reader. Three of the most common types of end matter are indexes, appendices and references.

Environmental scanning

Environmental scanning is the process of monitoring and detecting external changes in the environment. In essence, environmental scanning can be seen as a way of identifying new, unexpected, major and minor possible impacts on a business. Environmental scanning, however, needs to be systematic for two main reasons. First, indiscriminate collection of information is somewhat random and it may not be possible to distinguish the relevant from the irrelevant. Secondly, it provides managers with early warnings of changing external conditions in a measured and paced manner.

The key objectives of environmental scanning are:

- to detect scientific, technical, economic, social and political trends and events of importance;
- to define the potential threats, and opportunities for changes, implied by those trends and events;
- to promote future thinking in both management and staff;
- to alert the management to trends which are converging, diverging, speeding up, slowing down or interacting in some manner.

At the heart of environmental scanning is the notion that decision-makers need to be aware of the environment in which they operate. In this respect environmental scanning provides businesses with strategic intelligence which can help them frame their organizational strategies (see Figure 14). Environmental scanning should help a business to forecast in the light of the expectation of change.

Morrison, J. L., 'Environmental Scanning', in M. A. Whitely, J. D. Porter and R. H. Fenske (eds), *A Primer for New Institutional Researchers*. Tallahassee, FL: Association for Institutional Research, 1992, pp. 86–99.

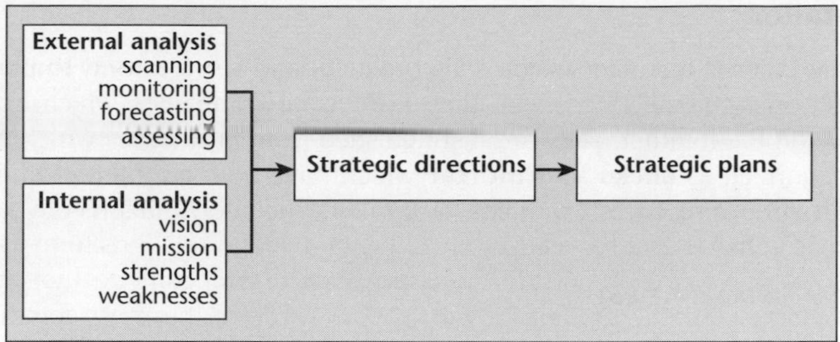

Figure 14 The role of external analysis in strategic planning

Source: J. L. Morrison, 'Environmental Scanning' (1992).

EPOS

EPOS, or Electronic Point of Sale, uses data which is captured electronically when a sale is made. The system relies on the presence of a bar code and an appropriate bar-code reader. When the sale is made, the salesperson scans the bar code, or in some cases, the shoppers do it themselves by using a portable reader. The bar code itself contains information including an identification of the item sold, the price and the store location. When coupled with a customer loyalty card, EPOS is able to match the purchases to the individual customer, thus enabling the business to target special promotions in line with the customers' buying habits.

The other major purpose of EPOS is to send the information to a computer which is linked to the purchasing facilities of the business. Having registered the fact that a product has been sold, the EPOS system, in conjunction with purchasing software, generates a re-order once a minimum order level has been reached. In this way a business can be assured that it has largely accounted for the stock which has left its shelves and that a process has been put in place in order for it to restock.

Brook, James, *Payment Systems: Examples and Explanations* (Examples and Explanations series). New York: Panel Publishing, 2001.

E-retailer

See **e-tailer**.

E-shopping

E-shopping is the process of buying products and services on-line via an **e-tailer** or through an **e-mall**.

E-tailer

An e-tailer is a retailer which sells products and services only through electronic channels. In effect, they are virtual companies which exist only on the internet. They are distinguished from businesses which are categorized as **clicks and mortar** which have both an internet and a high street presence. Examples of e-tailers include Amazon.com and Jungle.com.

See also **Dot-com Pure Play.**

E-testing

E-testing is essentially designed to reduce the risk of failures in web-based businesses and their associated applications. An e-testing programme will be applied to a business's on-line presence in order to identify performance, processes and security, as well as finding and eliminating defects. Businesses will often use e-testing specialists as an outsourced resource to essentially crash test their websites prior to going live on the internet.

Ethics/social responsibility

Ethics and social responsibility related to marketing have become increasingly important and much-debated issues in recent years. Essentially, there is an inherent conflict between the desires of business, industry, society in general and the consumer. All may have mutually exclusive goals and objectives. Ethical issues arise when one group's values conflict with those of another. In many cases there are multiple levels of conflict arising out of different sets of values.

The marketing industry has sought to pre-empt government intervention by establishing professional associations and accrediting bodies who are concerned with self-regulation, an example of which is the American Marketing Association (AMA), which suggests that marketing behaviour follows the rules set out in Table 21.

There is considerable conflict between the main purposes of marketing, the ethical criteria as stated by organizations such as the AMA, and the goal of making a profit. Given the fact that the major promotional objectives include accentuating the value of the product, the provision of information, the stabilization of sales, the stimulation of demand, and the differentiation of the product, it is clear from these inherent marketing responsibilities that it is difficult to retain an ethical balance.

Table 21 AMA recommendations

Guidelines	Description
Responsibility	The AMA urges those involved in marketing to accept responsibility for the consequences of their actions and activities. They are asked to consider their decisions, recommendations and subsequent actions in the light of satisfying and serving all stakeholders.
Honesty and fairness	The AMA urges marketers to show integrity, honour and dignity as professionals.
Rights and duties	The AMA suggests that there should be an inherent relationship between businesses and their customers firmly based on the notion of trust. Products and services should be safe and fit for the uses for which they were intended. They also stress that marketing communications should be truthful and that products and services should be sold in good faith. In the case of disputes, a grievance procedure should be established.
Organisational relationships	The AMA also suggests that those involved in marketing should be clearly aware that their actions are intended to influence the behaviour of others. In this respect, given their persuasive role, they should not encourage unethical behaviour or apply undue pressure to those they target.

Robin, D. P., and Reidenbach, R. E., 'Social Responsibility, Ethics and Marketing: Closing the Gap between Concept and Application', *Journal of Marketing*, 51 (January 1987), pp. 44–58.

www.ama.org

See also **American Marketing Association code of ethics.**

E

Exhibitions

Exhibitions or trade shows are events at which businesses display their products and services to their target markets. Many exhibitions, specifically trade shows, are aimed not at the general public but at business customers. There are a number of factors which may influence a business to consider attending an exhibition, including the location, the cost of stands, the other exhibitors, the type of visitor expected, and whether it is the norm for the industry in which they are trading.

Normally businesses will attend an exhibition in order to help maintain their market share, attempt to penetrate a market which they have interest in, develop their presence in a market, carry out market research or run a sales promotion.

Experimentation

Experimentation is a market research methodology during which one or more variables are changed, whilst others remain the same. This is so that **dependent variables** can be identified and the net effect on the other variables can be measured.

E-zine

An E-zine is an electronic magazine that can either be found on a website or be delivered to a user through email.

See also **e-marketing.**

Family branding

Family branding is a branding option which offers a business a head start in the launching of a new product. Customers are already aware of the family brand name and are therefore more likely to be inclined to risk purchasing the new product. Its association with accepted and trusted brand names, under whose umbrella it is launched, is a standard tactic of many businesses, such as Heinz.

Family life cycle

The 'family life cycle' is a market research term which considers age and life-cycle stage, but is essentially more multivariate as it defines such stages by the age, marital status, and employment status of the individual and by the age of the youngest child in the family.

Most life-cycle typologies are predicated on the basis of defining sequential stages through which a typical individual or family advances. In essence, these stages correspond to major changes in the pattern of development and help in reflecting the changing requirements and preferences of the individual or family. It is therefore possible to combine income trends and family composition to build up a picture of the demands which will be placed on that income over time.

The most commonly used form of life-cycle typology was developed by Wells and Gubar (1966). Given its venerable age, it is unsurprising that it is based on rather traditional family constructs. Their principal determinants are marital status and the presence or absence of children. There are nine stages in their typology, as shown in Table 22.

Wells and Gubar subsequently condensed their typology to three stages. The three life-cycle stages used are described in Table 23. Although this categorization is considerably simplified it does focus on the different demands and consumption patterns. Families which have reached the mid-point of the three categories have considerably different pressures on their income as children are present, they have less control over their budgets and consequently tend to spend more and borrow more.

Table 22 Life-cycle typology

Category	Description	Marketing implications
Bachelor stage	Young single people not living at home.	(a) Few financial burdens. (b) Fashion/opinion leader/led. (c) Recreation orientated. (d) Buy: basic kitchen equipment, basic furniture, cars, equipment for the mating game, holidays. (e) Experiment with patterns of personal financial management and control.
Newly married couples	Young, no children	(a) Better off financially than they will be in the near future. (b) High levels of purchase of homes and consumer durable goods. (c) Buy: cars, fridges, cookers, life assurance, durable furniture, holidays. (d) Establish patterns of personal financial management and control.
Full nest I	Youngest child under six	(a) Home purchasing at peak. (b) Liquid assets/saving low (c) Dissatisfied with financial position and amount of money saved. (d) Reliance on credit finance, credit cards, overdrafts etc. (e) Child-dominated household. (f) Buy necessities – washers, dryers, baby food and clothes, vitamins, toys, books etc.
Full nest II	Youngest child six or over	(a) Financial position better. (b) Some wives return to work. (c) Child-dominated household. (d) Buy necessities – food, cleaning material, clothes, bicycles, sports gear, music lessons, pianos, holidays etc.
Full nest III	Older married couples with dependent children	(a) Financial position still better. (b) More wives work. (c) School- and examination-dominated household. (d) Some children get first jobs; other in further/higher education. (e) Expenditure to support children's further/higher education. (f) Buy: new, more tasteful furniture, non-necessary appliances, holidays etc.

⇒

F

Table 22 Life-cycle typology (*continued*)

Category	Description	Marketing implications
Empty nest I	Older married couples, no children living with them, head of family still in labour force	(a) Home ownership at peak. (b) More satisfied with financial position and money saved. (c) Interested in travel, recreation, self-education. (d) Make financial gifts and contributions. (e) Children gain qualifications and move to Stage 1 (Bachelor Stage). (f) Buy: luxuries, home improvements e.g. fitted kitchens etc.
Empty nest II	Older married couples, no children living at home, head of family retired	(a) Significant cut in income. (b) Keep home. (c) Buy: medical appliances or medical care, products which aid health, sleep and digestion. (d) Assist children. (e) Concern with level of savings and pension. (f) Some expenditure on hobbies and pastimes.
Solitary survivor I	In labour force	(a) Income still adequate but likely to sell family home and purchase smaller accommodation. (b) Concern with level of savings and pension. (c) Some expenditure on hobbies and pastimes. (d) Worries about security and dependence.
Solitary survivor II	Retired	(a) Significant cut in income. (b) Additional medical requirements. (c) Special need for attention, affection and security. (d) May seek sheltered accommodation. (e) Possible dependence on others for personal financial management and control.

Duvall, E., *Family Development* (4th edn). Philadelphia, PA: Lippincott, 1971.

Hepworth, M., 'The Mid-Life Phase', in G. Cohen (ed.), *Social Change and the Life Course*. London: Tavistock, 1987.

Wells, William and Gubar, George, 'Life Cycle Concept in Marketing Research', *Journal of Marketing Research*, 3 (November 1966), pp. 355–63.

F

Table 23 The three life-cycle stages

Category	Description
Bachelor/Newly married	Head of household less than 45 years of age and has no children.
Full nest	Head of household is married/living with common-law partner and has dependent children, or is a single parent.
Empty nest/Retired	Head of household is over the age of 45 and has no dependent children.

Fast moving consumer goods

see FMCGs.

Fill-in

'Fill-in' is a market research term associated with questionnaires. Typically, sentences with options are given to the respondent, who then chooses the appropriate word to fit into the sentence to reflect their view on a particular issue. The fill-in technique is also used extensively in internet-based web questionnaires, where simple drop-down menus are generated at each fill-in point in a sentence. The respondent is able to click on the menu, scroll down, and select an appropriate word which best suits their answer.

Five Forces (PEST/SLEPT/STEEPLE)

This concept originally began with just four criteria, with the acronym PEST (Political, Economic, Social and Technological). These forces are seen as being the principal external determinants of the environment in which a business operates. In later years the Four Forces became five under the acronym SLEPT (Social, Legal, Economic, Political and Technological). The concept has now extended to include seven forces, using the acronym STEEPLE (Social, Technological, Economic, Educational, Political, Legal and Environmental protection).

The purpose of the 'Five Forces', or its variants, is to examine or audit where threats originate and where opportunities can be found. In other words, the broader STEEPLE acronym applies to the macro-environment (factors outside the organization). The main areas of interest within each letter are listed in Table 24.

Table 24 STEEPLE ('Seven Forces' acronym)

Letter	Description
S	Social and cultural influences, including language, culture, attitudes and behaviour which affect future strategies and markets.
T	Technological and product innovation, which suggest how the market is developing, as well as future developments in research and arising opportunities.
E (E1)	Economic and market competition, which consider factors such as the business cycle, inflation, energy costs and investments; an assessment is made as to how they will affect the level of economic activity in each market.
E (E2)	Education, training and employment, primarily the trends in these areas which may impact upon the availability of trained labour as well as the potential demands of new generations and probable expectations.
P	Political aspects, which focus on current and proposed policies which will impact on the business and the workforce.
L	Legal, which focuses on current and proposed legislation; of equal importance is the business's adherence to current laws and regulations.
E (E3)	Environmental protection, which addresses the business's current and future impact on the environment, working on the basis that environmental protection will continue to be a major issue in restricting and amending the ways in which a business operates.

See also **Porter, Michael.**

Porter, Michael, *Competitive Advantage.* New York: Free Press, 1985.

F

Five Ps

See **Seven Ps.**

FMCGs

'Fast moving consumer goods' (FMCGs) is a blanket description which covers products in great general demand by consumers. The category includes most food and drink products, as well as inexpensive electrical items.

Focus group

A focus group is a selected collection of individuals who are consulted as specialists during the market research process. As experts in their field they are considered to have useful and up-to-date information which could be of value to a business. In internet terms a focus group is a collection of online individuals who carry out online market research for organizations. The research can be in the form of e-questionnaires, **e-testing** and **mystery shoppers**.

Four Ps

See **Seven Ps**.

Fractional ad

A fractional ad (advertisement) is an advertisement that occupies less than a full page in a printed publication.

Fragmented market

A fragmented market is typified by a market situation in which no single business has a dominant market share. In a fragmented market the demands of the target segments are so disparate that it is difficult for a single business to provide them with a range of products and services to match their needs and wants. These markets offer a business the opportunity to gain a **competitive advantage** but individually each advantage is small as a result of the fragmented nature of the market.

Franchising

Franchising is a contractual and continuing relationship between a manufacturer, wholesaler or service organization and an independent business unit. The larger business provides management assistance and the right to use their trade mark, products and services in return for payments from the smaller business. The business providing the means by which the smaller one trades is known as a franchisor and the owner of the smaller business unit is called a franchisee. Collectively their association is known as a franchising system. There are two main types of franchising system. The most common is known as either product or trade name franchising, under which a supplier authorizes another business to use the trade name for promotional purposes, in order to sell a range of products and services.

Of equal importance as a franchising system is business format franchising, in which the parent company provides the smaller business with a proven formula and method of business operation. In both cases, not only does the franchisee pay an initial start-up fee (part of which pays for necessary training and orientation), but also two other payments are usually levied. The first payment is a percentage of the turnover or profits of the franchisee, paid usually on a quarterly or annual basis. The second payment relates to **cooperative advertising** in which the franchisee pays either a guaranteed minimum or a percentage of their turnover towards the general marketing and advertising costs of the franchising system.

Many businesses have turned to selling franchises in order to facilitate rapid expansion and provide instant injections of capital. Franchising also reduces the risk to the parent company because the franchisees are usually very motivated, as they are the ones who are taking the highest investment risk. Independent businesses tend to buy franchises in order to use an existing and proven trade name and business operation system. They can replicate the design of a business, use the technical and management skills of the parent company, and enjoy the promotional and distribution support already in existence.

In recent years franchising has become a heavily marketed area of operations and as a result of this growth there have been a number of problems arising out of franchising systems. Many businesses selling franchises project unrealistic incomes, do not provide the promised levels of support, encourage the sale of too many franchises in a given area, or unjustifiably terminate or choose not to renew a franchising agreement with an established business.

Franchising does offer long-term marketing potential to a business, as independent businesses can be encouraged to invest in a product or service concept, taking the lion's share of the risk. At the appropriate time the parent company can choose to buy back the franchise and return full control of the trade name to themselves, having established their products and services in the marketplace.

Notable successful franchises include Body Shop, McDonald's, Burger King, KFC and Prontaprint.

Raab, Steven S. and Matusky, Gregory, *The Blueprint for Franchising a Business.* Chichester: John Wiley, 1987.

Freelancer

The term 'freelancer' describes an individual who is casually employed by an advertising or marketing agency for a fixed period of time, or for the duration of a particular project or activity. Freelancers are usually highly experienced individuals in a specific area, such as copywriting or design and illustration. The availability of freelancers enables an agency to restrict its ongoing human-resource commitment to core workers and individuals, while having the flexibility to employ freelancers on an 'as and when' basis.

Frequency

The number of times the average person in a target market is exposed to an advertising message during a given period.

Frequency cap

An internet term relating to the number of times a single visitor to a website will be shown the same banner advertisement. Each visitor will be shown the advertisement a given number of times, before it is replaced by another advertisement in the same space.

Front matter

'Front matter' is a term associated with both advertising and publishing and refers to information, usually in text form, which precedes the main body of a document. Front matter is generally used as an introduction or a summary of the main information which will be encountered by the reader later in the document.

Fulfilment piece

A fulfilment piece is a single item which can be found in a fulfilment package. Collectively, fulfilment packages are promotional or informational items that are sent in response to a customer request. The term is most closely associated with advertisements which offer target audiences the opportunity to receive detailed information about a product or service.

Gantt chart

The Gantt chart was developed as a production control tool by Henry L. Gantt in 1917. Gantt was a US engineer and social scientist and developed this type of horizontal bar chart, which is now commonly used to illustrate a media schedule.

Gantt charts are also used in project management. They provide a graphical illustration of a schedule which assists the planning, coordination and tracking of each task within an overall project. Gantt charts can be simplistic horizontal bar charts, drawn on graph paper, or, as is more common, can be created using proprietary software, such as Microsoft Project or Excel.

Gap analysis

'Gap analysis' is both a general management and a strategy term as well as having its applications in marketing.

Gap analysis attempts to identify what is known as the 'performance gap'. It does this by comparing current objectives, which have been defined in the corporate goals, against forecasts (particularly of sales) which will arise from existing strategies. Businesses often encounter performance gaps when they switch their objectives, or when environmental conditions change, as well as through the relative success or failure of competitors.

It is standard practice to illustrate gap analysis in terms of a graph. This measures sales against time. Both the existing strategies and the new strategies are plotted and the difference between the two highlights the performance gap.

Gatekeeper

A 'gatekeeper' is a theoretical individual who is part of a **decision-making unit**. They are responsible for controlling the flow of information to the others in the group.

General Electric Screen Matrix (the General Electric (GE) business screen)

The GE Screen Matrix is essentially a derivation of the **Boston Growth Matrix**. It was developed by McKinsey and Co. for General Electric. It has been recognized that the Boston Consulting Group Matrix was not flexible enough to take into account broader issues.

The GE Matrix cross-references market attractiveness and business position using three criteria for each – high, medium and low. The market attractiveness considers variables relating to the market itself, including the rate of market growth, market size, potential barriers to entering the market, the number and size of competitors, the actual profit margins currently enjoyed and the technological implications of involvement in the market. The business position criteria essentially look at the business's strengths and weaknesses in a variety of fields. These include its position in relation to the competitors, and the business's ability to handle product research, development and ultimate production. It also considers how well placed the management is to deploy these resources.

The matrix differs in its complexity compared with the Boston Consulting Group Matrix. Superimposed on the basic diagram are a number of circles (see Figure 15). These circles are of variable size. The size of each represents the size of each market. Within each circle is a clearly defined segment which represents the business's market share within that market. The larger the circle, the larger the market; and the larger the segment, the larger the market share.

Generic brands

A generic brand is a product which is unbranded and the term usually refers to a standard consumer product which is in constant demand. Typical examples include milk, potatoes and aspirins.

Geo-demographic segmentation

Geo-demographic segmentation is a natural extension of **geographic segmentation** and suggests that it is possible to segment the market according to similarities in lifestyle, economic wealth, social class and other criteria.

The technique is especially useful in the identification of potential sales territories, sites for retail outlets, direct marketing and the distribution of sales literature. One of the most common forms of geo-demographic segmentation is the **ACORN** system, but latterly this has been

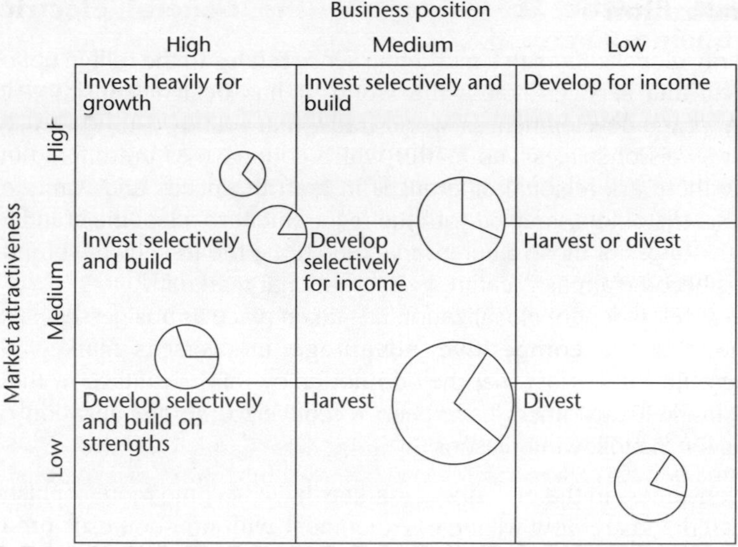

Figure 15 General Electric (GE) Matrix

all but replaced by more sophisticated systems including **MOSAIC** and **SUPERPROFILES**.

In the UK, many of the geo-demographic systems may lose their value and their appeal, as individuals will have the option to opt out of such data-gathering exercises previously gleaned from specific and almost universal figures collected via the UK electoral register.

Geographic segmentation

Geographic segmentation consists of dividing a country into regions, which normally become an individual salesperson's territory. In sales terms, larger businesses may well subdivide these areas and assign salespeople to specific parts of each area, with a regional sales manager to oversee operations, to control targets and to act as a link between the salespeople and the business.

In international sales and marketing, different countries may be deemed to constitute different market segments. Typically, geographic segmentation will consider cities, counties, regions, states or even nations as having broadly similar characteristics, usually expressed in terms of the prevalent culture of the area.

Globalization

The term 'globalization' in a marketing sense relates to the rolling out of products and services across the world. It has been a considerable feature of the development of world trade, that brands can now enjoy similar levels of success, no matter which country they are offered in. Clearly there are regional differences in both the needs and wants of overseas customers, coupled with the requirement to adapt the brand to meet the tastes of those different markets. None the less, global branding has become a major feature in international marketing.

The development of globalization has taken place as businesses have sought to find a **competitive advantage** in overseas markets to compensate for the fact that they do not enjoy this advantage in their home market. Customers have been receptive to the globalization of brands for the following reasons:

- Consumers in the majority of markets have become more sophisticated and are now willing to experiment with non-domestic products and services, as well as demanding products and services which they have consumed whilst abroad.
- This has been enabled by the gradual elimination of trade and travel barriers, coupled with strong political resolve to open most markets to competition.
- The globalization of brands has been coupled with the internationalization of both print and broadcast media, which carry advertisements for global brands.
- Given the fact that a domestic market may be saturated, businesses increasingly look for markets in which their products and services can continue to grow.

Keegan, Warren J. and Keegan, Mark C., *Global Marketing Management* (7th edn). Englewood Cliffs, NJ: Prentice-Hall, 2001.

G

Green marketing

In many respects green marketing can be considered as an attempt by businesses to make a proactive move before legislation and regulations force the business to adopt new product development, production and marketing strategies. Essentially, green marketing revolves around safety, satisfaction, social acceptability and sustainability, which are more commonly known as the 'Four Ss' of the green marketing mix (see Table 25).

The green marketing mix begins with the satisfaction of customer needs, whilst ensuring that both the product and the production are safe

Table 25 Green marketing's Four Ss

Green Ss	Description
Satisfaction	of the customers' needs
Safety	in respect of the product, production and other activities of the organization
Social	acceptability of the above
Sustainability	the ability of the organization to continue to operate as it currently does

with regard to the consumers, employees, society and the environment in general. The mix also recognizes that the product needs to be socially acceptable, in terms both of its production and of the way in which it is marketed and advertised. Finally, the product itself needs to be sustainable. In other words, the business needs to predict any imminent or future legislation and attitudes which may preclude it from producing and marketing its products and services in the way it currently does.

Allied to the green marketing mix are what are known as the internal and external green marketing Ps. The standard **Four Ps** of product, promotion, place and price are coupled with the overtly environmentally orientated need to provide information, examine processes, adopt appropriate policies and consider people, both internally and externally. There are also what are known as the 'external green Ps', which are:

- *Paying customers* – which looks at customers' needs in relation to green products and services, as well as information that they may require.
- *Providers* to the business in terms of how green their products and services are.
- *Politicians* – this concerns the increasing public awareness of green issues and how the political system is gradually, through legislation, impacting on the conduct of business.
- *Pressure groups* – this concerns addressing their main issues and identifying which groups of individuals are involved.
- *Problems* – this seeks to identify any past, current or future environmental issues that are attached to the business's operations.
- *Predictions* – this concerns the investigation of scientific research which may identify potential environmental problems in the future.
- *Partners* – this addresses how green or environmentally aware any other businesses with which the business has an association are.

G

This aspect considers how these partners are perceived and whether there will be any environmental problems arising out of their operations.

Wasik, John F., *Green Marketing and Management: A Global Perspective*. Oxford: Blackwell, 1996.

Growth stage

This is the second stage of the **product life cycle**. In the growth stage, the business seeks to build brand preference and increase market share. The implications for the **marketing mix** are as follows.

- *Product quality* is maintained and additional features and support services may be added.
- *Pricing* is maintained as the business enjoys increasing demand with little competition.
- *Place*: (distribution) channels are added as demand increases and customers accept the product.
- *Promotion* is aimed at a broader audience.
- *People*: market research looks at the opinion of customers and tries to make sure that the product lives up to what the customers are expecting as well as searching for new markets that may not be buying the product at the moment.

Onkvisit, Sak and Shaw, John J., *Product Life Cycles and Product Management*. London: Quorum Books, 1989.

Guerrilla marketing

Essentially, guerrilla marketing techniques are unconventional marketing activities that are designed for maximum impact with the use of scarce resources.

Jay Conrad Levinson is considered to be one of the originators of the concept having written *Guerrilla Marketing* (1984). He states that the need for guerrilla marketing can be seen in the light of three facts:

1. Because of big business downsizing, decentralization, relaxation of government regulations, affordable technology, and a revolution in consciousness, people around the world are gravitating to small businesses in record numbers.
2. Small business failures are also establishing record numbers and one of the main reasons for the failures is a failure to understand marketing.
3. Guerrilla marketing has been proven in action to work for small

businesses around the world. It works because it's simple to understand, easy to implement and outrageously inexpensive.

An ideal example of guerrilla marketing was carried out by BestOffer.com who received excellent free media coverage as a result of their unconventional marketing activities. When they launched in San Francisco, they promoted a 'Pain Free Parking Day' and gave away free parking, and when they launched in Los Angeles, they had 'Painfree Commuting Day' and gave away 20,000 gallons of petrol (gas). As a result of their activities they were able to generate over forty-five minutes of free television news coverage.

Levinson's site is www.gmarketing.com

Levinson, J. C., *Guerrilla Marketing*. New York: Houghton Mifflin, 1984.

Gutter

'Gutter' is a print-media and advertising term used to describe an area on a page. The gutter is the margin next to the fold in a publication. It is also the vertical centre of a double-truck or double-page spread. Text does not normally extend into the gutter area of a page; however, advertisements and illustrations often cover this area, giving the impression that the two pages of a spread are, in fact, one entity.

Halo effect

The term 'halo effect' has two distinctly different explanations. In general marketing terms, the halo effect refers to the theoretical transfer of goodwill from one product or service in a business's portfolio to another product or service. The theory holds that the established qualities and customer perceptions of a particularly well-known brand can be transferred by association to another brand, assuming, of course, that there are elements of the branding which allow this association.

The alternative definition of the halo effect is when customers' perceptions of a business, product or service are influenced in some way by the business's activities elsewhere and not directly related to that product or service. A business's stance with regard to a particular issue, such as concern for the environment, gives the impression that the business generally has that view related to all of its operations. The halo effect will transfer this positive image and improve customers' confidence in purchasing products and services from that business. Businesses will attempt to measure the net benefit from this halo effect in terms of its impact on sales.

Harris and Ogbonna

Harris and Ogbonna, writing in 1999, were concerned with the development of a market-orientated culture. Essentially, they extended the view of the Boston Consulting Group and proposed the notion that changes in the culture of an organization were inevitably caused by either internal or external environmental conditions. They recognized that the development of an organizational culture which aimed to be market-orientated would prove to be beneficial both to the customer and to the business: '[t]he organizational culture that most effectively and efficiently creates the necessary behaviours for the creation of superior value for buyers and, therefore, continuous superior performance for the business' (Narver and Slater, in Harris 1999, p. 86).

The move towards a market-orientated culture could either be a planned change, which had been fully thought through, or a revolutionary change as a result of sudden environmental changes. It was generally accepted by Harris and Ogbonna that a middle ground was, perhaps, the best way of progressing towards a market-orientated culture. They recognized that evolutionary change would not only meet long-term environmental changes, but also allow the business to gradually adapt.

Harris, Lloyd C. and Ogbonna, Emmanuel, 'Developing a Market Oriented Culture: a Critical Evaluation', *Journal of Management Studies*, 36:2 (1999), pp. 177–96.

Hiatus

'Hiatus' is an advertising and marketing term which refers to a period of time between scheduling advertising and marketing activities. Typically, this represents a period during which there is no visible presence of the business and its products and services in the media. The hiatus period, dependent upon the length of time involved, usually entails the business running general advertising not specifically designed to promote a product or a service, but to retain a degree of presence and awareness in the market.

Hierarchy of effects

The 'hierarchy of effects' is a marketing term which seeks to describe the buying readiness of a target audience. It follows the stages which a buyer passes through towards making a purchase. Its importance is in helping identify possible marketing activities which can be addressed at each stage to move the buyer further on in the process. The six stages – awareness, knowledge, liking, preference, conviction and purchase – are described in Table 26.

Clearly, what the hierarchy of effects misses is the after-purchase period, where it has become increasingly apparent, in marketing and in business in general, that a solid after-sales service programme can short-circuit the hierarchy of effects. Assuming that the customer has passed through these stages at least once, it is possible, by incorporating after-sales service into the overall programme, to ensure that the customer begins with preference or conviction and does not have to be taken through the earlier stages of the hierarchy of effects.

Hierarchy of needs

See **Maslow, Abraham.**

Table 26 Hierarchy of effects

Stage	Description and implications
Awareness	This stage recognizes that the customer may have little or no knowledge of the product or service. It is at this stage that marketing activities should revolve around building up a customer's familiarity with the product or service via a brand name.
Knowledge	This stage seeks to teach customers about a product or service's features, or, perhaps, to explain why the business is unique.
Liking	Based on the assumption that still, at this stage, the customer is indifferent to the brand – in other words, there is still no clear intention to purchase – marketing activities now focus on changing that perception to make customers feel that they could actually make use of the brand.
Preference	At this stage the crucial part of the process requires marketing activities to focus on amending customers' current buying habits and preferences. The marketing activity should attempt to distinguish the brand and convince the customer that the brand is more attractive than any alternatives offered by the competition.
Conviction	At this stage the customer is now reaching the point where they are about to make a decision or a commitment to make a purchase. The customer is still not utterly convinced, but is close enough to be persuaded by a salesperson or more compelling information, possibly through advertising or reviews of the product (achieved via Public Relations and other activities).
Purchase	At this stage the customer is about to buy the product or service. There can still be a postponement or delay, which may convince them to defer the purchase. At this stage marketing activities should impress on the customer that factors such as price should not be a huge consideration, as alternative payment methods (including credit, etc.) are available.

Hits

A hit is each single access request to a web server for either a file or a graphical file. A visitor to a website can, in fact, generate multiple hits per page download as the total depends on the number of associated files connected to the page. A visually rich web page would generate a large number of hits. If, for example, a web page had seven graphic images, the website would register eight hits, one for each of the images and a further hit for the html page itself.

Hooley, Lynch and Shepherd

Hooley, Lynch and Shepherd developed a typology which related business performance to different approaches to marketing. At the centre of their supposition they identified four different types of businesses:

- *Marketing philosophers* – which were businesses who saw marketing as having the key responsibility for identifying and meeting customers' needs. Marketing in these organizations was the guiding force behind all activities, and marketing itself extended beyond the normal associations of strictly being a sales support function.
- *Sales supporters* – which were organizations who considered marketing to be confined to a sales and promotional support function. Marketing itself was not necessarily involved in identifying or meeting customers' needs; this was the role of the sales department. Marketing simply supported this effort with appropriate and short-duration advertising and sales promotions.
- *Departmental marketers* – which were organizations that, whilst sharing many of the views of marketing philosophers, believed that marketing was restricted to a departmental function. Marketing was involved in identifying and meeting customers' needs, but this information was passed on and actioned by other areas of the organization.
- *Unsures* – which were organizations that were unclear about how they viewed marketing. Many had marketing departments or sections, but were not entirely convinced as to whether marketing was at the core of their activities. Marketing departments had been set up in these organizations simply because the business believed they needed one, but they were indecisive as to how to deploy the expertise.

Hooley, Lynch and Shepherd clearly believed that 'marketing philosopher' organizations were the ideal type of business and that marketing should not be restricted to a departmental function, or worse. From their research they suggested that marketing philosopher organizations enjoyed a higher return on investment than any of the other three types. 'Departmental marketer' organizations were somewhat average across the sample in their return on investment, whilst the other two groups of businesses performed significantly worse. The researchers identified the key characteristics of a marketing philosopher organization:

- They were more proactive than the other three groups in relation to future opportunities.
- They were equally proactive in new product development.
- They considered marketing training to be of great importance.
- Their marketing planning took a longer view.
- Those involved in marketing in these organizations held key positions within the business. In fact, in most cases, a representative from marketing was present on the board.
- Marketing was considered as a matrix function of the business in the sense that it had day-to-day working relations with other areas of the business.
- Marketing considerations were an integral part of the business's strategic plans.

Hooley, G., Lynch, J. and Shepherd, J., 'The Marketing Concept: Putting the Theory into Practice', *European Journal of Marketing*, 24:9 (1990), p. 723.

Horizontal marketing management

'Horizontal marketing management' describes a situation where independent businesses, who are working on the same level in a marketing channel, cooperate with one another. They form a loose association so that they can cooperate in buying and promotion in order to achieve **economies of scale**. In the UK, for example, horizontal marketing management can be seen at work when independent retail outlets combine their orders to manufacturers and run cooperative advertising to support one another. Without this additional muscle in an association of equals, each individual retail outlet would not enjoy the same degrees of discount from manufacturers, nor would they be able to afford the same level of advertising penetration into the market.

Horizontal publication

The term 'horizontal publication' is related both to the media and to advertising, as it describes a publication, print or otherwise, which has a broad range of editorial content. In this respect, the publication may well be attractive to those wishing to market products and services to a more general target audience. Horizontal publications are distinguished from vertical publications, as the latter have a far more focused, specialized and, possibly, niche audience.

House agency

See **in-house agency.**

Hybrid marketing channels

Hybrid marketing channels are essentially multi-channel distribution systems. A business may use two or more different forms of distribution channel in order to provide products and services to its customers. The stereotypical hybrid marketing channel system incorporates both direct and indirect distribution channels. In other words, the customers are given the opportunity to purchase products and services directly from the manufacturer or distributor, as well as using the more conventional distribution method of purchasing these products from retailers. Hybrid marketing channels have become common practice for the majority of computer hardware and software manufacturers and distributors.

Hybrid segmentation

Hybrid segmentation is both a market research and a general marketing term which describes a segmentation process that combines one or two segmentation variables to arrive at another form of segmentation. Standard segmentation relies on the identification of specific characteristics of a target market, perhaps relying on demographic information as its primary segmentation methodology. The expansion of the segmentation methodology to include factors such as lifestyle or other features, will provide the business with an alternative way of segmenting their markets. This additional approach may not have been a standard system used by the business in the past and may reveal other information about the target audiences that the business was not aware of until this point. Hybrid segmentation has therefore provided it with additional market data and a more focused view of the characteristics of its targets.

Ideation

Ideation is a market research term associated with new product development, as well as the framing of brand identities, images and product attributes. There are four different ways in which ideation can be approached, these are:

- *Brainstorming* – this encourages the participants to engage in free association.
- *Synectics* – this encourages the use of analogies to generate ideas.
- *Challenging* – this is the process of presenting alternative ideas in order to reformulate an original idea. Each idea is subjected to strongly opposing views, with the aim of reinforcing or replacing the original idea with a stronger suggestion.
- *Morphological methods* – which are variously known as decomposition/composition or mince-and-mix. These processes involve breaking down ideas or problems into sub-problems. These are listed in a matrix so that all the participants can see the elements involved. The participants then use and add to the list to reconstruct the idea, taking into account all of the various factors.

Image advertising

Image advertising focuses on the psychological or symbolic associations of a brand. Image advertising aims to build up a close association in the customers' perception of certain values and lifestyles linked to the brand. The process seeks to match the brand image with the image which the potential buyers wish to project, so that they closely associate with that brand when they consider their own image. The advertising will incorporate a common vocabulary, both in text and in image terms, with which the audience can clearly identify.

Most image advertising campaigns begin with a wider-pitched approach, incorporating features that will attract both the buyers already targeted and a broader targeted audience, who are yet to be convinced. Once the campaign has convinced the targeted buyers, it is assumed that a considerable proportion of the targeted general audience will have become receptive to the association. It is difficult to measure the shorter-term effectiveness of image advertising campaigns, as their sole measurement is not strictly related to the generation of sales. Image advertising requires a longer-term view which gradually imposes and matches points of view and associations on a wider audience.

Cafferata, Patricia and Tybout, Alice M. (eds), *Cognitive and Affective Responses to Advertising*. Lexington, MA: D. C. Heath, 1989.

Schmitt, Bernd H. and Simonson, Alex, *Marketing Aesthetics: The Strategic Management of Branding, Identity and Image*. New York: Simon & Schuster, 1998.

Impression

A web-based advertising term which represents the number of times a **banner ad** is shown to a user. In the majority of cases the number of advertisement impressions is reflected in the number of page impressions. In other words, the number of web pages visited by a user on a given website represents the page impressions, which will have one or more advertisements, thereby giving a total number of advertisement impressions.

Alternatively, the term 'impression' can be used to describe the number of commercial occasions or advertisements scheduled multiplied by the total target audience potential on each of those occasions. In the media, plans impressions are usually referred to as gross impressions. Therefore, an advertiser placing a printed advertisement on four occasions in a newspaper with a circulation of 10 million will have a gross impression of 40 million.

Incentive-base system

The term 'incentive-base system' has both an advertising and a sales application. Some advertising agencies have a relationship with their clients in which they are paid according to predetermined performance goals, rather than to another form of payment for their services. Normally, these performance goals will be related to empirical measurements of increases in sales or market share.

When the term is applied to sales, an incentive-base system refers to a payment process by which the salesperson is directly rewarded for the volume of sales generated. Traditionally, salespersons are paid a relatively modest basic rate of pay, which can be considerably improved by their sales performance. It is common practice to see the term OTE (On Target Earnings) quoted as the salary for a salesperson. This is an estimation of the sales potential of the job role, which is, in effect, an incentive-base system, alternatively known as commission- or performance-based.

Independent Television Commission

The Independent Television Commission (ITC) is a UK-based organization which regulates commercially funded television. It has a number of different functions, including:

- the issuing of licences to allow commercial television companies to broadcast both analogue and digital services into and from the UK;
- the setting of standards with regard to programme content, advertising, sponsorship and technical quality;
- the monitoring and penalising of broadcasters with respect to their output standards;
- the promotion and protection of the markets' environment in order to widen viewer choice and encourage innovation;
- to ensure that viewers receive the variety of services related to broadcasting on a fair and competitive basis;
- the responsibility to investigate complaints made by viewers and businesses and to publish the results of their findings.

Directly related to advertising and marketing, the ITC regulates commercial broadcasting through two codes – the ITC Standards Code and the ITC Rules on Amount and Scheduling of Advertising. The first code aims to ensure that television advertising does not mislead viewers, nor encourage harmful behaviour or give offence. The code also seeks to ensure that viewers are aware that they are watching advertisements and not programmes. It is in this regard that the second code seeks to ensure that the frequency and duration of commercial breaks are restricted. The ITC also ensures that commercial TV broadcast licence holders are made fully aware of the codes before allowing them to transmit. The ITC ensures that all output is monitored and can insist that advertisements which break the codes are either amended or immediately withdrawn.

In line with recent developments in UK television policies, an increasing number of programmes have attracted sponsorship. The ITC's Code of Programme Sponsorship aims to ensure that the sponsors do not exert influence on the editorial content.

The ITC also deals with complaints regarding advertising and sponsorship from viewers and other businesses and organizations. If an investigation is deemed necessary, then the broadcaster must provide information and evidence. All complaints are dealt with promptly and an advertising complaints report summarizes the outcomes of the investigation.

www.itc.org.uk

Towler, Robert (ed.), *Public's View*. London: Independent Television Commission, 2002.

Index numbers

Index numbers relate to a ratio which is used to describe the potential of a given market. An index number is created by dividing the percentage of users in a market segment by the percentage of population in the same segment, then multiplying these figures by 100. This can be used as a valuable base tool during market research in order to identify the comparative potentials of different market segments.

Indirect headlines

The term 'indirect headlines' is an advertising-related one. It refers to headlines which appear in an advertisement but that do not specifically identify a product or service. Neither are they specifically clear about the information which is being relayed in the advertisement message.

Indirect online contribution

'Indirect online contribution' is taken to mean an imprecise measurement of the influence of a website on a customer who subsequently makes an offline purchase.

Industrial advertising

Advertising targeted at individuals who buy, or influence the purchase of, industrial products or other services.

Infomercial

An infomercial is a paid-for television advertisement that seeks to provide viewers with detailed information about a product, service or issue. They are distinguished from normal television advertisements in respect of the fact that they are usually considerably longer and more detailed.

Hawthorne, Timothy R., *The Complete Guide to Infomercial Marketing*. Chicago, IL: Contemporary Books, 1998.

In-house agency

An in-house agency is an advertising agency that is set up, owned and operated by an advertiser. The in-house agency provides primarily the planning and execution of a business's advertising programme. It may be the case that the agency engages the services of **boutique agencies** or **freelancers** to supplement its own areas of experience and coverage.

Innovation-adoption model

The innovation-adoption model can be applied to both consumers and to businesses. When applied to consumers, the innovation-adoption model charts the process of gradual acceptance of a new product. For consumers the key stages are awareness, interest, evaluation, trial and adoption.

The innovation-adoption process in relation to businesses was developed by Everett M. Rogers and details the five stages of the innovation process, together with the associated activities at each of these stages, as can be seen in Table 27.

Rogers, Everett M., *Diffusion of Innovation*. New York: Free Press, 1995.

Table 27 Stages in the organizational innovation-adoption process

Innovation process stage	**Major stage activities**
I Initiation:	
1 Agenda setting	All of the information gathering, conceptualizing, and planning for the organizational adoption of
2 Matching	an innovation, leading up to the decision to adopt.
	The decision to adopt
II Implementation:	All of the events, actions, and decisions involved in putting an innovation into use.
3 Redefining/ structuring	(1) The innovation is modified and re-invented. (2) The relevant organizational structures are altered to accommodate the innovation.
4 Clarifying	The relationship between the innovation and the organization is more clearly defined as the innovation is put into full and regular use.
5 Routinizing	The innovation eventually loses its separate identity and is assimilated into the organizational routine.

Source: Rogers, *Diffusion of Innovation* (1995).

Inquiry test

An inquiry test is used as an integral part of advertising research. The test is designed to measure advertising effectiveness by calculating the number of inquiries or responses an advertisement has generated. An inquiry test may measure the number of telephone calls from potential customers, the coupons received requesting information, or the number of sales-promotion coupons clipped from the advertisement by customers, which have been redeemed at retail outlets.

Insertion advertising

Insertion advertising is a media publishing and advertising term which is used to describe a specific branch of print media-related advertising. Advertisers may choose, rather than paying for printed advertisements as integral parts of a magazine or newspaper, to have leaflets or fliers inserted into the publication. Normally an advertiser will pay a flat rate per thousand copies of the publication in which it chooses to have an insert placed. The pricing is usually based on the size or weight of the inserted document, as this will have a direct impact upon the distribution costs charged to the publisher of the magazine or newspaper.

Insertion advertising can be highly targeted, particularly in the case of regional or local newspapers. Specific postcode areas or smaller towns and villages can be specifically targeted with insertions. In this way the advertisers can choose to insert their sales literature into either all or some of the copies of the publication, dependent upon where those copies will be distributed.

Insertion order

Insertion order is a media buying or advertising term which is used to describe the confirmation that an advertiser will be purchasing advertising space in a publication. An insertion order traditionally referred to a paper document, rather like a standard order, which would confirm that the space had been booked. It is now not general practice to use paper-based confirmation of insertion orders, yet the term remains to describe the process.

Integrated marketing communication (IMC)

Integrated marketing communications represent a holistic view of marketing. IMC incorporates the planning, development, execution, evaluation and coordination of all marketing communications by a business. There is an inference that it ensures non-duplication of effort coupled with a standardized image. Businesses which have adopted IMC tend to show the following characteristics:

- a clearer awareness of where the target audience receives information, having assessed their media viewing, reading and listening habits and preferences;
- an understanding of the audience's current knowledge and an understanding that this level of knowledge will have an impact on their response;
- The use of a mixture of different promotional tools, each of which has specific objectives, but which collectively aim to work in conjunction with one another;
- a view that a consistent message needs to be relayed throughout all of the business's advertising, sales promotion, public relations and personal selling activities;
- a belief that in order to achieve the maximum impact on the market, there is a need to produce a continuous flow of information to the target audience, which is timed to the best effect.

The greatest problem with attempting to initiate IMC is that a business's internal organization may not yet be sufficiently developed or flexible in order to plan and coordinate effectively. An IMC programme can be evaluated on a number of different levels, but specifically relating it to advertising, personal selling, sales promotion and public relations, the following determinants can be considered:

- In relation to advertising, a series of well timed and related campaigns need to reinforce sales promotion and personal selling.
- The personal selling effort needs to be closely coordinated with the advertising programme. In other words, the sales department needs to be aware of the media schedule and of when advertisements will appear.
- Sales promotion materials, such as at the point of sale, need to be prepared in advance and coordinated with the advertising and personal sales efforts. If necessary, products need to be pushed through the distribution channel by offering incentives along that channel.
- Public relations work not only needs to coincide with the other three activities, but also needs to emphasize themes being drawn out in the advertisements.

Pickton, David and Amanda Broderick (eds), *Integrated Marketing Communications*. Englewood Cliffs, NJ: Prentice-Hall, 2000.

Interactive marketing

This is a relatively new branch of marketing, enabled by advertising media such as the internet or CD-Roms. The purpose of interactive marketing is to allow consumers to interact with the source of the message. Consumers are encouraged to actively seek information and respond to questions, thus allowing the business to send specifically targeted messages back to the consumer.

Sargeant, Adrian and West, Douglas C., *Direct and Interactive Marketing*. Oxford: Oxford University Press, 2001.

Internal analysis

Internal analysis can be seen as being a beginning point for the development of an **integrated marketing communication** system (IMC). The internal analysis involves the identification and analysis of the business's ability to plan product or service development, production and promotion. Internal analysis should identify any shortcomings in the business's present structure which may inhibit the adoption of IMC, and can provide information for the business in terms of training, additional personnel or outsourcing of expertise, as is appropriate.

The internal analysis tends to focus on the micro-issues which may affect the organization (such as relationships with customers, suppliers etc.). Once the internal analysis has been completed a more macro approach can be adopted which would include issues such as **PEST**.

See also **Five Forces.**

Internal marketing

At the centre of internal marketing is the desire to achieve change and have an impact upon attitudes and behaviours. Whilst external marketing seeks to assure customers of the value of the product and entice them to make regular purchases, internal marketing attempts to inform employees so that they understand, accept and adopt new processes.

In effect, internal marketing uses a modified communications plan, which features a fully functional flow of information, capable of amendment and revision as a result of feedback. The key stages are:

- Situation – determining the *target audiences*, and identifying channels of communication and the needs of each target audience.
- Objectives – generally using **SMART** (see p. 270).
- Strategy – what are the short-, medium- and long-term issues and strategic goals?

I

- Targets – all must be identified and provided for within the system.
- Promotion – direct communications, where target audiences are encouraged to contribute.
- Training – referring to training needed both by those engaged in delivering the internal marketing and by those within each target group, as required.
- Control – in order to ensure that achievement is measurable and the budget justified.

Ahmed, Pervaiz K. and Rafiq, Mohammed, *Internal Marketing: Tools and Concepts for Customer Focussed Management*. London: Butterworth-Heinemann, 2002.

Dunmore, Michael, *Inside–out Marketing: How to Create an Internal Marketing Strategy*. London: Kogan Page, 2003.

International marketing

'International marketing' is a rather collective term used to describe global marketing activities undertaken by certain businesses. International or multinational businesses will have identified target markets in a variety of different countries across the world. International marketing is designed to impose some kind of coordination between these disparate activities. It is not always appropriate to run either a simultaneous, or indeed a similar, advertising and marketing campaign in different markets. Given the fact that each market has its own peculiarities, seasonal fluctuations and specific customer needs and wants, the imposition of a standardized marketing system, incorporating identical advertising, is not always appropriate. None the less, international marketing can offer a business the opportunity to compare like with like in different overseas markets. It may be possible, for example, to compare response rates against costs, running similar advertisements or sales promotions in different countries. The purpose of coordination and planning is to establish the correct mix of activities for each overseas market and to learn lessons from similar markets when first entering a new overseas market.

Doole, Isobel, *International Marketing Strategy: Analysis, Development and Implementation*. London: Thomson Learning, 2001.

Interpretivist research

Interpretivist research is a form of consumer research which aims to understand the subjective meaning of an action. In this respect, interpretivist research addresses buying patterns and behaviours and seeks to understand the underlying meaning, or reasons, for particular forms of customer behaviour. The research, therefore, addresses issues such as customers' beliefs, attitudes and desires. As with most forms of market research, interpretivist research seeks to investigate the subjective in an objective manner.

Holt, Douglas B., 'Poststructuralist Lifestyle Analysis: Conceptualizing the Social Patterning of Consumption in Postmodernity'. *Journal of Consumer Research*, 23 (1997), pp. 326–50.

Interruption marketing

'Interruption marketing' is an internet term and is the direct antithesis of **permission marketing**. Typically, interruption marketing includes the posting of unwanted marketing communications to users (unsolicited emails) and the appearance of pop-up banner advertisements on websites.

Interstitial advertisement

'Interstitial advertisement' is an internet term to describe advertisements which appear between pages. A visitor to a website will view a page and then click to proceed to an associated page. Instead of being directly sent to the new page, the viewer is faced with an interstitial advertisement, which appears with a prompt to click and again to proceed to the chosen page.

Introduction stage

This is one of the first stages of the **product life cycle**. In the birth or introduction stage, the business hopes to build product awareness and develop a market for the product. The impact on the **marketing mix** is as follows:

- *Product* branding and quality level is established.
- *Pricing* may be low to build market share rapidly.
- *Place* (distribution) is selective (only available in certain places) until customers show acceptance of the product.
- *Promotion* is aimed at those willing to try something out before most other people. Promotion seeks to build product awareness and to educate potential customers about the product.
- *People* is concerned with finding out who the typical customer is and what other segments might be interested.

Island display

Island display is a term most closely associated with sales, merchandising and **point of sale**. An island display is, quite literally, a purpose-built or adapted structure in a retail outlet, which is used as a point of sale for a particular product or range of products offered by a single business. Normally purpose-built island displays will be of a temporary nature and, therefore, probably constructed of high-density cardboard or a similar, light material, which can be easily transported and erected. More permanent island display units are made from blockboard and are erected by the sales representative, who may also be responsible for monitoring the stocking levels on the display. Typically, the sales representative will make periodic visits to the retail outlet, to make an inventory of the current stock and replenish the missing stock up to an agreed level from their own mobile stock.

The island display may also be a moveable unit in the sense that it is built on wheels or rollers, or may, in itself, be a revolving carousel, which achieves the primary purpose of displaying the maximum amount of products in the minimum amount of space.

ITC

See **Independent Television Commission.**

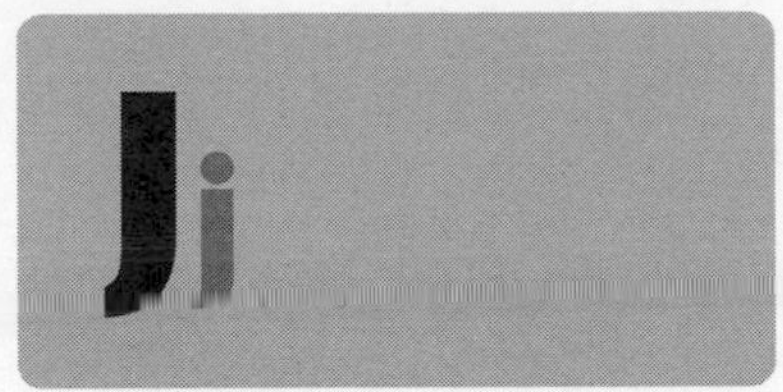

Jaworski and Kohli

Jaworski and Kohli wrote in 1990 regarding **market orientation**. They suggested that market orientation requires a business to collect a wide range of marketing intelligence information regarding customer needs, both now and in the future. Having collected this information, the business needs to disseminate this intelligence throughout the organization. Without these two prerequisites, the writers suggested that it was impossible to install a market-orientated approach in an organization.

Jaworski and Kohli recognized the fact that many businesses ignore the concept of market orientation. They do this on the basis that there is already an extensive demand for their products and services. Therefore, the business argues, there is very little need to shift towards market orientation whilst the demand remains strong. It is only when demand exceeds supply and there is more competition that businesses begin to seriously consider market orientation. The weaker the demand, the more inclined the business is to shift towards market orientation, often in a haphazard manner, in order to bridge the gap between supply and demand. It is only at this point that businesses begin to address the requirement of satisfying customers' needs rather than feeding a demand.

Kohli, A. and Jaworski, B., 'Market Orientation: the Construct, Research Propositions, and Managerial Implications', *Journal of Marketing*, 54 (April 1990), pp. 1–18.

Jingles

Songs or tunes about a product or service, that usually carry the advertising theme and a simple message.

Junk mail

'Junk mail' is often used as an alternative way of describing materials sent as a part of a **direct mail** shot. Professional **direct marketing** organizations that have systematic processes in place, and more precisely target recipients of direct mail, do not, strictly speaking, send out junk mail. The generally accepted definition of the term refers to unsolicited mail, which may or may not, depend on your stance, include all direct mail. Junk mail is generally typified by sales literature or product offerings, which are received by mail without any prompting or request made by the recipient. Often junk mail has no relevance for the recipient and in this case, as it is invariably consigned directly to the bin, it can be considered as junk mail.

Plusch, Jackie, *Junk Mail Solutions*. Phoenix, AZ: Clutter Cutter, 2001.

Kelly Repertory Grid

The Kelly Repertory Grid was developed in the 1950s by George Kelly, who was an educational psychologist. The grids are also known as 'Kelly's Triads'. The technique is used to describe how consumers perceive products, on the basis of the characteristics and attributes which they attach to those products. Typically, respondents will repeatedly be presented with three ideas, for example, three different brands. They are asked to separate the three as a pair and as a single. They are then asked to state what attributes and characteristics the pair shares compared with the single item. Next, the researcher discusses the respondent's views in detail. The researcher then rearranges the three ideas and asks the respondent to select a pair and a single once more, whereupon the whole exercise is then repeated.

The purpose of the research is to discover associations and connections made by the respondent, revealing ideas about the brands which may not have been considered up to this point.

The Kelly Repertory Grid was originally used clinically and in the workplace, for individuals who wanted to understand themselves. Kelly believed that people behave rather like scientists, constantly coming up with ideas and theories, and then testing them out. In that way an individual would build up their own model of the world in order to predict events and other peoples' behaviour. The Kelly Repertory Grid does not assign any measures or scores for particular traits when used as a personality questionnaire, as each individual has a unique model or view of the world.

Kelly, G. A., *The Psychology of Personal Constructs*. New York: W. W. Norton, 1955.

Kelly, G. A., 'Strategy of Psychological Research', in B. A. Maher (ed.). *Clinical Psychology and Personality: The Selected Papers of George Kelly*. New York: John Wiley, 1969, pp. 114–32.

Kelly, G. A., 'A Brief Introduction to Personality Construct Theory', in D. Bannister (ed.), *Perspectives in Personal Construct Theory*. London: Academic Press, 1970, pp. 1–29.

Kerning

'Kerning' is a printing and advertising term which is used to describe the reduction in the spacing between certain pairs of letters in order to improve their appearance. When fonts are created, each character has already been given a width that includes some space around that letter so that the characters do not run into one another when displayed or printed. Kerning involves amending this spacing and allowing the letters to be brought closer together, such as the letters A and V.

Key phrases/key words

Key phrases and key words are advertising-related and refer to the basic message being relayed to readers, listeners or viewers in an advertisement. The key phrases or words are often repeated or given a prominent position within the advertisement in order to stress their importance and relay the crucial message to the target audience, should the rest of the advertisement be forgotten. This is a means by which the advertisement can have a subliminal impact upon the audience's subconscious mind in order to aid recall.

Keyed advertisement

An advertising or **direct mail**-related term which refers to advertisements or sales literature which have coded letters or number sequences. In this way, the advertiser can identify the marketing or advertising vehicle which prompted the respondent to reply. Typically, advertisements in the media will feature, in an address, 'Department [*name of magazine*]'. In this way, advertisers can assess the independent response rates of individual advertisements, enabling them to calculate the cost of each response compared with the costs of the advertisement.

Kotler, Philip

Professor Philip Kotler is currently the distinguished Professor of **international marketing** at the Kellogg Graduate School of Management at Northwestern University. He has written a number of titles on marketing, including *Marketing Management: Analysis, Planning, Implementation and Control*, which is undoubtedly the most widely used marketing book in universities across the world. His other titles include *Principles of Marketing*, *Marketing Models*, *Strategic Marketing for Non-Profit Organizations*, *The New Competition*, *High Visibility*, *Marketing Places*, *Marketing for Hospitality and Tourism*, *The Marketing of Nations* and *Kotler on Marketing*. He is also the author of over 100 articles.

Kotler, in marketing terms, is a generalist, and has variously researched and written on areas as diverse as strategic marketing, marketing organization and planning, international marketing, **social marketing**, and marketing and economic development. He has been the recipient of various awards, including Honorary Doctorates at six different universities across the world, and has held his post at the Kellogg Graduate School since 1962.

Kotler, Philip. *Kotler on Marketing: How to Create, Win, and Dominate Markets*. New York: Free Press, 1999.

Kotler, Philip, *Marketing Management* (11th edn). Englewood Cliffs, NJ: Prentice-Hall, 2002.

Kotler, Philip, *Marketing Insights from A–Z: 80 Concepts Every Manager Needs to Know*. Chichester: John Wiley, 2003.

Kotler, Philip and Gary Armstrong, *Principles of Marketing* (9th edn). Englewood Cliffs, NJ: Prentice-Hall, 2000.

See also **markeing information system**.

Ladder of customer loyalty

The ladder of customer loyalty is a theoretical seven steps towards creating the ideal customer. The process can be seen as staged steps, which include suspect, prospect, customer, client, supporter, advocate and partnership.

See also **customer loyalty**.

Raphel, Murray and Raphel, Neil, *Up the Loyalty Ladder: Turning Sometime Customers into Full-time Advocates of your Business*. London: HarperCollins, 1996.

Laddering

'Laddering' is a market research term and is a technique adopted during **depth interviews**. The purpose of the technique is to gradually progress from questions and comments related to the product's characteristics to the characteristics of the respondent. The aim of the interviewing technique is to help identify the personal-construct theories of the individual and understand their underlying motivations. It is used both to examine the motivations and desires of the consumer and to help recognize the relationship between the consumer and the product. It assists the researcher in being able to frame the customer segmentation and then superimpose the product's characteristics. Laddering is particularly useful in new product development, particularly in cases where the business needs to ascertain the consumers' understanding and the relevance of the product to them, as well as their attitudes towards it.

Laggards

In the **innovation-adoption model** related to new products, laggards are the last group of consumers who are inclined to purchase a new product. They have an inherent suspicion of the new and prefer to use older, more established and personally reliable products, rather than risk investing in new product designs. Typically, they will enter the market as purchasers towards the end of the **maturity stage** of a **product's life cycle**.

Alternatively, they may wait until the product is in **decline**, which either confirms to them that the product's usefulness would have been short-lived, thereby underpinning their decision not to have purchased the product, or, alternatively, they can now pick up the product at a reduced price, due to it being remaindered or sold off prior to termination of production and distribution.

Rogers, Everett M., *Diffusion of Innovation*. New York: Free Press, 1995.

Lavidge and Steiner

Lavidge and Steiner produced their advertising hierarchy-of-effects model in 1961. It served to illustrate the way in which advertising worked and shows consumers passing through a sequential series of steps (see Figure 16). The first stage, which they named the cognitive stage, signifies initial awareness of a brand that has been advertised. The second, affective stage, signals the beginnings of preferences towards the brand, and the final, behavioural stage, signifies the actual purchase. Fundamental to their theory was the notion that advertising has a gradual effect. In other words, businesses need to recognize the fact that advertising in itself is not a quick fix solution and needs to be considered in the longer term. They consider it unlikely that advertising by itself would prompt an imme-

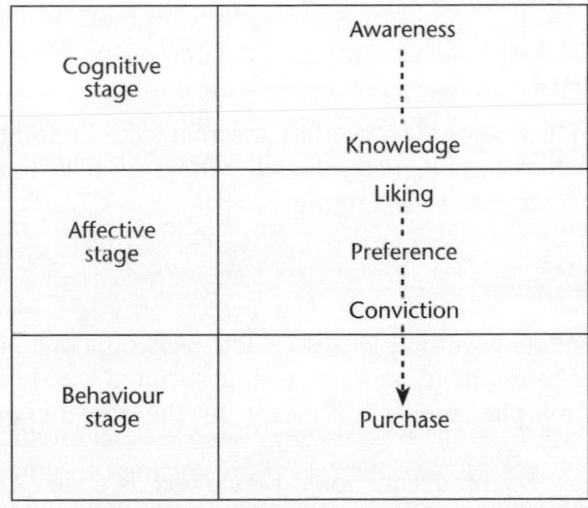

Figure 16 Lavidge and Steiner's hierarchy of effects

Source: Lavidge and Steiner (1961), p. 61.

L

diate behavioural response (purchase); but stress that it needs to fulfil the function of slowly building consumers towards that goal.

Lavidge, R. J. and Steiner, G. A., 'A Model of Predictive Measurements of Advertising Effectiveness', *Journal of Marketing*, 25:6 (1961), pp. 59–62.

Lead tracking

'Lead tracking' is a sales-related term which refers to the storing of information relating to contacts made with potential customers. Lead tracking involves not only the storage of this information, but also a process by which the business can ensure that these potential sale leads are followed up. Lead tracking software programs are commonly used by many businesses. Recent developments have also shown that businesses are adapting to web-based lead tracking, which updates information given to sales personnel regarding client leads and assigns the responsibility of following up each lead to an individual.

Bly, Robert W., *Lead Generation Handbook: How to Generate all the Sales Leads You'll Ever Need – Quickly, Easily and Inexpensively*. New York: Amacom, 1998.

Leading

'Leading' is a printing and advertising term which is used to describe the process of inserting spaces into text, usually between lines. The term is derived from traditional printing methods, when lead blocks would be fitted between lines of text.

Leave-behind

'Leave-behind' is a sales term used to describe sales literature, or other information, which has been literally left behind for a customer to read and assess following a sales meeting.

Levitt, Theodore

Although Theodore Levitt has written extensively on a number of different marketing issues, he is, perhaps, best associated with his writing on **marketing myopia** and the concept of the generic/**augmented product**.

Levitt argued that products should be viewed as a series of rings, at the centre being the generic product itself, the physical item that is either made or sold. Beyond this is another ring which he called the 'expected product', which comprises aspects of the product that are expected, including packaging, user instructions and guarantees. The next ring he describes as the 'augmented product', which is something unusual about the generic product, perhaps in the way it is handled or sold, such as an unrivalled customer-service provision. The final ring Levitt calls the 'potential product' and this concept examines how the product could be developed if all of its features were enhanced.

Levitt's other major contribution revolved around the concept of 'marketing myopia'. He believed that too many businesses began with their products rather than their customers. He argued that businesses needed to try to redefine the way they operated and focus on satisfying customers, and if need be, redefine their products and their ideas to match customer requirements. Famously he rounded on Hollywood, writing at the time of the advent of mass television. He recognized the Hollywood film industry as having missed an opportunity to expand its market into a general entertainment industry. Hollywood, he argued, looked very narrowly at the market and only sought to provide entertainment for cinemas, regarding television as a threat, rather than an opportunity.

Levitt also argued that for too long many businesses, in their product focus, had been preoccupied with producing more products at a lower unit cost, which led to what he described as 'undetected decay'. They failed to recognize that markets were constantly changing and that products were inevitably superseded by superior products. His definition of marketing was 'to discover, create, arouse and satisfy customer needs'. He went on to argue that the term 'growth industry' was something of a misnomer and that growth only actually occurs when a business recognizes an opportunity in a market and throws its resources into that market in order to stimulate growth.

Although written in the 1960s, Levitt's theories seem just as relevant today, if not more so. Certainly the speed at which markets grow and decline, along with their associated products, has increased.

Levitt, Theodore, 'Marketing Myopia', *Harvard Business Review*, 38:4 (July/August 1960), pp. 45–56.

Levitt, Theodore, *Marketing for Business Growth*. New York: McGraw-Hill, 1974.

L

Life cycle

See **product life cycle.**

Lifestyle

Lifestyle or psychographic segmentation is a market research method which suggests that individuals have characteristics that are reflected in the products and services that they buy. There are a wide variety of different lifestyle segmentation methodologies seeking to incorporate individuals' views and approaches to life which suggest the products and services that they may purchase. A typical example of lifestyle segmentation is the set of categories shown in Table 28.

Table 28 Lifestyle segmentation categories

Category	Description
Mainstreamers	This is the largest group of individuals as they are said to account for around 40% of the population. They have a tendency to purchase branded products as opposed to supermarket or own-label brands.
Reformers	This is a smaller group, but a significant one in terms of demanding changes in the products and services offered. As they are largely responsible for the purchases of supermarket brands and environmentally friendly items, they have driven many markets into providing substitute or replacement brands to accommodate their needs.
Aspirers	Aspirers are typified as being younger consumers who are ambitious and wish to be the first to own new designs or the latest version of a product or service.
Succeeders	These are individuals who consider products on the basis of how these fit into their general view of the world. They do not seek brands which are status symbols, but require reliability and usefulness.

Lifestyle research

Lifestyle research, or psychographic research, attempts to explain individuals' buying behaviour by analysing their attitudes, activities and opinions. Groups are categorized according to similarly held views and desires, which provide the researcher with clues as to how they will respond to particular products and services.

See also **lifestyle**.

Lifetime value

The concept of lifetime value aims to estimate, in various different ways, how much a relationship with a customer is worth to a business in terms of the purchases that they may make over a period of time. Typically, the following processes or calculations are made:

- The average profit per sale is calculated, which is equal to the total sales revenue less advertising, marketing and fulfilment expenses, divided by the number of sales.
- A calculation is then made as to how many times an average customer purchases from the business over a given period of time.
- The third calculation is the amount of profit that is made from that customer over the same period.

There are three commonly used formulae which can be used to calculate various aspects of a customer's lifetime value. These are:

Estimated average lifetime value = average sale × estimated number of times the customer reorders

Estimated average lifetime profit = average profit per sale × estimated number of times the customer reorders

Number of times customer reorders = number of sales made ÷ number of customers

Russ, Roland et al., *Driving Customer Equity: How Lifetime Customer Value is Reshaping Corporate Strategy*. New York: Free Press, 2002.

Likert scale

The Likert scale is named after Rensis Likert (1903–81) and is used particularly in questionnaires. The respondents are asked to mark their level of agreement with a series of statements related to an attitude which is being measured. They are usually asked to state their agreement or disagreement on a 5-point scale. Each degree of agreement is given a numerical value, usually 1–5, 1–7 or 1–9. In this way, the numerical value can be calculated for all the responses. Likert scales are usually constructed as described in Table 29.

Singh, Jagdip, Howell, Roy D. and Rhoads, Gary K., *Adaptive Designs for the Likert-type Data: An Approach for Implementing Marketing Surveys*. Cambridge, MA: Marketing Science Institute, 1990.

Link popularity

'Link popularity' is an internet marketing term which refers to the process by which search engines rank websites. Given the fact that

Table 29 Constructing a Likert scale

Stage of Procedure	Description
Gathering statements	The first step in creating a Likert scale-based questionnaire is to develop statements which allow respondents to express their reactions. Statements are usually worded so that respondents can react to them by marking their view at either one end of the scale or the other.
Formatting statements	Each of the statements is now given a graphic scale of between 5 and 9 (always odd) intervals along a continuum, which ranges typically from *Strongly Agree* to *Strongly Disagree*.
Scale administration	Clear instructions should be given to the respondents to either circle or mark the number in the scale which shows how close their view is to *Strongly Agree* or *Strongly Disagree*.
Scoring the scale	Normally *Strongly Disagree* would be valued as a 1 on the continuum, whereas *Strongly Agree* would variously be valued as either 5, 7 or 9, dependent upon the length of the continuum. The researchers total the score for each statement and the associated set of responses. The total score is then divided by the number of responses to that statement, producing an average score for each statement.

search engine providers wish to return valuable results to the user, they will inevitably rank websites by their popularity on the basis of their quality compared with others.

L

One way in which the popularity of a website can be assessed is to measure the number of site links to that website, the assumption being that a website with a large number of sites linking to it is more popular than one with only a few or none. Internet marketers will therefore attempt to induce as many websites as possible to carry a **banner ad** or link to their website so that this measure, used by search engines, will identify them as a popular site.

List broker

A list broker is an organization which acts as a collection point and repository of names and addresses. The organization will offer themed and sorted customer details, derived from a variety of different sources, including subscriptions, guarantee and warranty cards, and sales inquiries. An organization wishing to undertake a targeted **direct mail** campaign would be able to purchase likely prospects from the list broker.

List rental

The term 'list rental' is most closely associated with **list brokers**. List renting involves the purchase of a selected list of customer details to match the targeting criteria of a **direct mail** shot or campaign. Theoretically, the names and addresses, along with any other relevant details, are purchased on a one-off basis from a list broker, or, indeed, another organization that is prepared to share its customer details for a fee. It should be noted that the list is considered to be rented, on the basis that the provider of the list is constantly updating the details and that the purchase or use of the list at any given time is a snapshot of the information which is available.

Little Matrix (Arthur D. Little industry maturity/ competitive position matrix)

Arthur D. Little developed this matrix, which looks at the stages of industry maturity against the business's competitive position (see Table 30). In effect, the stage of industry maturity is very similar to the **product life cycle** criteria. The factors are used to assess the stage the business's products reached in terms of the state of the market, its relative efficiency as well as customer buying habits. Additional measures could include how easy it is to enter the market, as well as the technical demands of producing the products for the given market.

Table 30 Arthur D. Little competitive position/industry maturity matrix

		Stage of industry maturity			
		Embryonic	Growth	Maturity	Ageing
Company's competitive position	Dominant				
	Strong				
	Favourable				
	Tentative				
	Weak				

L

Location-based marketing

Location-based marketing is most closely associated with internet marketing and sales. The term describes the restriction of a special offer to customers in specified geographical areas. The term itself, however, can be applied to any advertising or sales-promotion campaign which limits the availability of the products and services on offer to particular parts of the country.

Logo

A logo is usually a graphic image which may or may not incorporate a business's name or initials. It is closely associated with **corporate image** and **corporate identity**. The purpose of a logo is to allow consumers to instantly recognize and associate with the organization and its products or services.

Thomas, Gregory, *How to Design Logos, Symbols and Icons: Twenty-Three Internationally Renowned Studios Reveal How they Develop Trademarks for Print and New Media*. Cincinnati, OH: North Light Books, 2001.

Longitudinal study

'Longitudinal study' is a **market research** term used to describe a series of surveys, or an individual survey, which is repeated at regular intervals. A longitudinal study will use the same **sample** of individuals, if possible, or will attempt to replicate the original sample in its composition. The purpose of longitudinal studies is to analyse gradual changes over a period of time.

L

Loss leader

'Loss leader' is a term associated with pricing policy and is a strategy which offers a product or service at a considerable discount. Although the discounting reduces profits in the short term, the strategy aims to attract additional customers who will, hopefully, remain loyal for the longer term. It is, therefore, a strategy which is often adopted by a business launching a product or service into a market for the first time. Loss leaders are used to introduce new customers to the product or service and the strategy is supported by other marketing activities, which aim to build a longer-term relationship with these customers.

Loyalty

See **customer loyalty**.

Loyalty programmes

Loyalty programmes have become an integral part of marketing and are characterized as being differentiated treatment towards existing customers, or those who purchase from the business on a regular basis. Loyalty programmes have become increasingly popular over the last few years, and aim to build a lasting relationship between consumers and the business. There is, however, considerable confusion over the definition and measurement of loyalty, and indeed the value of loyalty programmes. From an attitudinal perspective, loyalty programmes aim to establish an attachment to a business, a brand, a product or a service. Behaviourally, loyalty is typified by repeat purchases and recommendation. At the centre of all loyalty programmes is the desire to reduce the **churning** rate. But, underpinning this, regardless of any incentives offered, the business needs to assure consumers that they are receiving a level of service far superior to that of the competitors.

Unfortunately for the businesses who pioneered customer loyalty programmes, the concept has become more of an expectation than an additional incentive. Most businesses competing in the same market will offer, on the face of it, very similar customer loyalty programmes. The businesses are trapped into continuing to provide the customer loyalty programme on the basis that although it does not yield any advantage to continue, it offers considerable disadvantages if it is terminated.

There have been various attempts to frame a model of effective loyalty programmes. In essence, most recognize three key aspects or propositions:

1 The level of competition in most markets, and a business's need to collect, collate and analyse its customers to create customer profiles, have led to the development of customer loyalty programmes.
2 The effectiveness of a customer loyalty programme is dependent upon the structure of the market.
3 The use, validity and application of information derived from customer loyalty programmes have to provide tangible results and policies. This is typified by businesses being able to differentiate their products, and aspects of the programme, and show flexibility in order to cater for customers' differing preferences.

Loyalty value

An internet marketing term used to describe the **e-metric** calculation which a business assigns to the loyalty of its customers. Customer loyalty to an e-business can be measured in a variety of ways, including number of visits per month, number of purchases over a given period, and length of stay on the website.

Macro-marketing

Macro-marketing is a marketing approach which takes a broad view, encompassing the whole economy. It seeks to understand the way in which products and services flow from producers to consumers in a manner that closely matches the actual supply and demand in that economy or that **market**. In this respect, macro-marketing recognizes that in effectively matching supply and demand, it accomplishes the objectives of society in general.

Market

'Market' is a generic term used to describe a group of potential customers who have similar needs. These potential customers are willing to purchase various products and services in order to satisfy their needs. The term 'market' can be used to describe both consumers and other businesses, either as specific segments or as target audiences, whether they are part of a population in a given country, or more widely spread across the world. The term can equally be applied, therefore, to UK home owners and to airline operators – both are markets; one is focused primarily in a single country, with specific criteria, the other is a more global target, which includes operators, large and small, often located in other countries.

Market challenger

A market challenger is a business which holds a considerable **market share** in a **market**, but is actively trying to wrestle the control of the market from the **market leader**. Given the assumption that there can only be one market leader, businesses can adopt a number of different strategies. They can either launch outright attacks on the market leader, or pick on smaller businesses in that market, wrestle control of their market share from them, and build their own market share and potential to become market leader. Alternatively, a business which considers itself to be a market challenger could accept the status quo and adopt a less aggressive strategy, in which case, strictly speaking, they would be defined as **market followers**.

In order to be a successful market challenger, it is generally the case that they need to have a sustainable advantage, perhaps in terms of **product differentiation** or low costs. At the same time a market challenger needs to be as good as the market leader and be able to replicate, or better anything that the market leader is capable of doing. There also needs to be a reason why the market leader cannot effectively retaliate, otherwise a market challenger will often remain just that, or be forced to become a market follower. There are five tactics usually employed by market challengers in order to dislodge a market leader, these are listed in Table 31.

Market development

Market development is a marketing strategy which aims to increase sales by selling existing products into a new market.

Raymond, Martin, *Tomorrow People: Future Consumers and How to Read them Today*. London: Financial Times; Englewood Cliffs, NJ: Prentice-Hall, 2003.

Market follower

Market followers are businesses which do not necessarily wish to challenge the **market leader**. They may consider that they have more to lose than they have to gain by taking the market leader head-on. Market leaders, in any case, will bear the highest costs in terms of research and development, as well as advertising and the time it takes to build up demand for a product or service. Market followers wish to avoid these costs and the impact they may have on their profits. Market followers are typified by providing copies of, or in many cases improvements to, an original product offered by a market leader. They need to have the capacity to be able to produce new products and services which match the market leader's offerings as soon as is practicable.

Market followers are never likely to overtake the market leader, but they do enjoy high profits because of their lower development costs. Most market followers also replicate the way in which the market leader does business and position their products in a very similar manner.

Market leader

Market leaders are businesses which have the largest **market share** in a given **market**. Market leaders usually determine prices, promotional

Table 31 Tactics used by market challengers

Challenger's tactics	Description
Frontal attack	Usually this is the least likely to succeed as it requires the challenger to match the market leader's prices or advertising expenditure. As the market leader already has an advantage, it is more likely to simply respond in kind and beat off the challenge.
Flank attack	This more indirect approach is often more effective. The challenger strikes where the market leader is weak. Typically, specific market segments will be targeted where the market leader is not as dominant.
Encirclement attack	Essentially this is a longer-term development of the flank attack. The challenger establishes itself firmly in a specific market segment. Having gained superiority, and the knowledge that its position is secure, it then begins to fan out to cover the whole market. This is a gradual process and requires catching the market leader unaware.
By-pass attack	This is the most indirect challenge. The challenger focuses on the easier markets and diversifies into unrelated products in order to strengthen its position. Only when it is strong enough will it have the resources to match the market leader and attempt a more direct approach.
Guerrilla attack	Guerrilla attacks are typified by unpredictable targeting, akin to 'hit and run' tactics that aim to destabilize the market leader. The challenger will deploy price cuts, and short-term intensive advertising, and will seek to use public relations to damage the market leader. This is very much a stealth tactic and individually each of the attacks will not prove to be enough to undermine the market leader. Cumulatively the guerrilla attacks may succeed in taking the market leader's eyes off the ball so that another strike can be even more effective.

strategies and intensities and are also deeply involved in new product development. Market leaders are, in effect, a **benchmark** for any competitors who may choose to challenge them, avoid them, or simply imitate them. In all respects a market leader is recognized as such by its competitors, being seen as the dominant force in that market.

In most markets market leaders are constantly under pressure from **market challengers**, who seek different strategies to wrestle leadership. Market leaders tend to protect their market share in three main ways, as described in Table 32.

Table 32 Ways of protecting market leadership

Market leader's strategy	**Description**
Expand total demand	A market leader may choose to target new users in allied markets, perhaps by identifying new uses for the product. Another notable tactic is to encourage the rate of usage by existing customers by running sales promotion campaigns.
Protect and defend market share	This tactic, although defensive in its outlook, incorporates the aggressive use of promotion, distribution and new product development in order to ensure that customers remain aware of the fact that the business is the market leader. All other competitors must try to match the strength of the market leader, but invariably have little hope of being able to catch up.
Increase market share	It should be noted that market share and profitability are not the same issues and it may not be the market leader's short-term goal to increase profits. Market leaders will use new product development, advertising, pricing strategies, distribution incentives, mergers and take-overs, as well as expansion overseas, in order to increase their market share.

Being a market leader usually means that the business does enjoy a higher than average return on investment. It has been calculated that businesses with a market share exceeding 40% have an average return on investment of 30%. This is compared with businesses with a market share of less than 10%, who only enjoy a return on investment of around 10%. It is usually the case that the following assumptions can be made regarding a market leader:

Superior quality/new product development = market leader = premium pricing = higher profit.

Harari, Oren, *Leapfrogging the Competition: Five Giant Steps to Becoming a Market Leader*. Roseville, CA: Prima Games, 1999.

Market nicher

'Market nicher' is a term which describes a specialist supplier. **Niche markets** are, by their very definition, comparatively small compared with **mass markets**. Many niche markets, however, offer the potential for high growth and many are, in themselves, sufficiently large for a number of businesses to be attracted.

A market nicher will usually look for a market that is sufficient in size, with the potential for growth and profitability, but which is not currently receiving very much interest from potential competitors. The market nicher, with its specialist skills and resources, can serve the niche market and defend itself by building up strong **customer loyalty**.

Market nichers are usually relatively small businesses with limited resources. Alternatively, they may be parts of larger organizations which have been tempted into the market by the prospect of high profits and low competition. This is, in fact, a way in which **market challengers** can gradually build up sufficient resources in order to challenge a market leader.

Market nichers differentiate their products and services by their level of service, quality, rarity of offering, and price. Many successful market nichers are able to develop their niche markets sufficiently, and their associated products and services, to bring them into the mass market. A prime example of this is Body Shop, which successfully operated as a market nicher for a number of years before entering the mass market, whereupon it encountered, for the first time, a number of **market leaders** and potential challengers.

Sander, Peter and Sander, Jennifer Basye, *Niche and Grow Rich: Practical Ways of Turning your Ideas into a Business*. London: Entrepreneur Press, 2003.

Market orientation

Market orientation is an underlying marketing corporate philosophy. It is based on the creation, dissemination and use of market intelligence derived from **market research**. Integral to market orientation is the satisfying of customer needs and wants.

A market-orientated business will continually try to improve its position in a given market by carrying out market research. It will also attempt to be better placed to initiate proactive marketing, with the sole intention of meeting customer needs more efficiently than its competitors. There is a strong correlation between market orientation and the performance of a business.

Jaworski, Bernard J. and Kohli, Ajay K., 'Market Orientation: Antecedents and Consequences', *Journal of Marketing*, 57:3 (1993), pp. 57–70.

Kohli, Ajay K. and Jaworski, Bernard J., 'Market Orientation: the Construct, Research Propositions, and Managerial Implications', *Journal of Marketing*, 54:2 (1990), pp. 1–18.

Market penetration

This is a marketing strategy adopted by businesses in order to increase their sales of existing products in markets in which they already operate. Market penetration is usually achieved by an aggressive use of the **marketing mix**, which uses a balance of price cutting, sales promotions and advertising, enhanced distribution and new product development.

Market pioneer

A market pioneer should not be confused with the term **market leader**. Market pioneers are the first businesses to introduce major new products. Ideally they should be in a position which can allow them to exploit the fact that they are the only business able to offer this product or service. In practice, however, many market pioneers are not strong enough financially to exploit their advantage. Larger businesses which are market leaders in this or an associated market can move quickly to bridge the gap between their products and services and the pioneer's new inventions. A notable example of a business which is considered to be a market pioneer is the electronics company Phillips. It has systematically, over a number of years, been the first onto the market with a number of new products. These have been swiftly and effectively replicated by other businesses who are true market leaders in the electronics market. This illustrates that being a market pioneer is fraught with potential dangers: when Phillips launched the V2000 video recording system in the 1980s it failed to achieve a long-term market share against the later VHS system, which was inferior in many respects. Equally, the superior BETA system failed to outperform the VHS system.

Market research

There is considerable confusion as to the comparative definitions of market research and **marketing research**. Market research is, in effect, a subset of marketing research as it most usually describes consumer interviews and other procedures involved in marketing research. Whilst the generally accepted definition of marketing research encompasses all of the collection, recording and analysis of data related to the marketing of products and services, market research has a somewhat more limited definition.

Birn, Robin J. (ed.), *The Handbook of International Market Research Techniques*. London: Kogan Page, 2002.

Birks, David and Malhotra, Naresh, *Marketing Research: An Applied Approach*. London: Financial Times; Englewood Cliffs, NJ: Prentice-Hall, 2002.

Market segment

A market segment is a defined subset of individuals or businesses which can be identified as sharing similar characteristics. The group, or segment, must be able to be targeted by aspects of the **marketing mix** and must usually be large enough to warrant specific attention. Each segment, during **market segmentation**, is identified according to a series of criteria which best help to clearly describe the characteristics, buying behaviours, habits, attitudes and benefits sought.

Market segmentation

Market segmentation involves the identification of specific **target markets** for broader-based products and services, in order to enable a business to develop suitable **marketing mixes** for each of their target segments.

Market segmentation probably came into existence in the 1950s when **product differentiation** was a primary **marketing strategy**. By the 1970s, however, market segmentation had begun to be seen as a means of increasing sales and obtaining a **competitive advantage**. In recent years more sophisticated techniques have been developed to reach potential buyers in ever-more specific target markets.

Businesses will tend to segment the market for the following reasons:

- to make marketing easier in the sense that segmentation allows the business to address the needs of smaller groups of customers which have the same characteristics;
- to find niches, typically unserved or under-served markets, and to be able to target these buyers in a less competitive environment;
- to increase efficiency in being able to directly apply resources towards the best segments, which have been identified by the business.

Table 33 Measures of market segmentation

Segmentation criteria	Description
Size	The market itself needs to be large enough to warrant segmentation. Once a market has been segmented, it may be revealed that each of the segments is too small to consider.
Differentiated	There must be measurable differences between the members of the segment and the market in general.
Responsiveness	Having segmented the market, marketing communications need to be developed to address the needs of that segment. If a business cannot develop marketing communications which can contact this segment and have an impact upon it, there is little value in knowing about the segment in the first place.
Accessibility	Marketing communications need to be able to get through to the segment in order to be effective. There may well be a best single advertising medium or promotional device which can reach the segment and tell them the business's message.
Interest	Having established what benefits the segment is looking for, the business needs to be assured that this is precisely what the potential customers require and that the product or service matches these needs.
Profitability	A decision needs to be reached as to whether it is cost effective to reach these segments, considering the cost which may be incurred in running multiple marketing programmes alongside one another. Existing products or services may need to be redesigned in order to match the specific needs of the segment.

There are some common rules regarding market segmentation which determine whether the identified segments are significant enough or measurable. These are listed in Table 33.

In effect, there are two ways of segmenting a market. These are known as either *a priori* or *post hoc*. These two approaches are typified in the following manner:

- *A priori* is effectively based on a mixture of intuition, use of **secondary data** and analysis of existing customer database information. *A priori* segmentation takes place without the benefit of

Table 34 Information forming the basis of market segmentation

Measured variable	Description
Classification	Broadly speaking, classification actually encompasses demographic, geographic, psychographic and behavioural measures. It requires a system of classifying individuals and placing them into segments by using a mixture of these variables.
Demographic	'Demographic' features age, gender, income, ethnicity, marital status, education, occupation, household size, type of residence and length of residence, amongst many other demographically based measures.
Geographic	This broad range of variables includes population density, climate, zip or postcode, city, state or county, region, or metropolitan/rural.
Psychographic	Another broad range of variables which include attitudes, hobbies, leadership traits, lifestyle, magazines and newspapers read, personality traits, risk aversion, and television or radio programmes watched or listened to.
Behavioural	These variables encompass the current ways in which the target market views, buys and responds to products, services and marketing. The category includes brand loyalty, benefits sought, distribution channels used, and level of usage.
Descriptor	Descriptor variables actually describe each segment in order to distinguish it from other groups. The descriptors need to be measurable and are usually derived solely from primary research, rather than secondary sources of information. Descriptors will typically explain in shorthand the key characteristics of each segment and the members of that segment, so that these characteristics can be more readily exploited by subtle changes in the marketing mix. A descriptor variable may be featured as under 30, single, urban dweller, rented accommodation, medium to high income, etc.

primary research and may well produce relatively simplistic segmentation, such as male or female, young or old, regional segments, or buyers and non-buyers.

- *Post hoc* segmentation uses primary market research to classify and describe individuals within the target market, but segments are not defined themselves until after the collection and analysis period. The definition of each segment requires the placing of all members of the target market into specific segments.

There are a number of different types of information which are used extensively in market segmentation. These can be best described by category as in Table 34.

McDonald, Malcolm and Ian Dunbar, *Market Segmentation*. Basingstoke: Palgrave Macmillan, 1998.

Wedel, Michel and Kamakura, Wagner A., *Market Segmentation: Conceptual and Methodological Foundations*. Amsterdam: Kluwer Academic Publishers, 1999.

Market share

Sales figures do not necessarily indicate how a business is performing relative to its competitors. Changes in sales may simply reflect changes in the market size or changes in economic conditions. The business's performance relative to competitors can be measured by the proportion of the market that the firm is able to capture. This proportion is referred to as the business's market share and is calculated as follows:

Market share = Business's sales ÷ Total market sales

Sales may be determined on a value basis (sales price multiplied by volume) or on a unit basis (number of units shipped or number of customers served). While the business's own sales figures are readily available, total market sales are more difficult to determine. Usually, this information is available from trade associations and market research firms.

Market share is often associated with profitability and thus many businesses seek to increase their sales relative to competitors. Businesses may seek to increase their market share by the following means:

- Economies of scale – higher volume can be instrumental in developing a cost advantage.
- Sales growth in a stagnant industry – when the industry is not growing, the business can still increase its sales by increasing its market share.
- Reputation – market leaders have power, which they can use to their advantage.
- Increased bargaining power – a larger market share gives an advantage in negotiations with suppliers and channel members.

The market share of a product can be modelled as:

Share of market = Share of preference × Share of voice × Share of distribution

According to this model, there are three drivers of market share:

- Share of preference – can be increased through product, pricing, and promotional changes.
- Share of voice – the business's proportion of total promotional expenditures in the market. Thus, share of voice can be increased by increasing advertising expenditures.
- Share of distribution – can be increased through more intensive distribution.

From these drivers market share can be increased by changing the variables of the **marketing mix**.

- Product – the product attributes can be changed to provide more value to the customer, for example, by improving product quality.
- Price – if the **price elasticity** of demand is flexible, a decrease in price will increase sales revenue. This tactic may not succeed if competitors are willing and able to meet any price cuts.
- Distribution – adding new distribution channels or increasing the intensity of distribution in each channel.
- Promotion – increasing advertising expenditures can increase market share, unless competitors respond with similar increases.

Miniter, Richard, *The Myth of Market Share*. London: Nicholas Brealey Publishing, 2002.

Marketing audit

A marketing audit is an integral part of the marketing process which ensures that the basic objectives and policies of the marketing function of a business are being implemented and fulfilled. A typical marketing audit would encompass a systematic, often critical, but importantly unbiased review or appraisal of the marketing function. A marketing audit would examine the procedures, methodologies and individuals who are involved in implementing marketing policies.

Wilson, Aubrey, *The Marketing Audit Handbook: Tools, Techniques and Checklists to Exploit your Marketing Resources*. London: Kogan Page, 2002.

Marketing communications

'Marketing communications' is a generic term which is used to describe any form of communication with a business's publics. This description

M

includes **advertising, sales promotion, direct marketing, public relations** and any other personal selling, printed or broadcast message.

Fill, Chris, *Marketing Communications: Contexts, Strategies and Applications*. London: Financial Times; Englewood Cliffs, NJ: Prentice-Hall, 2001.

See also **integrated marketing communications.**

Marketing concept/philosophy

The fundamental marketing concept is that a business should attempt to satisfy its customers but produce a profit. There are, of course, various descriptions of what exactly marketing is and what the marketing concept entails. The Chartered Institute of Marketing, for example, defines marketing as 'the management process responsible for identifying, anticipating and satisfying customer requirements profitably'. The American Marketing Association defines marketing rather more precisely in describing it as 'the process of planning and executing the conception, pricing, promotion and distribution of ideas, goods and services to create exchanges that satisfy individual and organizational objectives'.

The marketing concept has really only been fully developed since the end of the Second World War. Marketing is now an important consideration in business planning and is seen as being a vital tool in an increasingly competitive market. Marketing is generally given the responsibility of identifying target markets and anticipating their needs and wants.

Figure 17 illustrates the position that marketing takes in the overall success of a business.

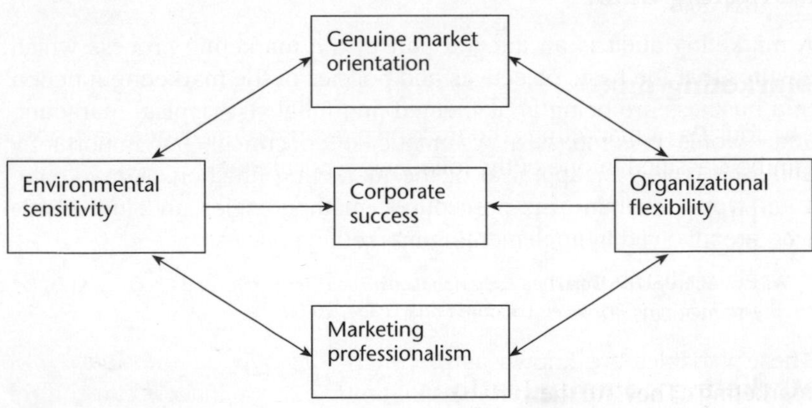

Figure 17 Marketing

Marketing information system (MkIS)

A marketing information system is, in effect, a 'marketing only' version of the more common management information system (MIS). An MkIS is a fully functional, self-contained system which uses decision support analysis to develop information from marketing intelligence and research, as well as internal records. Rather than being a software system as such, MkIS consists of people, equipment and procedures which aim to collect, sort, analyse, evaluate and distribute accurate information at the right time to those making decisions about marketing policies within a business (see Figure 18).

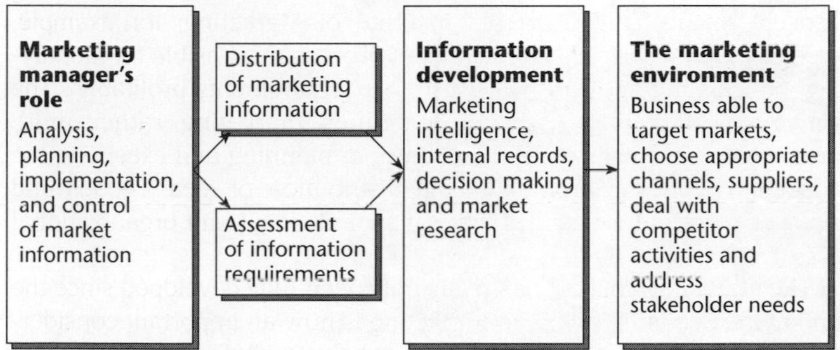

Figure 18 Model of a marketing information system

Source: Based on Kotler's MkIS model.

Kotler, Philip, Armstrong, Gary, Saunders, John and Wong, Veronica, *Principles of Marketing: European Edition*. London: Financial Times; Englewood Cliffs, NJ: Prentice-Hall, 2001.

Marketing mix

The four **Ps** of marketing. The major marketing management decisions can be classified in one of the following four categories:

- Product
- Price
- Place (distribution)
- Promotion

These variables are known as the 'marketing mix' or the 'four Ps of marketing'. They are the variables that marketing managers can control in order to best satisfy customers in the target market. The marketing mix is portrayed in Figure 19.

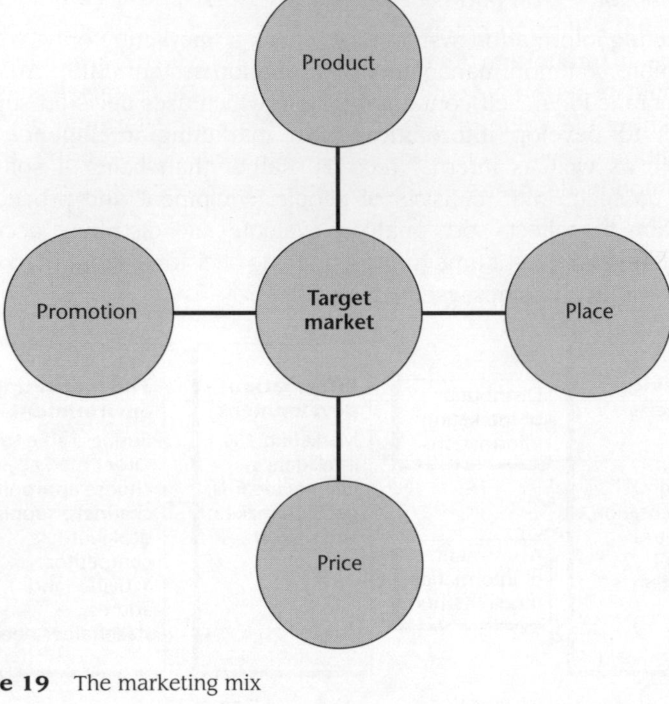

Figure 19 The marketing mix

The business attempts to generate a positive response in the target market by blending these four marketing-mix variables in an optimal manner.

- *Product* – The product is the physical product or the service offered to the consumer. In the case of physical products, it also refers to any services or conveniences that are part of the offering. Product decisions include aspects such as function, appearance, packaging, service, warranty, etc.
- *Price* – Pricing decisions should take into account profit margins and the probable pricing response of competitors. Pricing includes not only the list price, but also discounts, financing, and other options such as leasing.
- *Place* – Place (or placement) decisions are those associated with channels of distribution that serve as the means for getting the product to the target customers. The distribution system performs transactional, logistical, and facilitating functions. Distribution decisions include market coverage, channel member selection, logistics, and levels of service.

- *Promotion* – Promotion decisions are those related to communicating and selling to potential consumers. Since these costs can be large in proportion to the product price, a break-even analysis should be performed when making promotion decisions. It is useful to know the value of a customer in order to determine whether additional customers are worth the cost of acquiring them. Promotion decisions involve advertising, public relations, media types, etc.

Table 35 summarizes the marketing-mix decisions, including a list of some of the aspects of each of the Four Ps.

Table 35 Aspects of the Four Ps

Product	Price	Place	Promotion
Functionality	List price	Channel members	Advertising
Appearance	Discounts	Channel motivation	Personal selling
Quality	Allowances		Public relations
Packaging	Financing	Market coverage	Message
Brand	Leasing options	Locations	Media
Warranty		Logistics	Budget
Service/Support		Service levels	

See also **Seven Ps.**

Marketing myopia

The term 'marketing myopia' was coined by **Theodore Levitt** in an article published in the *Harvard Business Review* in 1960. The term describes a business that is product- or production-orientated and pays little heed to the market or the needs and wants of customers. A myopic organization will often not recognize or realize that market trends are changing and consequently it will run the risk of being caught out suddenly as a market, and consequent sales, decline.

Levitt argued that businesses should primarily consider the market and be prepared to amend or scrap products and services which do not precisely match the requirements of the customers.

Levitt, Theodore, 'Marketing Myopia', *Harvard Business Review*, 38:4 (July/August 1960), pp. 45–56.

M

Marketing plan

A marketing plan is a detailed document which aims to itemize and quantify actions which need to be taken in order to pursue marketing strategies. The components of a full marketing plan are as follows:

- executive/management summary or overview;
- objectives, including the business's mission statement, objectives and product or product-group goals;
- product or market background, detailing the product range, sales summaries and market overview;
- situation or **SWOT analysis**, showing the performance of current **marketing strategies**, and opportunities and threats, along with necessary analysis;
- marketing analysis, detailing the marketing environment, trends, customer requirements, **segments** and competitor analysis;
- marketing strategies, identifying the core **target markets** or segments, any of the business's advantages, and statements on product and brand **positioning**;
- sales forecasts and results – an estimate of the presumed sales figures, incorporating an analysis of the impact of the proposed marketing strategies;
- marketing programmes, which detail the marketing mixes, tasks and responsibilities;
- monitoring of performance, which details the controls and examines evaluation methods;
- financial implications, detailing the budgets, costs and apportionment, and expected returns on investment;
- operational considerations, featuring communications and research, development and production needs;
- appendices – various inclusions, but usually SWOT analysis, background data and market research findings.

The marketing plan has an associated cycle of development (see Figure 20).

1. The development or revision of marketing objectives (relative to performance), which reappraises the current marketing objectives.
2. Assessment of marketing opportunities and resources, which assesses existing or possible opportunities and whether financial resources are available to exploit them.
3. Revision/formation of marketing strategy – a revision, amendment or total rewrite of marketing strategies.
4. Development/revision of the plan for implementation and control –

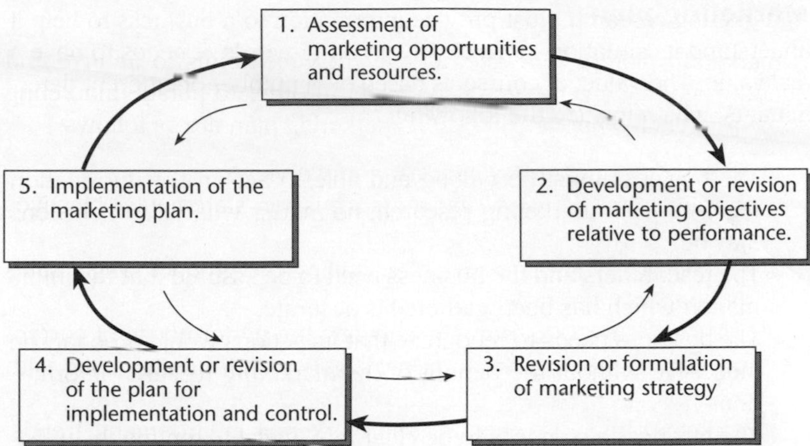

Figure 20 Marketing planning cycle

the creation of control systems or the review or improvement of existing ones to allow effective reports on progress.

5 Implementation of the marketing plan.

Canwell, Diane, *Marketing Campaigns*. London: International Thomson Publishing, 1998.

Westwood, John, *How to Write a Marketing Plan*. London: Kogan Page, 2000.

Marketing research

Marketing research attempts to adopt a scientific approach to building a clear picture of customers, the market and the competition and latterly it has been extended as an investigation into the wider environment in which the business operates.

Marketing research aims to discover, in a systematic manner using reliable and unbiased questions, ideas and intentions, as well as trends, which may affect a business, its markets and its customers. Marketing research processes data, analyses the data and interprets the facts, and is employed extensively in marketing management to help plan, evaluate and control marketing strategy and tactics.

Marketing research is often confused with **market research**, which has a considerably narrower definition. For the most part market research simply refers to consumer surveys, normally questionnaires, carried out face-to-face or over the telephone. Marketing research, therefore, can be seen as a broader church in terms of information gathering, collation and analysis.

Marketing research must provide information to a business to help it understand its situation more clearly. In other words, it needs to have a real value. The value, of course, is based on a number of different determinants, which include the following:

- The business must be willing and able to act on the information received from marketing research, no matter what its conclusions may be.
- The researchers and the business need to be assured that the information which has been gathered is accurate.
- The business needs to recognize that its actions would probably be indecisive without the benefit of the marketing research information.
- The business also needs to be clear that whilst accepting the validity of the information gathered, there may be a degree of variation or a margin of error.
- The business can also recognize that accurate and pertinent marketing research can reduce risk.
- The business needs to be cognizant that competitors' reactions may well react based on decisions made by the business arising out of their marketing research.
- Marketing research needs to be cost effective, in terms of both money and time. Any marketing research must be up-to-date, otherwise its value is limited, therefore any marketing research programme has to have a definite purpose and deadline.

The majority of marketing research projects are typified by following a clear series of tasks. These are:

1 Define the problem.
2 Determine research design.
3 Identify data types and sources.
4 Design data collection forms and questionnaires.
5 Determine sample plan and size.
6 Collect the data.
7 Analyse and interpret the data.
8 Prepare the research report.

See also **marketing research vs. market research** *and* **marketing research design**.

Birks, David and Malhotra, Naresh, *Marketing Research: An Applied Approach*. London: Financial Times; Englewood Cliffs, NJ: Prentice-Hall, 2002.

Marketing research design

There are a wide variety of different marketing research classifications and design methodologies. Broadly speaking, the marketing research design needs to closely mirror the objectives of the research. There are, in effect, three different forms of marketing research design which could be used by a business, as outlined in Table 36.

Table 36 Forms of market research design

Research type	Description and purpose
Exploratory research	Exploratory research is used primarily for the forming of hypotheses. This includes the clarification of concepts or explanations, the gaining of insights or the elimination of impractical suggestions. Normally exploratory research will begin by viewing existing market information and then move towards investigating individuals' experiences, usually through focus groups. Exploratory research does not need to find representative samples of individuals, as its primary purpose is to gain greater knowledge and insights into issues. Exploratory research does not test hypotheses, but it does develop them into workable suggestions.
Descriptive research	Descriptive research relies on a much more rigorous and representative research model. The purpose of most descriptive research is to help predict future demand, or to examine the characteristics of customers who already use a product. Descriptive research defines questions, identifies specific individuals to be questioned and ensures that a rigid analytical system is applied to the whole process.
Causal research	Causal research is concerned with cause and effect and, as such, looks at the relationships between different variables and how they impact on one another. Causal research usually requires a marketing research design to revolve around both field and laboratory experimentation.

Particularly in the field of descriptive research, there are several options in terms of marketing research design. A business may, for example, consider either a **longitudinal study** or a cross-sectional study. A longitudinal study looks at the same individuals over a given period of time and repeatedly measures their behaviour, noting any changes that occur. A cross-sectional study would seek to examine a specific sample of the population and make measurements over a period of time. The specific technique used is invariably cohort analysis, which tracks an aggregate of these individuals who experience the same event. Cross-sectional studies can also be combined with longitudinal studies in order to provide information which will assist long-term forecasting.

Creswell, John W., *Research Design: Qualitative, Quantitative and Mixed Method Approaches*. London: Sage Publications, 2002.

Punch, Keith F., *Developing Effective Research Proposals*. London: Sage Publications, 2000.

Marketing research vs. market research

The terms **marketing research** and **market research** are often incorrectly taken to mean the same thing. There is a technical difference between the two terms. Marketing research is a broader category, which actually includes market research. Marketing research can be used to describe any research activity related to marketing, including both **primary** and **secondary data** collection, analysis and dissemination.

Market research, on the other hand, primarily looks at customers' attitudes and opinions, market size and trends, and is typified by consumer surveys.

Marketing strategies

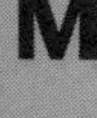

The term 'marketing strategies' refers to specific processes adopted by the marketing function of a business in order to achieve specific goals or objectives. A marketing strategy also encompasses the deployment of a business's resources in order to develop and maintain the business's market opportunities. At its core, marketing strategies seek to deploy a **marketing mix** in the most effective manner, not only to achieve the business's goals and objectives, but also to satisfy the customers' needs and wants.

Fill, Chris, *Marketing Communications: Contexts, Strategies and Applications*. London: Financial Times; Englewood Cliffs, NJ: Prentice-Hall, 2001.

Markov model

The Markov model or Markov chain has market research applications and is a complex mathematical sequence. The supposition is that each possible event and its outcome are dependent upon the outcome of previous events.

Andrei A. Markov developed the Markov model or Markov chain. He was a graduate of St Petersburg University in 1878 and returned to the institution as a professor in 1886. Initially Markov was concerned with number theory and analysis, developing an interest in integrals, approximation theory and other complex mathematical concepts.

In terms of marketing, the Markov model considers sequences of variables in which a future variable is determined. The process suggests that by investigating the cause and effect of sequences of events in the past, it is possible to predict future situations. In this way, the Markov model or chain can be applied in **marketing research** to predict future market trends and customer buying patterns.

Sheynin, O. B., 'A. A. Markov's Work on Probability', *Archive for History of Exact Science,* 39 (1988), pp. 337–77.

Maslow, Abraham

Abraham Maslow categorized human needs into five groups, which he arranged as a hierarchy (see Figure 21). Whilst Maslow's theory has been systematically applied in the field of human resource management, marketing has much to learn from the concept.

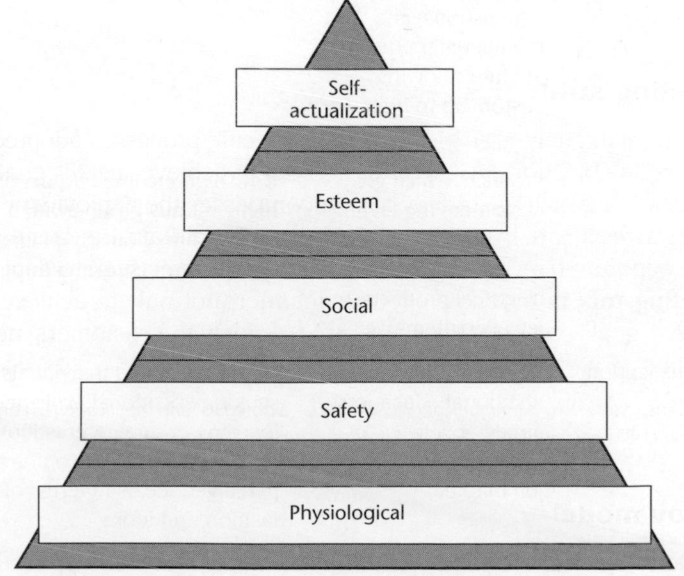

Figure 21 Maslow's hierarchy of human needs

M

Maslow's theory can be directly adapted to marketing as can be seen in Table 37.

Table 37 Maslow's categories as applied to marketing

Maslow needs category	Product suggestions	Target groups
Physiological	Products which give customers a sense of well-being, such as warming foods in winter	Grey market which has concerns over their health
Safety	Support services, including road-side assistance, insurance cover, private health care and extended warrantees	Safety-based products and services for those with children or valuables to protect
Social	Products which allow customers to maintain and improve their social lives, such as cheap-rate calls in the evening, reduced-rate internet connections, and membership privileges at clubs allowing customers to bring friends free	Networking solutions for people moving to new areas, contact with like-minded individuals (clubs and societies etc.), and groups set up for single people or single-parent families
Esteem	Products which give customers the feeling that they are successful, such as luxury cars, electrical products and jewellery items	New high income earners and higher status groups with a need to show outward signs of conspicuous consumption
Self-actualization	Higher, further or additional education aimed at self-improvement in the job market	Higher educated individuals seeking vocational skills and learning or adolescents looking for opportunities to conform to perceived ideals in terms of fashion and looks

Maslow, Abraham H. and Frager, Robert (eds), *Motivation and Personality*. Harlow: Longman, 1987.

Mass customization

Mass customization is an increasing trend and of considerable importance to marketeers. Mass customization involves the production of mass-produced, standard products, with slight variations or customizations for particular market or customer segments. As the manufacturing process has developed technologically, and become more flexible, it is possible to produce these personalized products without having a detrimental effect on profit margins. Indeed, these customized products can often warrant a premium price, providing a margin in excess of what had previously been enjoyed by the manufacturer. Manufacturers have therefore realized that mass customization is a means by which they can improve their profitability without the attendant loss of production or productivity.

See also **customization.**

Mass marketing

Mass marketing is typified by a product or production-orientated business which uses shotgun marketing tactics, rather than more precise targeted activities. Mass marketing is, to all intents and purposes, a blanket approach to all forms of marketing. The business does not differentiate between its different customer groups; it has ignored segmentation and does not consider it worthwhile to specifically address each individual **market segment**.

Mass marketing is best described as a business which chooses to use the same balance of its **marketing mix** in all situations.

Tedlow, Richard S., *New and Improved: The Story of Mass Marketing in America*. London: Butterworth-Heinemann, 1990.

Mass merchandising concept

The mass merchandising concept is, in effect, a sales promotion strategy which relies on the assumption that by charging lower prices for products and services, a business will achieve a greater sales volume and faster turnover. Because of the small margins involved, this strategy leaves little room for experimentation or error.

Maturity stage

This is the third stage of the **product life cycle**. At maturity, the strong growth in sales slows down. Competition may appear with similar products. Marketing efforts now switch to defending market share while maximizing profit. The implications for the **marketing mix** are:

- Product features may be improved to show that the product is different and better than competitors.
- Pricing may be lower because of the new competition.
- Distribution becomes more widespread and discounts may be offered to encourage customers to choose the product over competing products.
- Promotion focuses on the differences and quality of the product.
- People doing market research look at what customers would like improved, and at the features of competitors' products and services.

McKenna, Regis

Regis McKenna founded his first marketing business in the Silicon Valley in 1970, having worked in the electronics industry, within marketing departments. McKenna is credited with pioneering many marketing theories and practices which were originally applied to the technology market, but have now become part of the mainstream.

In 1985 McKenna suggested various marketing approaches to dealing with the different groups which had been identified by Everett Rogers in 1962 (*see* **adoption theory**). McKenna was also concerned with the identification of individuals within an industry who established and sustained standards for the whole market. His book *Relationship Marketing* was one of the first to tackle one-to-one marketing (1992). His latest book, *Total Access*, suggests that the future of marketing lies in computers and computer networks. He suggests that machinery will be able to fulfil the function of **market research**, customer care and customer fulfilment.

McKenna, Regis, *Total Access*. Cambridge, MA: Harvard Business School Press, 2002.

M

M-commerce

M-commerce is the blanket term used to describe the purchasing of products and services by customers using mobile communication devices, such as the mobile phone. M-commerce is strongly believed to be the next major growth area in marketing, despite the fact that mobile communications technology has not yet lived up to expectations in terms of its development and flexibility.

Dornan, Andy, *The Essential Guide to Wireless Communications Applications: From Cellular Systems to WAP and M-Commerce*. Englewood Cliffs, NJ: Prentice-Hall, 2000.

MEAL

MEAL is the shorthand form of Media Expenditure Analysis Ltd, a regular publication which shows the amount of advertising spending in a range of different media. Media Expenditure Analysis Ltd was created in 1967 and initially collected data on television and the national press. In 1980 Media Monitoring Services was launched to fulfil a similar role in business markets. The Media Register was launched in 1986 as competition to MEAL and in 1991 the two organizations merged to become Register Meal Ltd. Register Meal Ltd was acquired by A. C. Nielsen in 1992.

Media

'Media' is a collective term used to describe the intermediary or carrier of an advertising message. The media includes the print media (newspapers and magazines), internet (electronic magazines and publications), radio, TV and outdoor advertising (posters, billboards, etc.).

Media kit

A media kit is most closely associated with public relations. Typically a media kit would include copies of press releases, related information, photographs and, if appropriate or practicable, samples of the products or services featured. The purpose of a media kit is to provide the media with all the necessary information in order to write editorial copy on a specific event related to a business, such as the launching of a new product or service.

Media plan

A media plan is the schedule or outline of the advertisements and other activities that make up a marketing campaign. A media plan would involve initially analysing the different media in order to assess which of them would be the most appropriate channels for the messages that the business wishes to convey. A media plan allows a business to coordinate its activities in the promotion of its products or services so that it can assess whether the overall campaign is likely to be both consistent and effective.

Barban, Arnold M., *Essentials of Media Planning*. New York: Contemporary Books, 1994.

Scissors, Jack Z. and Barron, Roger B., *Advertising Media Planning*. New York. Contemporary Books, 2002.

Media release

See **press release**.

Media research

Media research is an integral part of a **media plan** as it involves the systematic investigation and assessment of various media options prior to placing orders for advertisement space. Typically a business would look at the media's existing audiences and compare them with its own customer profiles in order to achieve the closest possible match. An assessment would also be made as to the cost effectiveness of each of the different media. A business may choose to use a variety of different techniques, including **CPT** (cost per thousand) as a comparative measurement.

Jensen, Klaus Baruhn, *Handbook of Media and Communication Research: Qualitative and Quantitative Methodologies*. London: Routledge, 2002.

Merge/purge

The terms 'merge' and 'purge' are most closely associated with the management and maintenance of customer databases, specifically those which are to be used as the foundation of a **direct mail** shot. Given the normal procedures, which involve obtaining data from a variety of different sources, such as **list brokers**, a business will inevitably discover that a number of the data entries are either identical or incorrect in some way. Equally there may be reasons to delete certain data entries as a result of information received, such as the death of a customer or the knowledge that they have moved home. The merging process involves bringing all the data entries into a single database, which is then sorted using whichever criteria the business has adopted. The purging process begins with the elimination of duplicates and proceeds to delete any other data entries which are either incomplete or inaccurate.

The 'merge and purge' system is an integral part of **direct marketing**, which seeks to create accurate and highly targeted databases of potential customer prospects.

Micro-marketing

Micro-marketing is a dependent form of marketing which relies heavily on accurate **market segmentation**. Micro-marketing seeks to target specific and often relatively small groups of customers, through purpose-built promotions to that defined group. Typically the target markets may be defined geographically, demographically, behaviourally or psycho-graphically. In this way micro-marketing allows a business to concentrate on fulfilling the specific needs, wants and expectations of target groups without risking the message that it wishes to convey to them being lost in a more general marketing campaign.

Minority marketing

Effectively minority marketing is akin to **micro-marketing** or the activities of a **market nicher** in the sense that the business aims its products, services and promotions towards a **niche market**. Minority marketing is also used as an all-embracing description of marketing aimed at ethnic or national groups which form a minority in a particular country or region. Clearly there are specific alternatives and requirements of a business wishing to market to these groups, which may include advertisements in different languages and a different approach to the process of selling to accord with ethnic or national customs and traditions.

Halter, Marilyn and Susan Ralston (eds), *Shopping for Identity: The Marketing of Ethnicity*. New York: Schocken Books, 2000.

Schreiber, Alfred L. and Lenson, Barry, *Multi-cultural Marketing: Selling to the New America – Position your Company Today for Optimal Success in the Diverse America of Tomorrow*. New York: McGraw-Hill Education, 2000.

Mixed-mode buying

This is an internet marketing and sales term which is used to describe the process customers adopt when switching from online to offline or vice versa during the buying process.

MOSAIC™

MOSAIC™ is a proprietary national **geo-demographic segmentation** system. In effect, the system is a slightly more sophisticated version of **ACORN**. MOSAIC™ includes a neighbourhood classification system, rather like ACORN, which enables users to identify specific neighbourhoods in terms of their match with products and services.

The system was originally set up over 20 years ago and now extends to some 20 countries around the world. It is, perhaps, best known for its application in the USA, where, alongside the neighbourhood segmentation, classifications including **demographic segmentation** and **lifestyle** are incorporated.

MOSAIC™ was originally built using US census data, which breaks the neighbourhoods down into blocks of 500 households, of which there are

M

nearly 200,000 in the US alone. MOSAIC™ is used to predict consumer behaviour, lifestyles and attitudes, with the following objectives:

- that each of the segments is recognizable and meaningful;
- that each of the segments is statistically reliable;
- that each of the segments is homogeneous.

The system is validated using around 200 different variables and is regularly tested against other segmentation systems in order to evaluate various issues, including coverage, representation of minorities and the identification of different **clusters**.

www.ncsa.uiuc.edu

Multidimensional scaling (MDSCAL)

Multidimensional scaling is a **market research** method which uses a statistical technique to create a spatial structure from numerical data. Multidimensional scaling considers and estimates the differences and similarities between different factors in a study. A typical multidimensional scale may adopt features as shown in Figure 22.

See also **positioning** *and* **product positioning**.

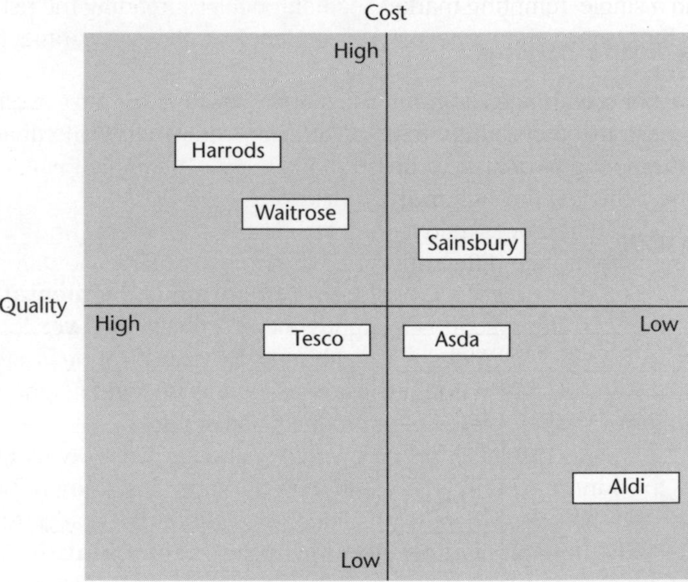

Figure 22 Features of a multidimensional scale

M

Multiple-choice questions

A true multiple choice question needs to incorporate three or more mutually exclusive possible responses. Any less than three, and the question would, technically, be a **dichotomous question**. Multiple-choice questions, as typically seen in printed, web-based or verbally delivered marketing research interviews, can require the respondent to indicate a single or multiple answers to the questions. The respondent needs to be given clear instructions as to whether they are required to give a single definitive answer or whether they can select two or more from the given list of possible responses. It is invariably good practice, in order to ensure that the respondent gives a truthful response, to include the category 'other', after which would be written 'please specify'. This allows the respondent to select a response which may have been overlooked in the questionnaire design.

Multi-segment strategy

A multi-segment strategy is a marketing strategy defined in a **marketing plan**, which seeks to use a different **marketing mix** for each segment. Multi-segment strategy seeks to combine the benefits which would be accrued to the business, of concentrating their marketing effort on a single, tempting market segment, whilst spreading the risk by approaching more than one market segment at the same time (see Figure 23).

The major advantages of a multi-segment strategy are that it offers the business the opportunity to dispose of excess production capacity whilst attempting to achieve a broad market coverage, which would be otherwise achieved through **mass marketing**.

The major differences between multi-segment strategy and mass marketing is that price differentials between brands offered to different

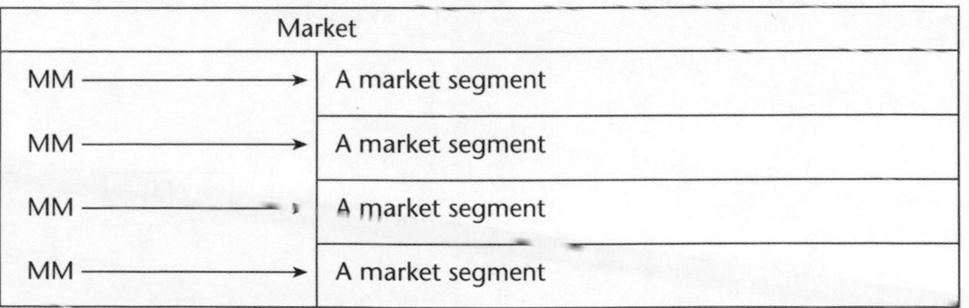

Figure 23 A multi-segment marketing strategy

market segments can be maintained and that consumers within those target segments may be willing to pay a premium price, provided the brand is tailor-made for their needs and wants.

The strategy also has a number of drawbacks, which include the possibility of the business needing to initiate a wider variety of production processes in order to tailor-make products for each specific market segment. Since the business will also be launching a marketing campaign to each market segment, there are increased costs involved, which may stretch the resources. Equally, different channels of distribution may be required and there may be a necessity to change the packaging and overall look of the brand. In order to ensure that multisegment strategy is successful, each market segment needs to be assured that the products being offered are distinctive to them.

Mystery shopper

A mystery shopper is an individual who is employed directly or indirectly by a business to make periodic checks on the services, processes and quality of its activities. Mystery shoppers will not announce themselves as such when visiting an outlet. They will judge various criteria, including customer service, efficiency, friendliness, layout, appearance, as well as the quality and range of products and services on offer. Immediately after their visit mystery shoppers complete a questionnaire based on their observations and this information is then passed on, either to the business or to agents working on behalf of the business, to suggest improvements.

Newhouse, Dr Ilisha S. and Larson, Joanna, *Mystery Shopping Made Simple: A Tutorial to the Mystery Shopping Industry*. New York: McGraw-Hill, 2002.

Nader, Ralph

As well as standing as a Green candidate in the US Presidential elections in 2000, Ralph Nader has devoted most of his career to championing the rights of consumers. He has been variously described as a consumer crusader or public defender and is undoubtedly the US's toughest customer.

Nader began his association with the consumer movement in 1965, when, as a lawyer, he wrote *Unsafe at Any Speed*, a scathing attack on the US car industry. New car safety laws were passed in the US the following year. Nader is arguably responsible for at least eight major US Federal consumer protection laws and he has been involved in campaigns on subjects as varied as safety belts and hotdogs.

Nader's Center for Study of Responsive Law, established in Washington in 1969, has helped foster the creation of several consumer groups, including the Public Interest Research Groups, which has produced hundreds of reports and guides, as well as lobbying decision makers and the media. In 1971 Nader established Public Citizen, which has a current membership of over 100,000.

He is particularly concerned with the growth of multinational businesses and how they refuse to be responsive to customers' needs. In this respect, through his various organizations, Nader actively seeks redress on public liability and negligence issues. Businesses across the US and beyond have discovered, to their great cost, that ignoring Nader, his supporters and organizations, is a virtual impossibility.

Gorey, Hays, *Nader and the Power of Everyman*. New York: Grosset & Dunlap, 1975.
McCarry, Charles, *Citizen Nader*. New York: Saturday Review Press, 1972.

Narrowcasting

'Narrowcasting' is a term most closely associated with the relaying of advertising and promotion messages to small, but clearly defined groups of individuals. For the most part, the term has tended to be used in internet marketing campaigns where specific target groups can be easily targeted (such as subscribers or users of particular websites), but the term is equally valid for marketing or advertising campaigns aimed at any small target group by the use of defined media.

In the field of the broadcast media, narrowcasting refers to situations where the programmer or producer assumes that only a limited number of people or a specific demographic group will be interested in the subject matter of a programme. This is the very nature of most cable television's programming strategy as they follow the format or characteristics of specialized magazines. Most US cable television programmes or channels emphasize one subject or a few closely related subjects, and therefore only appeal to a narrow segment of the potential viewing market.

Waterman, David, '"Narrowcasting" and "Broadcasting" on Nonbroadcast Media: A Program Choice Model'. *Communication Research* (Newbury Park, California), February 1993.

Narver and Slater

In 1990 Narver and Slater wrote that 'the organisational culture that most effectively creates the necessary behaviours for the creation of superior value for buyers and, thus, continuous superior performance for the business' was **market orientation**. They defined market orientation as having three components which were:

- customer orientation – which they defined as 'the sufficient understanding of one's target buyers to be able to create superior value for them continuously';
- competitor orientation – which they described as where 'a seller understands the short-term strengths and weaknesses and the long-term capabilities of both the key current and the key potential competitors';
- inter-functional coordination – which suggested that the activities and the structures within an organization need to be simultaneously deployed in order to ensure market orientation.

They added two decision criteria – long-term focus and profit objective. They finally decided that there were 15 measurable criteria within their five components, which they referred to as MKTOR (Market Orientation). Six factors were identified for customer orientation, four for competitive orientation, five for inter-functional coordination and three each for long-term horizon (focus) and profit emphasis.

Narver, J. C. and Slater, S. F., 'The Effect of a Market Orientation on Business Profitability', *Journal of Marketing* (October 1990), pp. 20–34.

Slater, S. F. and Narver, J. C., 'Does Competitive Environment Moderate the Market Orientation–Performance Relationship?' *Journal of Marketing*, 58:1 (1994), pp. 46–55.

N

Network marketing

Network marketing is variously known as either multi-level marketing or referral marketing and is, in effect, a more 'hands-on' version of **viral marketing**. Network marketing is a logical development of pyramid selling as money changes hands from level to level of the distribution network, whereas viral marketing is a more word-of-mouth system that simply extends the coverage of a product or service.

The concept and structure of the operation encompasses not only the direct selling of products and services on behalf of a supplier, but also the active recruitment of others who will also sell and who ultimately recruit new sellers. Every person an individual recruits (and those the recruits subsequently recruit) will provide an income stream for the recruiter, the recruiter's recruiter, and so on.

The system often promises far more than it can deliver. One of the largest network marketing operations, the US-based Amway (which also owns the web-based business Quixtar Inc.) has millions of 'distributors' worldwide. On average, these distributors earn around $700 per year from their association with the business, but spend $1,000 per year on Amway products. In effect, network marketing is a legal form of **pyramid selling**.

Fitzpatrick, Robert L. and Reynolds, Joyce, *False Profits – Seeking Financial and Spiritual Deliverance in Multi-level Marketing and Pyramid Schemes*. Scottdale, PA: Herald Press, 1997.

New product development

New product development not only involves the creation of new products and services, along with allied research, but also involves product improvement and modification. New product development is concerned with the formulation of new product and service ideas which are normally taken to the prototype stage, encompassing **marketing research** regarding the future prospects of the product, as well as early indications of customer suggestions and attitudes.

Rosenau, Milton D., Griffin, Abbie, Castellion, George A. and Anschuetz, Ned F., *The PDMA Handbook of New Product Development*. Chichester: John Wiley, 1996.
Ulrich, Karl T. and Eppinger, Steven D., *Product Design and Development* (2nd edn). New York; McGraw-Hill/Irwin, 1999.

New product launch

The term 'new product launch' is equally applicable to both products and services and can be a complex marketing communication exercise.

N

Normally there are four stages in the product launch phase of bringing a new brand onto the market. These are:

1 pre-launch;
2 launch;
3 post-launch;
4 expansion stage.

These four phases require considerable pre-planning and coordination. Amongst the many aspects which a business will consider are the following:

- How the product or service fits into the overall **corporate image** and **branding**.
- The use of this image and branding across all proposed promotional activities.
- Internal staff training to bring them up to speed on the features of the new product or service.
- The preparation in-house, or via an agency, of the necessary sales literature and promotional materials.
- The organization of public relations campaigns, particularly during the pre- and post-launch period.
- The media buying and scheduling of any associated advertising campaign.
- The development of sales-promotion programmes, both to the consumers and to potential suppliers, the latter of which needs to be in place before the launch
- The possible use of a **direct marketing** campaign to establish an early indication as to the demand for the product.
- The deployment of sales staff to target specific groups.

Cooper, Robert Gravlin, *Winning at New Products: Accelerating the Process from Idea to Launch* (3rd edn). New York: Perseus Publishing, 2001

Niche marketing

Niche marketing involves targeting a specialist area of the market. Traditionally, businesses will target very clearly defined **market segments** which are not currently being directly targeted by larger organizations. The attractiveness of being able to offer tailor-made products to match the needs and wants of these niche markets is typified by the fact that there is little competition and that premium prices can often be levied. Many niche markets remain just that – a specialist area which will not necessarily attract the attention of a larger business. Many other niche markets have been developed to such an extent that inevitably they draw the attention of larger competitors. Similarly, some niche markets have actually been expanded to such an extent, and the products and services to them sufficiently recognized, as to develop into what is, essentially, a **mass market**. Certainly many products and services which were initially aimed at a niche market have now spread successfully into the mass market.

Marketing and selling into niche markets requires a considerably different approach to mass-market selling. Given the fact that there are fewer potential customers, there is little room for error in being able to provide precisely what the customer demands.

Milder, David N., *Niche Strategies for Downtown Revitalization: A Hands-On Guide to Developing, Strengthening, and Marketing Niches*. New York: Alexander Communications Group, 1998.

Nielsen Retail Index

The A. C. Nielsen Retail Index is a proprietary system, also known as the Retail Measurement Service, which has become an industry standard. Data is collected from over 80 countries and includes product sales, **market share**, **distribution price** and other information. The data is collected by bar-code scanning by auditors, providing a sample of information on products including food, household goods, health and beauty, durables, confectionery and beverages. Businesses use the system to help them gauge product **penetration**, performance, the effectiveness of **promotions**, and **price sensitivity**.

The system was originally introduced in 1933 as the Food and Drug Indices but is now a comprehensive system incorporating sales and merchandising information. **Point of sale** information is gathered in supermarkets, petrol stations, convenience stores, pharmacies, independent retailers and other **distribution** channels.

www.acnielsen.com/services/retail

N

Noise

'Noise' is a general marketing term used to describe all of the other marketing communications which are present at any one time whilst a business is trying to deliver its own marketing messages. The noise, in other words competing marketing messages, seeks to block all other messages and collectively they run the risk of undermining one another and achieving little.

The term is also used to describe a situation which arises out of this general noise. It is often the case that the intended message from a business to its potential audiences does not reach them as accurately as it would have hoped. Typically, businesses will transfer their message into a specific medium, then relay the message via that medium to their audiences. When the audiences receive the message they may not necessarily interpret it in the way that was intended. This is partly due to the business having chosen, possibly, the wrong medium, but it is exacerbated by the fact that there is other noise deflecting the impact and attention towards the message itself.

Shimp, Terence A., *Promotion Management and Marketing Communications*. London: Thomson Learning, 1993.

Non-price competition

Non-price competition, as the name suggests, is competition that is based on factors other than price. The primary task is initially to establish differentiating criteria which mark the product or service as being sufficiently unlike those offered by competitors. Normally 'non-price competition' would imply that a product offered convenience, taste or a degree of prestige. Businesses have recognized that pricing-based competition, in the medium to long term, does little to benefit either organization. Competition based on pricing can temporarily increase **market share**, but in the longer term customers begin to expect lower prices and alternative measures need to be sought in order to maintain market share. Price-cutting merely achieves a cut in the contribution of each unit and may detrimentally affect profitability.

Non-price competition has, therefore, become an important battlefield for many markets. It is typified by the concept of adding a degree of value to whatever the business is offering its customers. Typically these would include some or all of the following:

- customer loyalty cards;
- additional services;
- home delivery systems;
- discounts in allied product areas;
- extended opening hours;
- customer self-scanning of products;
- incentives for purchasing off-peak, or out of season;
- internet shopping.

Metwally, M. M., *Price and Non-price Competition: Dynamics of Marketing*. London: Asia Publishing House.

Non-probability sample

A non probability sample is a **marketing research** technique. A **probability sample** is preferable, as this sampling technique tends to imply that the results derived from the marketing research will be applicable to, and representative of, the larger population. It is sometimes not possible, however, to carry out probability sampling, in which case a non-probability sample, although the respondents will be drawn from the relevant research population, is another alternative. There are a number of different types of non-probability samples, which include **quota sampling**, purposive sampling, snowball sampling, and accidental or convenience sampling.

Purposive sampling uses individuals who have similar characteristics to those in the designated research population. They will not usually be selected at random, but will be targeted as they are easy to contact or may be clustered in one area. Snowball sampling is traditionally used when the research population is actually difficult to find. When the characteristics of the people to be included in the sample have been established, some are found and then asked to suggest other individuals who could be included in the sample. The final alternative, variously known as accidental, convenience or available sampling, relates to those who agree to take part and are available at the right time. In practice this sampling technique, as it is not representative in any way, tends to be used just for pilots or exploratory marketing research.

Observation research

Observation research is a **marketing research** technique which actually incorporates a number of different marketing research procedures. Researchers will literally observe personally or remotely interactions and experiences normally related to sales personnel and customers. Observation research tends to be used to measure the actual nature of a customer's experience when he or she interacts with the business. Observation research includes the following areas:

- **Mystery shopping** – which deploys individuals to pose as customers in order to see how sales employees deal with queries and complaints.
- Mystery calling – which uses individuals who pose as customers to make telephone calls to the business to see how problems or queries are dealt with.
- Customer flow analysis – which usually employs the use of remote cameras to see areas, particularly of a retail outlet, which attract attention or suffer from congestion.

An organization could use observation to collect information and answer questions about the following areas:

- Environment and facilities – Is everything working properly, clean and tidy, well presented?
- Service standards – Are specific standards being met, all the time, every time?
- Politeness and helpfulness of staff – Do staff have good skills with the customers?
- Product knowledge – Do staff understand the features, functions, and benefits of the products/services offered?
- Procedures knowledge – Staff may know what to do, but do they know how?
- Test purchases – Do staff sell effectively?
- Refunds and complaints procedures – How are customers treated when returning products, and how are customer complaints handled?

- Product support – Are new products being promoted effectively?
- Promotional materials – Are sales leaflets and brochures being displayed effectively?
- Help lines, support lines – How well does the business perform when dealing with customers on the telephone?
- Price audits – Are prices competitive?
- Legal checks – Are staff observing laws and the business's own recommended safety checks?
- Websites – How well does the business perform when dealing with customers online?

Odd–even pricing

Odd–even pricing may be part of a business's **pricing strategies** which attempt to influence a buyer's perception of the price. There is considerable debate as to how customers perceive specific prices and in many respects odd–even pricing is very much akin to **psychological pricing**. Some businesses may opt for odd pricing, typically £19.99 or £99.99. This is based on the assumption that customers perceive the price as 9 rather than 10. Other businesses have recognized the value of even pricing and set their price points at £5, £10, £15 or £20. The inference here and the consequent buyer perception is that the business is not trying to fool them and that it recognizes the customers' intelligence in not being fooled.

Nagle, Thomas T. and Holden, Reed K., *The Strategy and Tactics of Pricing: A Guide to Profitable Decision Making* (3rd edn). Englewood Cliffs, NJ: Prentice Hall, 2002.

Off-peak pricing

Off-peak pricing is another **pricing strategy** which attempts to stimulate demand by price reduction during periods when demand is traditionally low. Off-peak pricing is also referred to as 'seasonal pricing', which is not to be confused with discounting in the sense of running sales, for limited periods, to reduce stock levels.

Omnibus survey

An omnibus survey is usually a piece of **marketing research** which has been carried out by a market research organization. Typically, an omnibus survey would be a syndicated, regular survey in which businesses or clients can purchase questions to go into the survey at a price per question. An omnibus survey is, therefore, an ideal way of reaching a large sample of established respondents at a considerably lower cost than launching an independent marketing research exercise. Omnibus surveys are ideal vehicles for businesses who only wish to ask a limited number of questions. They can generally be assured of receiving information from a large and representative sample of their target population.

On-pack offer

On-pack offers are sometimes referred to as being 'self-liquidating premiums'. Typically, a self-liquidating premium requires the customer to make an initial purchase of one or more products in order to receive a discount, via a clip-out coupon, for subsequent purchases. Self-liquidating premiums are just one type of on-pack offer. Other alternatives may be increased volume (such as 25% extra free), the collection of coupons to receive free or discounted gifts, or an inducement on the pack which offers a free or discounted allied product at the time of purchase.

Open-ended questions

There are two close associations with the term 'open-ended question', one relating to sales and another which describes a particular form of question used in **marketing research** on a questionnaire.

As a sales-related device, open-ended questions are used by salespersons to gather information and establish a rapport, trust and credibility with the customer. Sales professionals are often urged not to ask questions which can allow the customer to supply them with a simple 'yes or no' answer. They are encouraged to engage and involve the customer in the sales discussion. Open-ended questions allow customers to explain their requirements and concerns, so that the salespersons can tailor their sales technique to allay any problems or suspicions regarding the product or service.

O

Open-ended questions are also used in questionnaires and whilst they are more difficult to analyse than other types of questions, they can provide the market researcher with valuable insights into the true feelings of the respondent. Typically, a blank space will be left on a questionnaire which allows and prompts the respondents to put in their own words their answer to a carefully designed question.

Opportunity cost

'Opportunity cost', although strictly speaking an economics term, can be equally applied to marketing and advertising. Each time a business chooses to pursue a particular form of marketing activity it has made that choice, having investigated all of the other options. Given the fact that it is unlikely, even with the largest marketing budgets available, that a business can pursue all forms of **marketing research** simultaneously, some options have to be discarded. Opportunity cost argues that the potential benefits which could have been enjoyed by choosing a particular marketing activity have to be considered if they are not chosen and an alternative action is preferred. In other words, opportunity cost examines the real cost of an action in terms of the next best alternative that has been forgone.

Opt-in email/mail

An internet marketing term closely associated with **permission marketing**. Customers or potential customers (prospects) give permission to the business to send them marketing communications. Typically, this opt-in option would appear when the visitor is prompted to click a box on a web-based form or questionnaire. Opt-in is also applied to a customer applying for the regular delivery of a newsletter. Opt-in is distinguished from opt-out, where the customers or prospects have decided that they no longer wish to receive marketing communications, and have selected the 'unsubscribe' link.

The issue is further complicated by the terms 'double opt-in' and 'double opt-out'. 'Double opt-in' refers to situations where users who have already opted-in receive a confirmation email stating that they have made this choice. The user is prompted to reply to the email in order to confirm the relationship and that marketing communications can now be sent. 'Double opt-out' involves a similar process: after the user has decided to unsubscribe or receive no further marketing communications from the business, a confirmation email is generated. The user must send a reply to the automated email in order to confirm that opt-out has been selected.

The opt-in process is equally applicable to conventional postal mailings as part of **direct marketing/direct mail** campaigns.

Orders per 1000 (OPM)

'OPM' is a direct marketing term which in its abbreviation confusingly refers to millions; none the less, the term refers to the number of confirmed orders (which are then subsequently processed) per 1,000 contacts with potential customers as part of a **direct marketing** campaign. OPM is used as a primary initial measure of the success (or relative failure) of the direct marketing exercise.

Osgood's Semantic Differential Scale

Osgood's Semantic Differential Scale requires the researcher to evaluate the direction and intensity of a respondent's attitude towards a product. It is useful for measuring attitudes and uses a 7-point double-ended scale. Typically it uses opposite adjectives, statements or phrases, which may be bi-polar (such as good–bad) or mono-polar (such as sweet–not sweet). An example is shown in Figure 24.

As with other forms of semantic differential scales, exploratory research is often employed to identify relevant attributes. The normal procedure is to mix bi-polar and mono-polar scales so that the respondent does not develop a set process of responses. Equally, the adjectives, statements and phrases can be reversed in order to help offset this tendency.

Indicate on the scale below which adjective best describes *Key Concepts in Marketing*

Good	0	0	0	0	0	0	0	Bad
Non-rigorous	0	0	0	0	0	0	0	Rigorous
Analytical	0	0	0	0	0	0	0	Descriptive
Interesting	0	0	0	0	0	0	0	Boring
Challenging	0	0	0	0	0	0	0	Routine
False	0	0	0	0	0	0	0	True
Negative	0	0	0	0	0	0	0	Positive

Figure 24 Illustration of a Semantic Differential Scale

O

Webb, J. R., *Understanding and Designing Marketing Research*. London: Academic Press, 1992.

Own label/brand

The term 'own label' or 'own brand' refers to products or services which have been created by a retailer. A wide variety of different products and services are developed using the retailer's own name, and are seen as a viable alternative, in terms of both implied quality and price, to traditional branded products.

Packaging

Packaging entails the development of a product's container, label, design and overall identity. The packaging of a product is considered to be a very important consideration as it is the first impression that a customer receives of the product prior to purchase.

Packaging needs to fulfil a number of different functions, including, of course, protection for the product whilst it is within the **distribution channel**, or storage, as well as while it is waiting on a retailer's shelves prior to purchase. In this respect there are a number of prerequisites, including ensuring that the product contents do not part company with the packaging prior to purchase (spillage, or damage to the product). In the past, packaging merely involved the printing of a trader's name or the product's name on a relatively functional or plain packaging material. Packaging now has identifiable **logos**, slogans and names. Packaging reinforces advertising campaigns by allowing the customer to recognize the image that has been portrayed, and also assists **point of sale** merchandising and **brand image**.

Increasingly, there have been concerns regarding packaging, involving environmental and recycling issues. 'Green packaging', which involves the use of recycled material, the opportunity to recycle, or more biodegradable materials, has begun to be used extensively.

Hine, Thomas, *The Total Package: The Secret History and Hidden Meanings of Boxes, Bottles, Cans, and other Persuasive Containers*. Boston, MA: Little Brown, 1997.

Packaging tests

Packaging tests tend to be an integral part of the pre-launch period of **new product development**. Businesses may already have preferred and well-tested packaging techniques for their products. Indeed, their packaging may be an integral part of their overall **brand image**. None the less, innovative packaging designs are often employed specifically to stand out from other products and services which may be available to the customer. A packaging test would therefore involve the initial design of a prototype packaging for a particular product. It would then be assessed to measure its durability and suitability for the task. Alongside these tests there would also be a process of eliciting potential buyers' responses to the way in which the packaging appears. They would be encouraged to suggest the suitability of the packaging, as well as noting points about the packaging which might attract them or cause them concerns.

Risch, Sarah J., *Food Packaging: Testing Methods and Applications*. Washington, DC: American Chemical Society, 2000.

Paid circulation

A media, advertising and publishing term used to describe the actual number of copies of a magazine or periodical which are purchased rather than the number printed. It excludes copies which have been given away free for promotional purposes. This figure can be seen as an alternative to having the magazine independently audited. The figure would, commonly, include all subscriptions and sales on demand.

Paid listing

'Paid listing' is an internet marketing term used to describe an advertisement which appears on the first page of a search engine's results. To the user, it appears that the result is highly placed and a good match for their search criteria. The advertisement is, in fact, a paid-for advertisement. This is used by Google and Yahoo as an additional income stream.

Panel

Panels are often used in **marketing research** as an information-gathering technique, involving asking a sample group of individuals a series of questions over a period of time. The method is often used to assess shifts in attitudes and opinions. In marketing there are three identifiable types of panels which are often used, these are:

- *Consumer purchasing panel* – where customers' purchases and attitudes to particular products or types of products are collected.
- *Test panel* – where groups of people are asked to field-test new products before their launch.
- *Audience panel* – which monitors the viewing or listening patterns of TV and radio audiences, using a computerized system.

Table 38 lists the advantages and disadvantages of using panels.

Table 38 The advantages and disadvantages of panels

Advantages	Disadvantages
They are a good trend indicator.	Regular panels can be disrupted by deaths or non-attendance.
They are useful for analysing changes and assessing them in relation to external factors that may have influenced them.	Panels tend to attract more intelligent individuals and there is a tendency for the less articulate to be excluded.
Detailed information can be collected on the habits and attitudes of individuals, which provides valuable background information.	Panellists may adopt uncharacteristic behaviour during the panel discussions.
	Selecting and recruiting panellists can be expensive and time-consuming.
	Panellists will have to be replaced periodically.
	Panellists will expect some form of reward.

Wansink, Brian and Sudman, Seymour, *Consumer Panels*. London: Butterworth-Heinemann, 2002.

Pareto Analysis

Vilfredo Pareto (1848–1923) was an Italian economist and sociologist, known more widely for his theory on mass and elite interaction as well as his application of mathematics to economic analysis.

The fundamental concept of Pareto Analysis, or the Pareto Principle, is that a business derives 80% of its income from 20% of its customers. In other words, this 20% of loyal customers is the foundation upon which a business can build its profits and its **market share**. On the reverse, the remaining 80% of their customers only provide businesses with 20% of their income. This is largely due to the fact that these customers are irregular purchasers, and are far more prone to **brand switching**. Marketing aims to ensure that the profitable 20% of customers retain their **customer loyalty** and that gradually, significant numbers of the remaining 80% are transformed into loyal customers, thus increasing market share and profitability.

P

Party plan

Party plans are a form of **direct marketing** particularly used for cosmetics, plastic ware, kitchen ware and jewellery. Party organizers are recruited by a business, and receive a gift and/or a percentage of the sales achieved at the party. The party organizer, or host, is encouraged to invite friends or neighbours to the party, where the products are displayed and demonstrated. Party plans have become an integral part of many businesses' strategies and they have adopted this **distribution channel** as an alternative to offering their products and services through more conventional means.

Clarke, Alison J., *Tupperware: The Promise of Plastic in 1950s America*. Washington, DC: Smithsonian Institution Press, 2001.

Pay-per-click advertising

See **pay-per-click search engine.**

Pay-per-click search engine

A pay-per-click search engine charges website owners every time a browser clicks on the link to their site from the search page. In many respects, this is a more efficient and reasonable means of payment to the search engine as the charge is made per visitor to the website, rather than according to the subsequent page impressions.

Penetration

'Penetration' is a general marketing term used to describe the gradual process of achieving a foothold in a particular market. Penetration involves establishing a product or service in a given market, or the development of a **market share** which has, hitherto, been comparatively small. The greater the penetration into the market, the larger the market share and hence the more influence the business may have over that market. One of the many **marketing strategies** or **pricing strategies** is **penetration pricing**.

Penetration pricing

Penetration pricing is an aggressive form of **pricing strategy**. A business sets the prices for its products and services deliberately low enough to attract as many customers as possible in the shortest possible time. The sole purpose of penetration pricing is to undermine the pricing structure of competitors and to wrestle as much **market share** from them as is practicable in the shortest period of time. Having established a viable market share by adopting this policy, a business will then review its pricing strategies and may well revert to a more traditional pricing structure. Penetration pricing can be seen as the direct opposite of **price skimming**.

Perceived value pricing

This form of **pricing strategy** requires a business to have already established perceptions of customers in relation to the benefits or qualities of a particular product or service. Customers will have their own perceptions of whether the product or service offers them value in proportion to the price demanded by the business. Providing a balance is established, and that the price and the customers' perceptions of the value of that price are near to equal, then this can form the foundation of a business's pricing structure.

Permission marketing

Permission marketing is also known as request marketing and involves **direct marketing** approaches to customers who have expressed an interest in receiving further information, news and updates from a particular business. Permission marketing is used in several different areas of marketing and across a wide variety of different industries. Conventional forms of permission marketing relate to the continued contact with customers who have requested brochures, or sales literature, on a previous occasion but may not have yet purchased products or services from the business. Alternatively, they may be lapsed customers who are still on a business's database.

Permission marketing has developed considerably over the last few years alongside the increased intensity of business use of the internet. It is closely associated with concepts such as **opt-in email** or other positive customer-initiated contacts with a business. Permission marketing practitioners distinguish their form of marketing from the more intrusive forms of **direct mail**, or emailing unsought sales messages to customers. Permission marketing, by its very nature, infers that the customers have a basic form of interest in what the business is offering and that they welcome the periodic contact with the business.

Godin, Seth and Peppers, Don, *Permission Marketing: Turning Strangers into Friends and Friends into Customers*. New York: Simon & Schuster, 1999.

P

Personal interviews

Personal surveys are also known as face-to-face or personal interviews. These involve actually asking questions of the respondents in person in the street or at their workplace. It can be a very useful way of collecting information for **market research**. The strengths and weaknesses of personal interviews appear in Table 39.

Table 39 An assessment of personal interviews

Strengths	Weaknesses
The interviewer can help the respondents by prompting them.	The cost of transportation to and from the interview.
The interviewer can see the respondents' reactions.	The travelling time to the interview.
The respondents have time to think and give better answers.	There is a risk that the interviewer might suggest answers.
The respondents can be interviewed in their own surroundings.	Organizing personal interviews across the country can be difficult and expensive.
The respondents will give the interviewer their full attention during the interview.	It is often difficult for the interviewer to be sure that a respondent is the right sort of person needed for the survey.

Personal selling

Personal selling is a face-to-face communication and sales technique aimed at persuading a customer to purchase a product or service. It is distinguished from advertising, sales promotions and other promotional tools as they are, generally speaking, impersonal selling techniques. The personal selling or personal communication sales technique, although costly in comparison with other methods, replicates normal human interaction and allows the salesperson not only to provide information, but also to arouse in the customer a desire to purchase the product. It is a measure of the importance placed on personal selling that in the US alone, 1.5 million people are involved in personal selling, compared with less than a third of that figure in advertising. Personal selling is particularly useful in the following circumstances:

- when the product or service has a high unit cost or is technical and requires a demonstration;

- when the product needs to be tailor-made for the customer, particularly in the case of pensions or insurance;
- when the product is relatively unknown in the market and is, perhaps, in the introductory stage of its life cycle;
- when the business may not have sufficient resources to sustain a heavy advertising campaign;
- when the market is particularly concentrated geographically, with several large customers.

See also **selling, inside** *and* **selling, outside.**

Singer, Blair and Kiyosaki, Robert T., *Sales Dogs*. Boston, MA: Little, Brown, 2003.

Personalization

Personalization is a growing area of sales and marketing, as it seeks to provide individual customers, or groups of customers, with adapted versions of a basic product. Specific changes or amendments can be made to the standard offering – for example, customers can buy a regular model of a vehicle but determine the colour, the trim and the internal colours and layout. Personalization has become possible as businesses adopt more **market orientation** in their approach and adapt their production systems to produce products and services on demand, rather than stockpiling supplies in the anticipation of sales. Personalization allows marketing to focus on the individuality of each of the products, and the options and choices available to each and every customer.

Kasanoff, Bruce, *Making it Personal: How to Profit from Personalization without Invading Privacy*. Chichester: John Wiley, 2001.

PEST

See **Five Forces.**

Piggyback

The term 'piggyback' has several allied definitions which are all related to linking a product or a service with another product or service. A piggyback promotion, for example, would offer a voucher, or perhaps a free sample of another product. Piggyback selling involves the immediate sale of an allied item as the result of the initial purchase, and in **direct marketing** and **direct mail** shots piggybacking involves the inclusion of additional sales literature in an already agreed package of information.

PIMS (Profit Impact of Marketing Strategies)

PIMS is a **marketing research** programme which is a database of information on some 3,000 business units of 200 different businesses. The information is used to analyse marketing performance and in assisting the formulation of **marketing strategies**.

Buzzell, Robert D., *The PIMS Principles: Linking Strategy to Performance.* Basingstoke: Macmillan, 1987.

Place

'Place' is one of the four original elements of the **marketing mix**. Place focuses on how a product or service is supplied to the customer. In other words, the focus of place is on the **distribution channels** and the timing of that distribution along the route to the end user.

Plug

'Plug' is a semi-slang term used to describe the mentioning, endorsement or testimonial of a product, service, brand or business by the media without charge.

Point of purchase

The point of purchase is the place in which customers physically buy products and services. In most cases points of purchase are retail outlets and include, therefore, counter displays, window displays, banners and other focus points within the premises. 'Point of purchase' offers businesses the opportunity to encourage impulse buying. In many respects, point of purchase is a somewhat more viable term than the interchangeable **point of sale**.

Point of Purchase Advertising Institute, *Point of Purchase Design Manual.* Hearst Books International, 2002.

Point of sale

The narrow definition of 'point of sale' is literally the area immediately surrounding the cash register in a retail outlet. There are opportunities, as customers are queuing to purchase a product or service, to sell them additional items as impulse buys. In practice, however, the term 'point of sale' has little difference from **point of purchase** and, as such, includes outdoor signage, window displays, counter pieces, display racks and self-service containers.

Austin, Thomas E., *New Retail Power and Muscle: Remarkable Weapon to Win the War at the Point of Sale*. BRG Publishing, 2000.

Porter, Michael

Michael E. Porter is currently a professor at the Harvard Business School and is considered to be the leading authority on **competitive strategy** and competitiveness. He graduated with an MBA from Harvard in 1971 and a PhD in 1973. He has written some 16 books and 75 articles, including *Competitive Strategy: Techniques for Analysing Industries and Competitors* (1980), *Competitive Advantage: Creating and Sustaining Superior Performance* (1985), *The Competitive Advantage of Nations* (1990) and *On Competition* (1998).

Over the years he has received a number of awards, including the Adam Smith Award from the National Association of Business Economists. Porter serves as an advisor to several different countries and has led major economic studies in countries as diverse as New Zealand and Peru.

Porter, Michael E., *Competitive Advantage: Creating and Sustaining Superior Performance*. New York: Free Press, 1985.
Porter, Michael E., *The Competitive Advantage of Nations*. New York: Free Press, 1990.
Porter, Michael E., *On Competition*. Boston, MA: Harvard Business School Press, 1998.

Porter's Five Forces model

Michael Porter's classic Five Forces model (see Table 40) appeared in his 1980s book *Competitive Strategy: Techniques for Analyzing Industries and Competitors*. It has become the standard analysing tool for many businesses.

Table 40 Porter's Five Forces – simple model

Force	Description
Industry competitors	Rivalry amongst existing businesses
Potential entrants	Threats of new entrants into market
Buyers	Bargaining power of buyers in the market
Substitutes	Threat of substitute products/services
Suppliers	Bargaining power of suppliers to businesses in the market

P

Table 41 Porter's Five Forces

Five Forces	**Description**	**Implications**
Threat of new entrants	The easier it is for new businesses to enter the industry, the more intense the competition. There may be factors which may limit the number of new entrants, which are known as barriers to entry.	Customers may already be loyal to major brands. Incentives may be offered to customers in order to retain them. Fixed costs will be high and there may be a scarcity of resources. Businesses and customers may find it expensive to switch suppliers and take the attendant risks.
Power of suppliers	This measures how much pressure suppliers can place on businesses within the industry. The larger the supplier and the more dominant, the more it can squeeze a business's margins and profits.	In some markets there are few suppliers of particular products as there are no available substitutes. Switching to other suppliers may prove difficult, costly and risky. If the product is extremely important to the buyer they will continue to purchase it. In many cases the supplying industry has a higher profitability than the buying industry.
Power of buyers	This is a measure as to how powerful customers are and what pressures they can apply to a business. The larger and more reliant customers are, the more likely they are to be able to affect the margins and volumes of a business.	There may be a small number of buyers who purchase large volumes of products and services. Buyers may be tempted to switch to an alternative supplier. If a product is not at the core of their business or requirements, buyers may choose not to purchase for a period of time. The more competitive the market, the more price sensitive the customers may be.

⇒

Table 41 Porter's Five Forces (*continued*)

Five Forces	Description	Implications
Threat of substitute products	This is a measure of how likely it is for buyers to switch to a competing product or service. Assuming the cost of switching is low, then this will be a serious threat.	Businesses should be aware that similar products, if not exact substitutes, may tempt the buyer to switch, temporarily at least, to another supplier. If, for example, a supermarket chain is offered considerably cheaper alternatives to plastic shopping bags, they may be tempted to move over to cardboard boxes or paper sacks.
Competitive rivalry	This measures the degree of competition between existing businesses in an industry. It is usually the case that the higher the competition, the lower the return on investment. Margins are pared down to the lowest levels.	Assuming there is no dominant business, then many of the competitors will be of a similar size. There will also be little differentiation between competitors' products and services. The more stagnant the industry, in terms of market growth, the higher the possibility that competitors will focus on taking customers away from other businesses, rather than attempting to develop the market themselves.

The Five Forces shape every market and industry and help a business to analyse the intensity of competition, as well as the profitability and attractiveness of the market and industry. The Five Forces can be best explained as in Table 41.

Porter, Michael E., *Competitive Strategy: Techniques for Analyzing Industries and Competitors*. New York: The Free Press, 1980.

P

Position charge

'Position charge' is an advertising and media-related term which refers to an additional payment levied on an advertiser or an advertising agency on behalf of their client for the specific positioning of an advertisement on a page. It is generally believed that magazine and newspaper readers, for example, are inclined to look at right-hand pages first. Specifically, their attention will be drawn to the top right-hand corner of a right-hand page. Therefore, by extension, this is the most desired position on any given page. A premium will normally be charged by the publisher if the advertiser wishes their advertisement to appear either in a specific position on a page or on a specific page, perhaps close to an editorial or article which in some way relates to the advertisement.

Positioning

Positioning is most commonly associated with the term '**product positioning**'. In this sense positioning attempts to establish an image, or a view, of the product or service in the minds of the target customers. Positioning may also be applied to the business as an entity. Marketing may be used to establish in the minds of customers, competitors and the industry in general, the overall stance, identity and image of the business, based on criteria such as quality, service, innovation or price.

The basic positioning map can be seen in Figure 25. A completed positioning map is given in Figure 26.

See also **product positioning.**

Ries, Al, and Trout, Jack, *Positioning: The Battle for your Mind – How to be Seen and Heard in the Overcrowded Marketplace.* New York: McGraw-Hill, 2001.

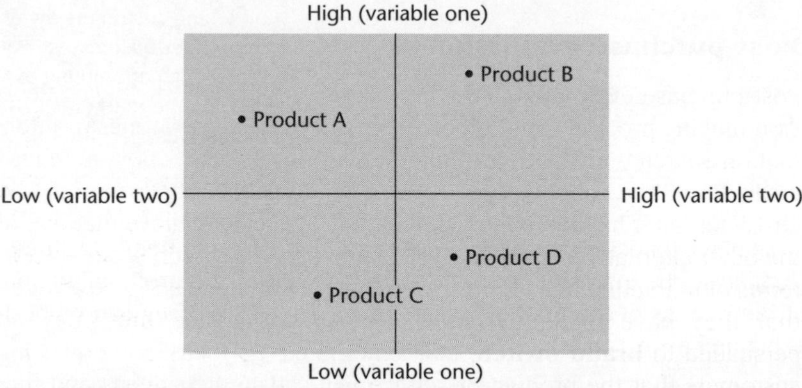

Figure 25 A basic positioning map

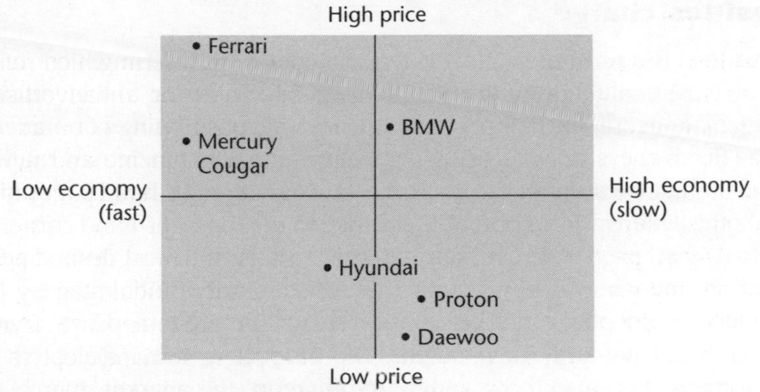

Figure 26 A completed positioning map

Positivist research

Positivist research tends to use qualitative data and it presupposes that there is some underlying true reality. In other words, the positivist approach is an attempt to predict phenomena or events which will occur, based on the evidence which has been gathered. There is a close correlation in positivist thinking that, providing objectivity and rigorous research techniques have been employed, then direct conclusions can be established which are quantifiable and accurate.

See also **qualitative research**.

Lacity, Mary C. and Janson, Marius A., 'Understanding Qualitative Data: a Framework of Text Analysis Methods', *Journal of Management Information Systems*, 11:2 (Fall 1994), pp. 137–56.

Post-purchase evaluation

Post-purchase evaluation is the last stage in a customer's buying decision making process (need recognition and problem awareness – information search – evaluation of alternatives – purchase – post-purchase evaluation). The concept itself arises from **cognitive dissonance**. The customer, after having made the purchase, may now believe that one of the other alternatives that were on offer would have been preferable. In terms of marketing, it is at this stage that customers need to be assured that they have made the right decision, otherwise they may be persuaded to **brand switch**. Marketing needs to focus on convincing customers that the product or service will satisfy their needs and that they have made the correct decision.

Post-test

'Post-test' is a term most closely associated with advertising. Post-tests involve the evaluation of the effectiveness of advertising at the end of a particular advertising campaign. There are various measures of the relative effectiveness of advertising campaigns, including increased market or customer awareness, an increase in sales or increases in inquiries and other interest from potential customers.

The term 'post-test' can also be applied to the period immediately after the launch of a new product or service. In the initial stages of a product's entry onto a market, a business will be concerned with trying to ascertain not only how quickly the product is being accepted by customers, but also how much information the market has been exposed to regarding the product. In this sense, a post-test can measure the launch marketing activities and assess whether any lessons are to be learned in future launches, or whether some form of remedial action needs to be put in place in order to further establish the product in the marketplace.

Postal research

Postal surveys (questionnaires sent out by mail) are often used by a business or a market research company to obtain information from customers. The strengths and weaknesses of postal surveys are summarized in Table 42.

Postal walk (unaddressed mail)

The term 'postal walk' is most directly applicable to **direct marketing**, **direct mail** and the hand delivery of sales literature. A postal walk is literally the households which a single postal worker delivers to on the normal delivery route. By using a mixture of analysis techniques which determine the type of households within a given postcode or zip code area, a more focused delivery of sales literature can be achieved through choosing appropriate postal walks.

Predatory pricing

Predatory pricing is a **pricing strategy** adopted by some businesses in order to inflict financial damage on competitors by forcing them to cut their profit margins and match the unfeasibly low prices the business is offering. This is an extremely aggressive and often short-term policy, used to drive competitors out of a market. Invariably it is adopted by

Table 42 Evaluation of postal surveys

Strengths	Weaknesses
They are relatively easy and inexpensive to set up and control.	Not that many respondents bother to fill in the questionnaire and send it back.
Respondents can give thoughtful and considered responses.	You cannot be sure that the person it was sent to actually filled in the questionnaire.
Respondents have the time to think about their answers.	Sending out the questionnaires and waiting for them to return can take a long period of time.
Because there is no interviewer involved, the respondents actually put down what they think and not what they think the interviewer wants to hear.	Because there is no one there to thank them for bothering, the respondents might not feel that their opinions actually matter.
It doesn't matter where the respondent is, the questionnaires can be mailed to anyone, anywhere.	Respondents can read through the questionnaires first and choose answers that mean that they don't need to fill in later parts of the questionnaire.

businesses who already have a substantial **market share** and enjoy considerable **economies of scale**, allowing them to temporarily offer products and services at prices well below the market norm. In recent years predatory pricing has become a feature in a number of areas, particularly with regard to supermarkets, where basic stock items, such as bread, baked beans and tinned tomatoes, have been offered at virtually cost price. Extreme cases of predatory pricing do in fact aim to drive competitors out of business. If this purpose is revealed and proven, the strategy is deemed illegal.

P

Pre-launch

Pre-launch is the period immediately prior to a product or service appearing in the market. The pre-launch period is critical as it requires, as far as marketing is concerned, that all campaigns and associated activities be in place and ready for customers to be able to know about the product and make easy purchases. The pre-launch phase usually involves a considerable degree of **public relations** in the form of **press**

releases to alert the media and other interested parties to the imminent launch of the new product.

Premiums

Premiums are distinct from premium pricing as a form of **pricing strategy** as they offer products or services either free, or at a lower cost, in order to provide an incentive to customers to buy.

Press release

Press releases, or news releases, are an integral part of **public relations**. They are written and designed in order to provide the media with an easy to translate, newsworthy story regarding the business or their products and services. Press releases are sent to reporters and editors in the hope that some editorial space will be assigned to the story. Typically, press releases will include quotes, have a personal angle, and may be accompanied by relevant photographs or other illustrative material, in order to reduce the amount of legwork that needs to be done to follow up and present the story in the media.

See also **media kit.**

Northmore, David, *How to Get Publicity for Free: How to Write a Press Release, Contact the Media, Gain Radio and Television Interviews and Organise Press Conferences.* London: Bloomsbury, 1993.

Press tour

A press tour is a specific event organized by the **public relations** personnel of a marketing department. A press tour, or visit, consists of inviting members of the press, either to the business's premises, or to a neutral venue, in order to coincide with a special event, such as the launching of a new product or initiative.

Prestige pricing

Prestige pricing is a **pricing strategy** which relies on the business, through marketing, having established a perception in the minds of customers that the product or service has notably superior levels of quality, exclusivity or service. Prestige pricing may also be referred to as 'premium pricing', as products or services have a pricing structure often somewhat different from that of the competitors. The business trades, and relies heavily, on the customers' continued and engrained perceptions of the product, for which they are prepared to pay a considerably higher price than for other alternatives available.

Pre-test

Pre-tests are a form of **marketing research** usually carried out on behalf of those who have framed the content of an advertising campaign. A pre-test research activity will revolve around attempts to evaluate and assess the potential effectiveness of elements within the advertising campaign. Notably the focus will be upon the clarity of the messages contained within the advertisements and whether those who would become the targets of the advertising campaign perceived the messages in the same way as those who wrote them.

Price

Price is one of the four original Ps of the **marketing mix**. Effectively, price covers the money charged for a product or service, or more explicitly, the sum of money which customers are prepared to pay for a product, based on their own valuation of the benefits they will receive. Price is an integral element of the marketing mix and there are a number of determining factors, which can be categorized into three areas:

- *Cost* – including the variable costs, fixed costs and proposed mark-up.
- *Competition* – the number of direct competitors, lower-priced segments in the market or substitutes available from other industries.
- *Customers* – past prices, just or fair prices, perceptions of quality, and price expectations.

Price bundling

Price or product bundling is the sale of two or more separate products in a single package. Price bundling is the sale of two or more separate products in a package at a discount, where there is no attempt to integrate the two products. The bundling does not create added value for the consumer as the two products are not directly associated. This is why a discount is offered to motivate consumers to buy the bundle.

In 1988 Microsoft began bundling several software programs under the title Microsoft Office. Up until this time customers had been able to purchase Word, Excel, Access and PowerPoint as separate products.

They may not necessarily have required or desired all of these products. None the less, they were now able to purchase all of the software at a discounted rate compared with the individually priced items. The result was that Microsoft enjoyed an enormous sales increase and was propelled towards market dominance.

Product bundling can be differentiated from price bundling in the sense that two or more separate products are integrated in some way, which implies that the Microsoft experiment was both a price bundling and a product bundling exercise. Other examples of product bundling tend to add value to the consumer's purchase, such as integrated stereo systems, which offer compactness.

Bakos, Yiannis and Brynjolfsson, Erik, 'Bundling Information Goods: Pricing, Profits and Efficiency', *Management Science*, 45:12 (1999), pp. 1613–30.

Price elasticity

Price elasticity, or price elasticity of demand, measures the responsiveness of quantity demanded to a change in price. The most commonly used formula compares the proportion in change in quantity divided by the proportion in change in price. The effects are summarized in Table 43.

Table 43 Effects of price elasticity

Elasticity	**Demand is price elastic: $|h_p| > 1.0$**	**Demand is price inelastic: $|h_p| < 1.0$**
Price reduction	Expenditure increases	Expenditure decreases
Price increase	Expenditure decreases	Expenditure increases

Tellis, Gerard J., *The Price Elasticity of Selective Demand: A Meta-analysis of Sales Response Models*. Cambridge, MA: Marketing Science Institute, 1988.

Price sensitivity

Price sensitivity is a measure of how customers may react to changes in the costs of the products and services they purchase. It is a term closely associated with **price elasticity** and it is largely determined by a difference in the perceived value of a product or service or the number of competitors in a market.

Price skimming

Price skimming is a **pricing strategy** which is the direct opposite of **penetration pricing**. Price skimming allows a business to set a high price for its products and services that may only be acceptable to a proportion of its customers (see Figure 27). Specifically these customers are the ones who value the product highly and, importantly, have the means to continue purchasing it.

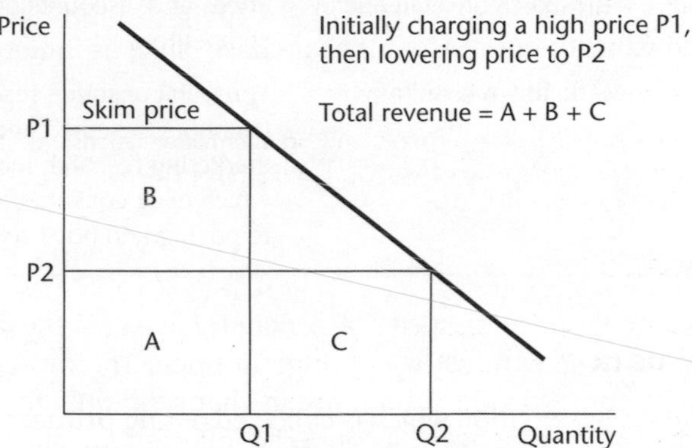

Figure 27 Price skimming. The diagram shows that at P1, the skim price, quantity sold is comparatively low. Should the business reduce its price to P2, then Q2 sales can be included in the overall equation. Having maintained a skim price at P1 for a period of time before reducing to P2, the business enjoys a total revenue that is the sum of A, B and C, as shown on the diagram.

Pricing research

Pricing research is a form of **marketing research** which investigates **price sensitivity** and price perception. The information and sources, as well as the key stages of pricing research, are summarized in Table 44.

The purpose of pricing research is to enable a business to have a more market orientated **pricing strategy**, by identifying what associations consumers make with different prices and product variations.

Pricing strategies/policies

There are innumerable pricing strategies which can be adopted by business in order to fulfil specific marketing objectives. The most common are summarized in Table 45.

Nagle, Thomas and Holden, Reed, *The Strategy and Tactics of Pricing.* US Imports and PHIPES, 2001.

P

Table 44 Pricing research

Factor	Source	Details
Costing	Accounts and production	Costing information would include the cost of raw materials, production, distribution and warehousing.
Competitors	Sales force or retail audits	Prices and discounts offered by competitors.
Consumer	Marketing research	Through consumer research, telephone research and other marketing research methods, which elicit consumers' attitudes to pricing and price sensitivity.

Primary data

Primary data is information which is collected during **primary research**. It is differentiated from **secondary data** or **secondary research** by virtue of the fact that it has been specifically collected for the purpose of the study which is ongoing. Typical forms of primary data include:

- customer demographics and socio-economic characteristics;
- customer lifestyle or psychological characteristics;
- customer attitudes and opinions;
- customer awareness and knowledge;
- customer buying intentions;
- customer motivation.

Normally primary data is either collected using direct communication with the respondents, verbally or in writing or by using email, or **observation research** can be used to collect a variety of primary data information.

P

Sayre, Shay, *Qualitative Methods for Marketplace Research*. London: Sage Publications, 2001.

Primary research

Primary research is concerned with the collection of **primary data**. By inference the term suggests that any data collected during this **marketing research** exercise should consist of fresh and hitherto uncollected, collated or analysed information.

Table 45 Pricing strategies

Pricing strategy	**Explanation**
Market penetration pricing	Low prices, particularly when a product is first launched, in order to obtain a significant penetration into the market.
Market skimming	High prices to support heavy advertising and sales promotion. Involves a higher than usual profit margin on each unit sold.
Average price	Basing pricing on the average for the industry.
Product mix	A pricing strategy associated with setting prices along a product line, which successively offers more features or higher quality for a higher price.
Optional	The practice of setting price according to optional or accessory products which are offered together with the main product.
Captive	Setting a premium price on products that must be used with a popular main product.
Product bundle	Combining several products and offering the whole bundle at a discounted or reduced price.
Discount	Offering a variation in price for those who settle their account quickly, or offering seasonal discounts to encourage customers to buy at times when demand is low.
Discriminatory	Setting the price within a set of parameters, negotiated with each individual customer, dependent upon quantity purchased, location, timescales or product type.
Psychological	Setting prices which appear to be fundamentally better or more appealing to the customer.
Promotional	Offering temporary pricing structures to increase short-term sales, such as loss leaders or prices attached to special events, cash discounts for frequent purchasing or reduced prices for local stockists, where delivery is not a particular concern.
Cost plus	Setting the price at a set proportion or percentage above the cost of production and all other associated costs.

Daymon, Christine and Holloway, Immy, *Qualitative Research Methods in Public Relations and Marketing Communications*. London: Routledge, 2002.

Prime time

'Prime time' is a media and advertising term used to describe the periods during which television or radio broadcasts receive the largest number of viewers or listeners.

Probability sample

A probability sample is a sample of respondents chosen during a **marketing research** activity who are not only believed to represent the larger target population, but are also capable of producing results which can suggest that in all probability a series of future events will occur.

See also **non-probability sample**.

Hansen, Morris H., Hurwitz, William N. and Madow, William G., *Sample Survey Methods and Theory: Methods and Applications*. Chichester: John Wiley, 1993.

Problem child/question mark/wild cat

One of the four **Boston Growth Matrix** categories variously named as 'problem child', 'question mark' or 'wild cat'. Almost all new products start life being launched into high- rather than low-growth markets, as the perception is that high-growth markets will eventually generate a greater return. However, the drain on resources at this stage can be enormous. Initially the volume of the product sold will be low and significant marketing expenditure will be required to raise market awareness and stimulate volume sales.

If a problem child product's sales can be made to grow faster than other competing products, then it will move into the **star** category. If the product is not supported and for a time has a static market position, it will eventually lose sales to competing products and fall into the **dog** category.

Product

A product, which is often, in marketing terms, a wholly transferable description of a service, is something that can be offered to the market for consumption or acquisition in order to satisfy a need or a want. 'Product', as a term, is also closely associated with the **marketing mix**.

There are a number of dimensions related to a product which fully describe its exact nature; these include the basic product, materials used, components, usage, performance, features, quality, design, reliability and technical sophistication. In addition to the overall description of a product, it is also prudent to consider service, technological advice, maintenance and repair. There are a number of different product types, which include consumer goods, speciality products, raw materials, components and industrial services.

Product adoption process

A series of five stages in the acceptance of a product: awareness, interest, evaluation, trial and adoption.

Product differentiation

See **brand differentiation** (p. 000).

Product life cycle

The product life cycle is a widely accepted model which describes the stages that a product or service, or indeed a category, passes through from its introduction to its final removal from the **market** (see Figures 28 and 29). The model suggests that the **introduction stage**, or the launch, of the product, during which the product sells in small numbers and marketing activities are expensive, is superseded, if successful, by three other stages. The **growth stage** is characterized by higher sales, greater profitability, but crucially, more competition. At the **maturity stage**, providing a product has managed to survive, stable sales and a higher level of profitability are enjoyed. The final stage, known as the **decline** stage, shows that the product is finally declining in terms of demand and associated profits. Optionally, it is possible to insert a further stage between maturity and decline, denoting a period of the product's life cycle when competition has reached a stage which makes it difficult to sustain the original product. Indeed, it may be the case that the product is already growing stale. This saturation period marks a slight downturn, which can be adjusted by a re-launch or a repackaging of the product, otherwise it will begin its inevitable slip into the decline stage.

At the decline stage, the business needs to carefully consider its policy towards the product or service, as it is not merely a question of letting the item fade away over a period of time (perhaps when stocks are finally exhausted). An **abandonment** policy must be put in place which takes into account the ramifications in terms of its impact on staffing levels, deployment of human and other resources, as well as its impact on the market, suppliers and distributors.

Shaw, John J., *Product Lifecycles and Product Management*. Westport, CT: Greenwood Press, 1989.

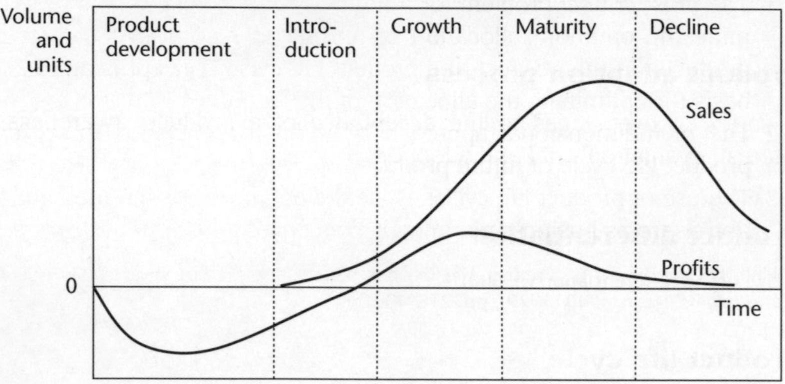

Figure 28 The standard product life cycle graph showing the phases of the life cycle and the association between profits and sales over the cycle

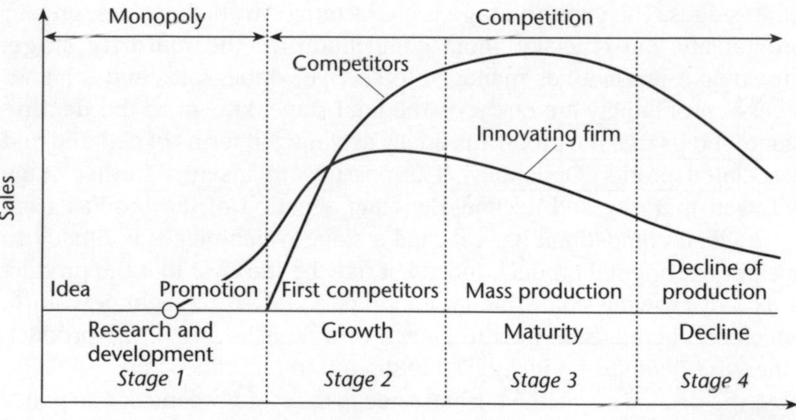

Figure 29 This is a more complex view of the product life cycle, which illustrates the dangers often faced by product innovators in developing new product ideas only to lose the potential of sales as a result of the actions of competitors.

P

Product life cycle management

Rink and Swan (1979) presented product life cycle patterns (see Figure 30), which afford an opportunity to consider whether a business is able to influence or manage the shape of the curve. Specifically, the implicit ideas of the various shapes offer the following opportunities:

1. The most critical problem for a multi-product business is to determine the optimum allocation of its limited resources to various products. In this respect, the product life cycle concept is an ideal basis for optimizing the allocation of the resources.
2. The multidimensional approach is useful in conceptualizing the product life cycle of future products.
3. The use of product life cycles is ideal when brought into the equation as far as business planning is concerned.

Rink, D. and Swan, J., 'Product Life Cycle Research: a Literature Review', *Journal of Business Research*, 40 (1979), pp. 219–43.

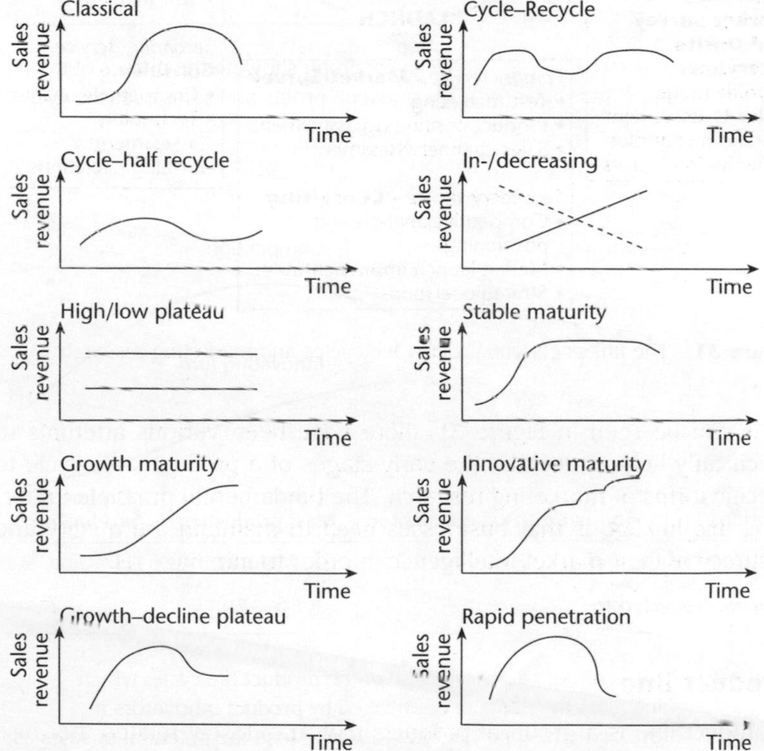

Figure 30 Product life cycle patterns (Rink and Swan, 1979)

Product life cycle marketing research process

The link between **product life cycles** and **marketing research** is best seen as an underlying concept that seeks to link various forms of marketing research which are appropriate to each stage of a product's life cycle. A product's life cycle moves from original idea or conception to design, launch, growth, maturity and final decline.

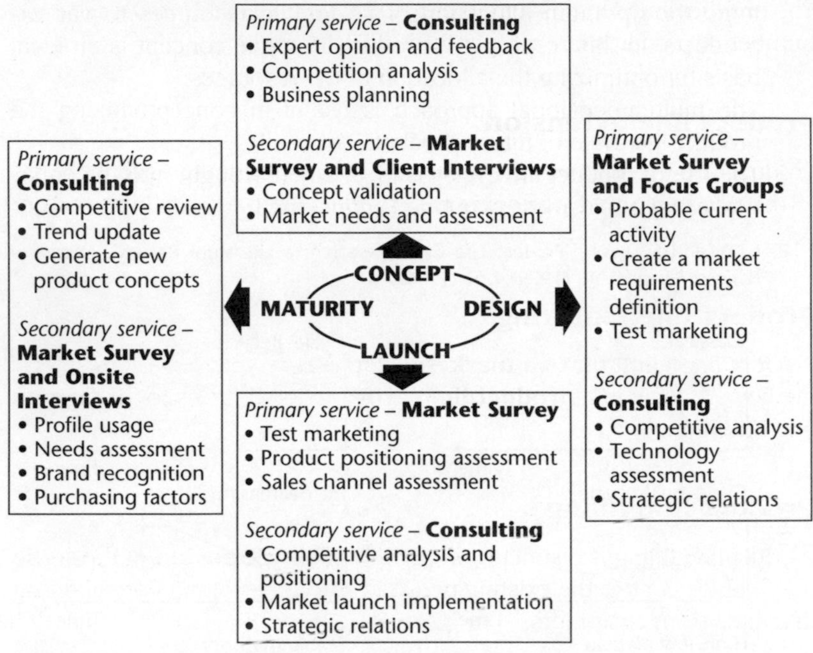

Figure 31 The links between product life cycles and marketing research

P

As can be seen in Figure 31, there have been various attempts to specifically link particularly the early stages of a product's life cycle to specific forms of marketing research. The fundamental principle underlying this linkage is that businesses need to maintain the quality and accuracy of their market intelligence in order to minimize risk.

www.sresearch.com

Product line

A product line is a group of products that are closely related, because they function in a similar manner, or are sold to the same customer groups, or are marketed through similar **distribution channels**, or have similar pricing structures.

Ries, Al, and Ries, Laura, *The 22 Immutable Laws of Branding: How to Build any Product or Line into a World-class Brand.* Profile Business, 2000.

Product line depth

The product line depth is a marketing term which is used to describe the number of products in each **product line**.

Product line extension

Product line extension is the means by which businesses add products to the **product mix** by bringing new products into an existing **product line**.

Product line featuring

Product line featuring is a **marketing strategy** which involves selecting key products in a **product line** as the major vehicles for promotion and attention.

Product line filling

Product line filling is distinct from **product line extension** in the sense that it plugs gaps in the existing **product line** to accommodate differing demands from customers.

Product line pricing

Product line pricing is a **pricing strategy** which features a series of steps in price between products in a **product line**. Normally the price differentials are based on customers' perceptions of the products in terms of their features and benefits, as well as on influences arising out of an analysis of the competitors' prices.

Product line stretching

Product line stretching is essentially an amalgam of both **product line extension** and **product line filling**. The process involves literally extending the scope of the **product line** beyond what is currently on offer and, perhaps, taking the product into associated markets and applications.

Product line width

The product line width is the number of **product lines** in a business's **product mix**.

Product mix

'Product mix' is a marketing term which is used to describe a business's entire selection or assortment of different products and **product lines**.

Product placement

See **brand placement.**

Product portfolio

'Product portfolio' is, essentially, a very similar term to **product mix**. However, it is something of an extension of this concept, as not only does it describe the products and **product lines** owned by the business, but it also describes the business's desire to satisfy the needs of target markets, as well as its goals in terms of profitability and other objectives.

See also **product portfolio analysis.**

Cooper, Robert G., Edgett, Scott J. and Kleinschmidt, Elko, J., *Portfolio Management for New Products*. New York: Perseus Books, 1998.

Product portfolio analysis

Product portfolio analysis is probably most closely associated with attempts to assess the market growth rate and a product's relative **market share**. Product portfolio analysis is a key marketing activity in determining the direction and intensity of **marketing strategies**.

Product positioning

Product positioning is certainly best described in terms of using a **multidimensional scale**. A product's position incorporates many different aspects, features and benefits that may be directly or indirectly associated with the product itself.

In Figure 32, the various brands marked A–E are plotted on a multidimensional scale and placed in positions which **marketing research** has elicited as representing the perceptions of customers or consumers, probably both users and non-users. A business will use a positioning

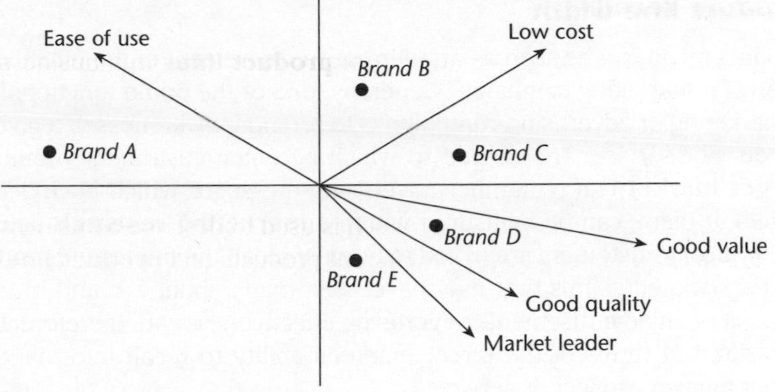

Figure 32 A multidimensional scale

strategy for each **segment** it wishes to target. In other words, it will compare perceptions, both implicit and explicit, against those of each of the key competitors. Positioning a product requires a number of suppositions – these are:

- that the product, service or brand has objective and/or subjective attributes;
- that potential purchasers may consider one or more of these attributes during the buying process;
- that any respondents have actually considered the attributes of each of the competing products and are, in some way, able to state where they would place a specific brand within the parameters established for the positioning process.

Product positioning is also useful in a pre-launch phase and, indeed, during the design of new products and services. Typically a business will seek to identify the prime desired characteristics and attributes of successful brands by using a multidimensional scale to product-position these **market leaders**. It will then seek, in its development of the new product or service, to replicate the best features, in order to allow the brand to be in an advantageous position once it hits the market.

Marketing strategies need to be specifically designed in order to match the perceived product position of a given brand. In other words, the **marketing mix** needs to support the product position and not seek to undermine it.

Feig, Barry, *Marketing Straight to the Heart: From Product to Positioning to Advertising.* New York: Amacom, 1997.

P

Product recall

Product recall can be seen as an ultimate measurement of the effectiveness of a marketing campaign. Generally, one of the prime functions of a marketing or advertising campaign is to promote awareness of a given product or service. The degree to which potential customers within a **target market** can remember advertising messages which have been aimed at them, can be measured within a **marketing research** activity. Typically customers are asked to literally recall the names of brands, and associated claims that may have been made about a brand in the context of an advertisement. Advertising effectiveness can, therefore, be measured in terms of the target market's ability to recall information about a given product or service.

Product repositioning

Product repositioning refers to a situation when a business deems it necessary or desirable to adjust the **product positioning** of one of its products or services. This is generally a rather difficult task as it requires an amendment to the brand's image and re-education of consumers in order to make them perceive the product or service in an entirely different manner. A brand, for example, may have been originally positioned to imply value for money. However, as the market has developed, other products from competing businesses may have moved into this part of the market and effectively undermined the 'value for money' concept upon which the product positioning was established. The original brand can therefore be repositioned through an extensive marketing and advertising campaign to project a different image or position, which may incorporate quality or exclusivity.

P

Product research

Product research is a **marketing research** activity which is concerned not only with the design, development and testing of new products, but also with the modification or improvement of existing products. Typically, product research would include comparative tests against competing products, concept testing, idea generation and screening, product simplification or elimination, and **brand positioning**.

Gorchels, Linda, *A Product Manager's Handbook: The Complete Product Management Resource*. Chicago, IL: Contemporary Books, 2000.

Kahn, Kenneth B., *Product Planning Essentials*. London: Sage Publications, 2000.

Profit impact of marketing strategies

See PIMS.

Profit per order (PPO)

PPO is a direct marketing term which describes the actual profit made by the business after having taken into account all of the expenses incurred in attracting a customer to make an order.

Projective technique

Projective technique is used in **marketing research** when subjects, or respondents, are requested to carry out specific tasks for a particular reason, when they are, in fact, being assessed and evaluated for another reason which is unknown to them.

Promotion

'Promotion' incorporates a number of different marketing techniques, including advertising, **personal selling**, **public relations** and sales promotion. In essence, promotion incorporates any communications between businesses and potential customers.

Promotion is also an integral part of the **marketing mix**. There are several associated factors which influence the selection of promotional methods, these are:

- promotional objectives;
- cultural and legal constraints;
- infrastructure available to support the promotional effort (within the organization or its agents);
- the development of the market (in terms of accessibility and sophistication);
- distribution infrastructure;
- availability of suitable media;
- activities and intentions of the competition.

Promotional budget

A promotional budget is the total amount of financial resources which a business allocates to its promotions over a period of time. There are a number of different ways in which a business allocates or estimates its promotional budget. These are summarized in Table 46.

Table 46 Approaches to the promotion budget

Method	Description
Affordable approach	This approach is essentially a production-orientated method. The business calculates gross margins, determines its required net profit and then deducts all other costs and expenses. The remainder can be allocated to the promotional budget.
Objective and task approach	This approach looks at the objectives and calculates the funds which are required to meet them. It is often difficult to build into the budget any eventualities that may unexpectedly occur.
Competitive parity approach	This budgeting technique uses the competitors as a benchmark and requires the business to spend as much as, if not more than, the competitors are spending.
Percentage of sales approach	Based on either historical or predicted sales figures, an agreed percentage per sale is allocated to advertising.
Historical approach	This approach is based on what has been spent in the past and is ideal for a stable market. It does not take into account what may or may not need to be spent and may often lead to the business spending more than is necessary.
Experiment and testing approach	Different levels of expenditure are allocated to each test market. Awareness and sales can then be measured and compared. This is a far more scientific approach to the allocation of the budget.
Modelling and simulation approach	This approach employs mathematical techniques to build models to help forecast performance against different media plans and advertising expenditure. This is, perhaps, the most scientific approach as it takes into account the relationship between cost and response.

Promotional mix

The term 'promotional mix' describes the combination of two or more elements, which may include advertising, **personal selling**, **public relations** and sales promotion. These four elements are very much the traditional components of the promotional mix. In addition to these, other techniques are now increasingly added to the overall promotional mix. The additional components include:

- branding;
- corporate image;
- customer service;
- direct marketing;
- exhibitions;
- internal marketing;
- merchandising;
- packaging;
- sponsorship;
- email/internet;
- word of mouth.

Soares, Eric J., *Promotional Feats: The Role of Planned Events in the Marketing Communications Mix*. Westport, CT: Greenwood Press, 1991.

Prospecting

Prospecting relies on the establishment of a comprehensive database which helps identify lists of potential customers. Various criteria are set as to the likelihood of customers wishing to purchase products or services from the business. Customers are ranked in order of their suitability and are systematically contacted by the sales force.

Psychographics

This is a **marketing research** and **market segmentation** technique used to measure **lifestyles** and to develop lifestyle classifications. The technique relies on measuring customers' AIO (activities, interests and opinions). Psychographic segmentation is a workable means of dividing large markets into smaller groups according to individuals' lifestyles, activities, opinions and beliefs.

See also **lifestyle**.

Kahle, Lynn R. and Chiagouris, Larry (eds), *Values, Lifestyles and Psychographics*. Hillsdale, NJ: Lawrence Erlbaum, 1997.

Kahle, Lynn R., *Cross-national Consumer Psychographics*. London: International Business Press, 2000.

P

Psychological pricing

'Psychological pricing' is a general **pricing strategy** term which encompasses all techniques that attempt to elicit a certain reaction from consumers, based on the **price** of the product. Psychological pricing includes **prestige pricing** and **odd–even pricing**.

Public relations

The basic function of public relations is to establish and maintain a mutual understanding between a business and its publics. Typically, public relations activities will include the preparation of press kits, holding seminars, making charitable donations and sponsorships, community relations and lobbying.

Broadly, public relations has the following objectives:

- establish and maintain the prestige and reputation of the business;
- support the promotion of products and services;
- deal with arising issues and opportunities;
- establish and maintain goodwill with customers, employees, government, suppliers and distributors;
- deal promptly with unfavourable publicity.

In effect, public relations seeks to transfer a negative or null opinion of the business into knowledge or a positive attitude. Public relations can be seen as distinctly different from advertising, as can be seen in Table 47.

Table 47 A comparison between public relations and advertising

Public relations	**Advertising**
Informative	Informative and persuasive
Subdued messages	Immediate impact
No repetition	Repetition
Credibility	Less credible
Newsworthy	Not necessary
Low cost	High cost

Mazur, Laura and White, Jon, *Strategic Communications Management: Making Public Relations Work*. Reading, MA: Addison-Wesley, 1994.

P

Publicity

Publicity is a part of **public relations** which focuses on providing news, mainly to the media, about the business or its products and services.

Pull quote

'Pull quote' is both an advertising and a publishing term. A pull quote itself is used to attract attention, especially in a long article or a text-dense advertisement. Literally, a small section of text, or a phrase, is pulled out and quoted in a larger typeface; usually it will be framed and placed within the article, often spanning two or more columns. A pull quote is also known as a 'call out'.

Pull strategy

'Pull strategy' is a term which is simultaneously related to both distribution and advertising. Literally, as the term implies, advertising and marketing aim to motivate end users to demand a product or service. They then approach the retailer, who is then persuaded to stock the products and services in question.

As can be seen in Figure 33, pull and **push strategy** can be used simultaneously to force products and services through distributors to the end users.

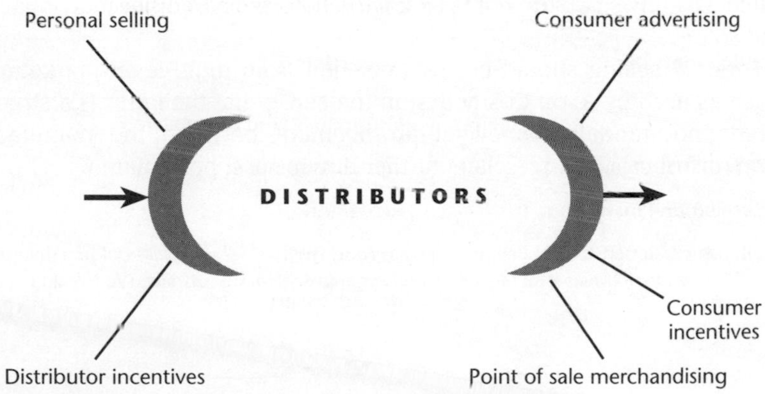

Figure 33 Pull and push strategies

Push strategy

An alternative to, or perhaps used in conjunction with, a **pull strategy** is a push strategy, which aims to provide encouragement to distributors to stock and therefore make available products and services to end users. The principal objective of a push strategy is to offer incentives, usually through **personal selling** techniques to distributors to encourage them to stock and display products and services, thus achieving the goal of pushing the products and services through the distribution channel to the end user.

Pyramid selling

Pyramid selling or pyramid schemes are, essentially, illegal and fraudulent money-making operations which require recruits to give money to recruiters and then enlist new recruits to pay them.

The system is called a 'pyramid' scheme as it resembles a huge three-divisional triangle with a single individual at the top. In a short period of time, if the initiating individual recruits ten people, who each recruit ten, who then recruit ten more and so on, the pyramid becomes vast. It also becomes extremely lucrative to those at the top of the pyramid, who receive a share of the income of each recruiter they have recruited. At the bottom of the pyramid, it becomes increasingly difficult for people to find new recruits in order to recoup the recruiting costs they have paid.

The system works on the basic premise of greed; the schemes, although illegal, are active on the internet in the form of buying 'market reports' from an individual who has sent an unsolicited email. The purchase allows you the rights to sell the reports on to other individuals, and so on.

Pyramid selling should be distinguished from multi-level marketing (such as used by Avon Cosmetics) in the sense that the latter is a structured and mutually beneficial arrangement between the manufacturer/distributor and re-sellers further down the supply chain.

See also **viral marketing**.

Fitzpatrick, Robert L. and Reynolds, Joyce, *False Profits – Seeking Financial and Spiritual Deliverance in Multi-level Marketing and Pyramid Schemes*. Scottdale, PA: Herald Press, 1997.

Qualitative research

Qualitative research is a **marketing research** approach which largely revolves around interview methods. It is distinct from **quantitative research** in the sense that its sample is far smaller, but the depth of the information is greater. Typically qualitative research techniques would include **depth interviews** and group discussions. Qualitative research would be used for a number of different research projects, including exploratory, diagnostic, evaluative and creative work. Its strengths and weaknesses are summarized in Table 48.

Table 48 An evaluation of qualitative research

Strengths	Weaknesses
• Depth and detail on each individual respondent may be high	• Fewer people studied. • Less easy to generalize.
• Openness – respondents tend to be more prepared to be open if a personal approach is used.	• Difficult to aggregate data. • Highly dependent on researchers' skills.
• Can help avoid pre-judgements.	• Setting where a respondent is questioned may affect results.

Seale, Clive, *The Quality of Qualitative Research*. London: Sage Publications, 1999.
Silverman, David, *Interpreting Qualitative Data*. London: Sage Publications, 2001.

Quantitative research

Quantitative research is a **marketing research** approach which entails the collection and analysis of data, primarily in numerical form. Quantitative research tends to be the preferred option when a researcher is looking to test the existence of relationships between variables, or looking at specific attributes in a population, which may be based on measurements derived from a sample. Quantitative researchers tend to assume that within a range of probabilities, providing they use appropriate and objective research, then a definite anticipated outcome can be established. The key to effective quantitative research is to minimize the possibility of error or bias. The criteria used in order to evaluate the quality of the quantitative research can be seen in Table 49.

Table 49 Criteria used to evaluate quantitative research

Criteria	Description and implications
Construct validity	Does the study actually measure the attributes and variables which were the intended purpose of the survey?
Reliability	Was the data-collection methodology sound enough to provide accurate and consistent measures?
Internal validity	Were extraneous variables eliminated and were rival explanations controlled?
External validity	Was a sound sampling strategy employed, given the time constraints and the information accessed?

Creswell, J. W., *Research Design: Qualitative and Quantitative Approaches*. San Francisco, CA: Sage, 1994.

Nardi, Peter M., *Doing Survey Research: A Guide to Quantitative Research Methods*. London: Allyn & Bacon, 2002.

Q

Questionnaires

Questionnaires are used in a wide variety of different circumstances in **marketing research**. Questionnaires may be designed for the respondents to use personally or for the researcher to complete on their behalf, either face-to-face or by telephone. In all cases questionnaires need to have clear and accurate questions which are structured in a meaningful manner. Equally, questions should have an intended meaning that is the same to anyone who reads it. In other words, questions should be unambiguous. There are a wide number of different types of questions which could be used in a questionnaire. These can be best summed up in terms of their types and applications as in Table 50.

In designing a questionnaire, it is imperative that the researcher immediately engages the respondent. Easy questions should be asked

Table 50 Types of question used in questionnaires

Question type	**Purpose**	**Example**
Open ended	To encourage the respondents to answer in their own words.	What do you think of . . . ?
Unaided recall	To avoid asking a leading question and to allow the respondent to explain.	How did you choose this course and university?
Dichotomous	Offering two or perhaps three choices of answer.	Typically Yes, No or Don't Know.
Multiple choice	Also known as cafeteria questions, which offer the respondent a range of answers listed either alphabetically or from one extreme to the other.	What are your impressions of the President of the United States? (Tick all that apply)
Semantic differential, or thermometer	These questions ask respondents to rate their response on either a numerical or a descriptive scale.	*See* **Osgood's Semantic Differential Scale** (p. 214).
Checklist	Basically a memory prompter which would incorporate a number of features that the respondents could tick to show their agreement. This requires the questionnaire to contain all possible likely associations.	What are your impressions of our new advertising campaign? (Questionnaire would now list features such as *interesting, boring, funny, informative* etc.)

first and more difficult questions later. It seems to be the general consensus of opinion that the questions of the greatest importance should be about one third of the way through the questionnaire. Above all, the questions need to be clearly worded and designed in such a way that they will provide the answers necessary to solve the research problem.

Behling, Orlando and Law, Kenneth S., *Translating Questionnaires and Other Research Instruments: Problems and Solutions.* London: Sage, 2000.

Oppenheim, Alan V., *Questionnaire Design.* London: Continuum International Publishing Group, 2000.

Peterson, Robert A., *Constructing Effective Questionnaires.* London: Sage, 1999.

Q

Quota sample

Quota sampling is used extensively in **marketing research**. The basic purpose is to identify the correct proportion of respondents who have the same agreed characteristics as the target research population. Typically, interviewers will be given quotas of particular groups of people that they are required to interview. If, for example, the research population is known to consist of 70 per cent women, of whom 50 per cent are over 55, then this quota will be explicitly stated to the interviewer. They will be required to interview a proportionate sample in line with the quota-sample criteria. There can be complex criteria used in quota sampling, which may encompass age, gender or type of household. The quota sample aims to make the survey as representative as possible and to help eliminate sampling errors.

There is another variant of quota sampling, called non-proportionate quota sampling, which does not require the interviewer to match the proportion in the research population. Interviewers are simply instructed to interview a minimum number of individuals in each particular identified group.

Barnett, Vic, *Sample Survey Principles and Methods*. London: Edward Arnold, 2002.

Random sampling

Random sampling is a **marketing research** technique in which a sample of respondents is chosen to represent the target research population. On the basis that each individual approached by a researcher has an equal chance of being chosen, the likelihood of bias is seemingly reduced.

Rank order scaling

Rank order scaling is most closely associated with **marketing research** as it is used to ask respondents to literally rank specific attributes or characteristics of given **brands**. A typical example may appear as follows:

> Based on your own experience, or what you have seen or heard from others, please rank the following types of vehicle according to their reliability. Please place a '1' next to the car that you feel is the most reliable and a '2' next to the car which is the next most reliable, and so on. Please do not give the same ranking to two cars.

Rating point

Rating points are an alternative way of calculating the cost of advertising, particularly in the broadcast media. Whilst many charges are based on **CPT** or the **ABC**, an alternative measure is to establish a rating according to the number of individuals, or audience, associated with a given programme, within which, or near which, the advertisement will appear. If, for example, a television programme was given a rating of 11.0 then it means that the programme reaches 11 per cent of the homes in a given country which are able to receive television programmes. In the US for example, an approximation of the number of households is 94 million, therefore an 11.0 rating would reach 10.3 million homes. If the business ran its advertisements 10 times, then according to this rating they would have achieved 103 million gross rating points.

Webster, James G. and Lichty, Lawrence W., *Ratings Analysis: Theory and Practice.* Hillsdale, NJ: Lawrence Erlbaum, 1991.

Rating scale

See **semantic differential scale.**

Raw data

Raw data is variously known as source or atomic data. This is **marketing research** information which has not yet been processed. Typically, to follow the analogy, once the data has been processed, it is called cooked data.

Raw data can be derived from a number of different sources, for example, an **electronic point of sale** terminal in a supermarket. Before the data is processed and allocated to each customer in terms of what they have bought, when they have bought it and at what price, it remains raw data. Typically, raw data will be put into a database to allow it to become accessible for processing and analysis.

Reach

'Reach' is also known as 'cumulative audience' and is a **marketing research** term used to describe unduplicated audiences for broadcast advertisements, over a number of airings. The key aspect of reach is that it calculates the audience figures on the basis that each individual is only counted once.

Reactive marketing

Reactive marketing is a **marketing strategy** which can be seen as a response to or a defence against activities carried out by the competition. As such, reactive marketing can be seen as the direct opposite of proactive marketing, which involves a more systematic planning, implementation and control of marketing strategies and activities.

Recall

See **product recall.**

Recency

Recency is a concept which fundamentally questions the value of advertising. The premise is based on the fact that no matter how much advertising attempts to impart knowledge about a specific brand to any given audience, they are unlikely to respond unless they are paying attention.

In other words, the audience will only react when they are ready to buy and will only show any degree of interest when they have reached this point. It therefore follows that no matter what the impact or intensity, or, for that matter, what the strength of the brand is, consumers will not respond without a reason or impetus to do so.

Recency, Frequency and Monetary Value (RFM) model

RFM is a technique used in **direct marketing** where customers on an organization's database will be scored on each of the three variables. They will be given a score of either 1, 2 or 3. A score of 1 would indicate that the customer ranks very low in that category, whilst a score of 3 shows a high-ranking position. Table 51 summarizes the three considerations.

Table 51 Recency, Frequency and Monetary Value (RFM) model

Measurement	Description	Example
Recency	This is the time that has elapsed since the customer's most recent purchase. A customer who has made a purchase in the past few days will have a score of 3.	1 = Customers who made a purchase more than 48 months ago. 2 = Customers who made a purchase more than 12 months ago but fewer than 48 months ago. 3 = Customers who made a purchase in the last 12 months.
Frequency	This is the number of purchases made by the customer over a pre-determined period of time, again the higher the number of repeat purchases in this given period, the more likely the customer will be to score 3.	1 = Customers who made a single purchase in the past 60 months. 2 = Customers who made two purchases in the past 60 months. 3 = Customers who made three or more purchases in the past 60 months.
Monetary	This is a measure of the customer's average purchase value – the higher the value of each purchase made (averaged), the more likely that the customer will be given a score of 3.	1 = Customers with an average purchase amount up to £2,000. 2 = Customers with an average purchase amount from £2,001 to £4,000. 3 = Customers with an average purchase amount greater than £4,000.

A customer who receives a ranking of 3, 3, 3 is considered to be a very valuable customer, whereas a customer with a ranking score of 1, 1, 1 is deemed to be a less valuable prospect for the business.

Novo, Jim, *Drilling Down: Turning Customer Data into Profits with a Spreadsheet.* Booklocker.com 2002.

Reference group

A reference group is closely associated with **marketing research**, as it describes a group of individuals who have a standard series of characteristics against which all other groups can be compared. Reference groups are also often referred to as **control groups**.

Reference groups are used as a standardization tool when making comparisons and are, in effect, a blueprint of the ideal, or sometimes, totally contradictory individuals who will become part of a research programme.

Reference groups can also be used to determine and list key characteristics of behaviour and values.

Frey, Lawrence R., Gouran, Dennis, and Poole, Marshall Scott, *The Handbook of Group Communication, Theory and Research*. London: Sage Publications, 1999.

Reintermediation

'Reintermediation' is an internet term which refers to the reassembling of buyers, sellers and business partners who formed a traditional supply chain, into a web-based set of linkages. In effect, the term is the reverse of 'disintermediation' which aims to cut out the middle-men in e-commerce transactions.

Relationship marketing

Relationship marketing attempts to develop a long-term relationship with customers on the premise that it is far cheaper to retain existing customers than it is to attract new ones. There are a number of factors involved in relationship marketing, which tend to frame the exact nature of how it works within a given organization; these are:

- a primary focus on customer attention;
- an orientation towards product benefits rather than product features;
- an emphasis on commitment and contact with customers;
- the adoption of a total quality approach;

- the development of ongoing relationships with customers;
- the deployment of employees at various levels to maintain contact;
- the cultivation of key customers,
- the emphasis on trust, honesty and promise keeping

Egan, John, *Relationship Marketing*. London: Financial Times; Englewood Cliffs, NJ: Prentice-Hall, 2001.

Payne, Adrian, Christopher, Martin, Peck, Helen and Clark, Moira, *Relationship Marketing for Competitive Advantage: Winning and Keeping Customers*. London: Butterworth-Heinemann, 1998.

Remnant space

'Remnant space' is an advertising term that is used to describe areas of a publication which have been earmarked to contain advertisements. Each publication has a date by which advertisements must be booked in order to ensure their insertion in the next issue. Often some of this advertisement space remains unsold and is therefore offered at a considerable discount, either by the sales team directly associated with the publication, or by a third party taken on as a subcontractor to fill the space. Remnant spaces do not offer the same degree of flexibility as other advertisement space as they may be on undesirable pages or in less effective positions on a given page.

Repositioning

See **product repositioning**.

Research design

Research design is a very necessary precursor to carrying out any form of **marketing research**. Usually it involves four steps, which are:

- the formulation of a strategy which will resolve a particular question;
- the collection and recording of the information;
- the processing and analysis, as well as interpretation, of the findings;
- the publication of the results.

In the research design process there are eight various options, each pair being mutually exclusive, as shown in Table 52.

Creswell, John W., *Research Design: Qualitative, Quantitative and Mixed Method Approaches*. London: Sage Publications, 2002.

Table 52 Research design options

Quantitative Statistically based and considered scientific.	**OR**	*Qualitative* Individually based and often called humanistic.
Interpretive Studies meaning and analyses content. Is abstract and conceptual.	**OR**	*Functional* Studies behaviour and effects, looking at cause and effect.
Experimental Manipulates independent variables followed by the measurement of a dependent variable. Considered scientific.	**OR**	*Naturalistic* Studies processes as they occur, usually through observation.
Laboratory Carried out in an artificial environment controlled by the researcher.	**OR**	*Field* Carried out in a normal environment amidst day-to-day life.
Participant Borrowed from anthropology where the researcher participates in the activities.	**OR**	*Non-participant* Observer operates outside the situation and simply observes.
Overt Respondents are aware that they are being observed or measured.	**OR**	*Unobtrusive* Subjects are unaware that they are being observed.
Cross-sectional Measurements are carried out at one point in time. Both the past and the future are ignored.	**OR**	*Longitudinal* Involves repeated measurements of the same group of people over a period of time to track changes.
Basic Intended to look at theoretical issues. Application is not considered important.	**OR**	*Applied* Pragmatic approach, where the focus is on addressing problems.

Response rate

This is a **marketing research** term used to describe the number of respondents who have completed questionnaires compared with the number of questionnaires sent out. The response rate is usually expressed as a percentage and can also be used to measure the number of individual questions that have been answered.

Retention rates

See **customer retention**.

Rink and Swan

See **product life cycle management**.

Rollout

Ideally, a business, or an advertising agency, will pre-test or trial a marketing or advertising campaign prior to the launch. The effectiveness and initial reactions of a sample of the target audience, or **test market**, may require the amendment of certain aspects of the campaign. Once this process has been completed, the campaign is then launched or rolled out as planned.

Run of paper

'Run of paper' is an advertising and publishing term used to describe the positioning of an advertisement at the publisher's discretion. The advertising space is purchased, as usual, at a lower rate than would have been demanded for a preferred position.

Run of schedule/station (ROS)

ROS is similar in concept to **run of paper** except that it refers to the broadcast media. Typically, a television or radio broadcaster would have sold the best positions with the largest audiences first, but will seek to fill less desirable advertising positions with ROS advertisements.

ROS is also known as Best Time Available (BTA), which offers an advertiser the best positions that are left after the best spots have already been sold. ROS advertisements attract a lower charge than those guaranteed to be broadcast at premium times.

Sagacity

Sagacity is a term used to describe a refinement of the **market segmentation** technique, which seeks to group or identify the **family life cycle**. The system suggests that individual family groups have different behavioural patterns and associated aspirations at various stages. There are four stages of the life cycle which are identified using the sagacity concept; these are:

- dependent – which refers to individuals under 24 who still live at home with their parents;
- pre-family – who are the under-35s who have their own households but do not have children;
- family – who are individuals or couples under 65 who have one or more children in the household;
- late – who are adults, whether couples or individuals, whose children have left home, or householders over 35 with no children.

Notably, sagacity not only considers the stage of the life cycle but also takes into account the age and the income of the groups.

Sales promotion

Sales promotion is taken to mean any marketing activity which involves the promotion of sales, excluding advertising. It has close connections with merchandising and is more commonly known as **below the line**. More commonly, sales promotion is also associated with the shorter-term techniques employed by a business such as special offers and price reductions.

Robinson, William A., *Best Sales Promotions*. Chicago, IL: Contemporary Books, 1987.

Schultz, Don E., Robinson, William and Petrison, Lisa A., *Sales Promotion Essentials: The 10 Basic Sales Promotion Techniques and How to Use Them*. Chicago, IL: Contemporary Books, 1997.

Sales territories

A sales territory or territories is a defined geographic area, **market segment** or product group to which individual sales personnel are assigned. These individuals, within their territory, probably under the leadership or supervision of a sales manager, are responsible for developing sales and maintaining close customer relations.

Scholm, Charles C., *Planning and Managing Sales Territories*. Alexandria, VA: LRP Publications, 1990.

Salting

Salting is a technique often adopted by **list brokers** in order to monitor the use of database information which has been sold or rented to a third party. In order to ascertain whether or not the database and its related information is being misused, fictitious names are inserted deliberately into the database. The names, addresses or contact details of these individuals will route back to the original creator of the database, allowing the list broker to check that an unauthorized third party is not using the database sold to another business.

See also **seeding**.

Sample

A sample is taken to mean a representative proportion of the entire population of a given target group. Clearly, many **marketing research** activities cannot have sufficient scope to involve all those who may be in a specific target group. A representative sample, therefore, needs to be identified, which can provide an indication as to how the whole target group feels or reacts to given questions, products or services.

See also **quota sample** *and* **random sample**.

S

Sampling error

Sampling errors occur when the **sample** selected during a **marketing research** activity is incorrect in some way and is not representative of the whole target group. Equally, sampling errors can occur when incorrect conclusions are drawn from the limited number of respondents who may have been included in the original sample. Normally, as part of the marketing research process and, indeed, the **research design**, an estimation of the sampling error (which may have occurred by chance) is factored in as a cautionary note following the analysis and interpretation.

Sampling frame

A sampling frame is an integral part of **research design** and needs to be established before the **marketing research** truly gets underway. A sampling frame seeks to control, specify and structure the data for each **sample** and may well be prescriptive in terms of the source of any data. A sampling frame is usually a numbered list from which the random sample can be chosen.

Screening

Screening is a concept closely allied to **new product development**. It involves the methodical checking of a new or modified product or service against predetermined and identified key success factors. Products or services which do not match the essential criteria are eliminated as early as possible in their development. This process assists a business in terminating the development of products or services at the earliest possible stage in order to avoid the waste of resources associated with a product that may well fail in a market.

Seasonal rating adjustment

Seasonal rating adjustments can be applied to a number of different areas associated with marketing. In essence, the adjustment takes into account seasonal factors (such as peak or off-peak) that may positively or adversely affect sales, **response rates** or other measures. Adjustments based on seasonal variations are also incorporated into media costing (clearly with prime advertising periods revolving around such times as Christmas, etc.). By taking the seasonal adjustments into account, the marketing department is able to identify the underlying trends beneath the figures.

Secondary data

In **marketing research**, secondary data, or **secondary research**, is seen often as a viable alternative to **primary data** or **primary research**. Typically, secondary data can be described as being either internal or external sources of information. Internal data includes information which is already held by the business commissioning the marketing research study and may include sales invoices, customer records and warranty cards, etc. A vast amount of other secondary data is, of course, available external to the business in the form of published or commercially available data. Typical examples would include a government census or a **syndicated research** set of findings.

Secondary data certainly has an advantage in terms of cost and time. However, it is often the case that the available secondary data does not match the **research design** in terms of its objectives. It may also be the case that the data has aged to the extent that it is no longer relevant and that it would be foolish to base any decisions on that data. It is also notoriously difficult to verify the accuracy of secondary data, particularly if it has been republished and it is not clear how that information was initially gathered. There is often no indication as to the degree of error that may have crept into that research.

There are, however, several ways of evaluating secondary data – these are by asking:

- Is the data specifically useful for the research study?
- How current is the data?
- Is the data dependable and has it been verified?
- Is there any bias?
- What methodologies and specifications were employed?
- What was the objective of the original data collection?
- What is the nature of the data available in terms of variables, measurement and categories?

Secondary research

Secondary research involves the gathering of **secondary data**. Secondary research is usually concerned with the scanning and collection of relevant publications, literature and other data sources. It is usually accepted that secondary research is an easier form of **marketing research** to manage than **primary research**.

Stewart, David W. and Kamins, Michael A., *Secondary Research: Information Sources and Methods* (2nd edn). London: Sage Publications, 1993.

Seeding

Seeding is a concept most directly related to the use of **direct mail** lists purchased from **list brokers**. It is alternatively known as **salting**. A seed is literally an inclusion, on a mailing list, of a number of check names and addresses. These can be monitored to show usage, speed of delivery, or the improper use of the list by an unauthorized third party. The check names and addresses are also referred to as 'sleepers'.

Segment

See **market segment**.

S

Segmentation

Segmentation is a process used in marketing to break down the markets into smaller groups, each of which may require a distinctly different *marketing mix*. Each of the segments requires four preconditions. It must be:

- measurable – enabling the segment to be determined in terms of its size and characteristics;
- substantial – in that the segment is large enough to warrant the expenditure of time and resources;
- accessible – so that both the promotion and the product itself can reach the members of that segment;
- actionable – so that the segment offers the business the opportunity to deal with it using available resources.

There are many different forms of segmentation. Broadly, these are split into two different categories, aimed at either consumer or industrial segments:

- consumer segments – benefits sought: demographic, geographic, personality and lifestyle; purchase frequency and point; socio-economic, usage rate and user status;
- industrial segments – benefits sought: demographic, geographic; purchasing organization type; usage rate and user status.

See also **market segmentation.**

Dibb, Sally and Simkin, Lyndon, *The Market Segmentation Workbook*. London: International Thomson Business Press, 1996.

Myers, James H., *Segmentation and Positioning for Strategic Marketing Decisions*. New York: McGraw-Hill, 1996.

Wedel, Michel and Kamakura, Wagner A. (eds), *Market Segmentation: Conceptual and Methodological Foundations*. Amsterdam: Kluwer Academic Publishers, 1999.

Self-liquidating offer

See **on-pack offer.**

Self-mailer

'Self-mailer' is a term associated with **direct mail**. It is a piece of sales literature which can be delivered to the recipient without the need to insert it into an envelope or other outside packaging. Typically, a self-mailer will take the form of an over-large postcard.

Selling, inside

'Inside selling' is a generic sales-related term which describes the situation when the customer approaches the business, either in person or via the telephone, in order to make a purchase.

Selling, outside

Outside selling is the opposite of **inside selling** and is a situation where sales personnel approach a customer in order to persuade them to purchase products and services. This can be face-to-face or via the telephone (**telemarketing**). Generally, the term is applied to situations when manufacturers or distributors approach other business users, notably distributors and not necessarily the end users (consumers).

Semantic differential scale

A semantic differential scale is often used on **questionnaires** as part of a **marketing research** programme. It asks the respondent to use a 5-, 7- or 9-point rating scale which has two bi-polar or mono-polar adjectives or statements, one at each end.

See also **Likert Scale** *and* **Osgood's Semantic Differential Scale** .

Snider, James G., *Semantic Differential Technique*. Chicago, IL: Aldine Publishing, 1969.

Seven Ps

The Seven Ps are a development from the original Four Ps (product, place, price, promotion). Generally, the Seven Ps are taken to be:

- product;
- price;
- place;
- promotion;
- process – the steps needed to fulfil the **marketing mix**, including evaluation, modification and supervision;
- physical evidence – the tangible results or benefits of the marketing mix, as predicted in any forecasts made;
- people – either taken to mean the individuals involved in the marketing mix implementation (personnel/agencies/freelancers) or the net impact and changes made to the target audiences (compared with their views/status etc. prior to the implementation).

Davies, Peter and Pardey, David, *Making Sense of Marketing: Workbook 3 – Determining the Marketing Mix*. Basingstoke: Macmillan, 1990.

S

Shelf talker

Shelf talkers are encountered at either the **point of sale** or the **point of purchase** as they are printed material which is attached in some way to the shelves of the retail outlet. They are positioned alongside a particular brand to facilitate self-selection and obviate the need to rely on sales personnel to direct individuals to a particular **brand**. Shelf talkers will either be produced and distributed by the manufacturer or source of the brand to the retail outlets (as part of the delivery of the products, with the hope and intention that the stockist will use the shelf talker), or they are produced by the stockist to highlight a special promotion.

Shell directional policy matrix

The Shell directional policy matrix (see Table 53) was developed by Shell Chemicals in 1975. It remains a useful means of looking at an organization's competitive capabilities and future opportunities for profits.

Table 53 Shell directional policy matrix

		Prospects for sector profitability		
		Unattractive	**Average**	**Attractive**
Organization's competitive capability	**Weak**	disinvest	phased withdrawal	double or quit
	Average	phased withdrawal	custodial	try harder
	Strong	cash generation	growth	leader

The matrix aims to identify strategies that are resilient and viable in relation to the future, where each of the strategies is evaluated for its robust ability to cope with a number of future problems or challenges. The matrix allows an investigation into the opportunities for market growth, the quality of the market, the competitive and environmental situation, when set against the opportunities for profit. The profitability aspect looks at investment opportunities whilst the competitive capability examines the business's ability to deal with situations as they may arise.

Ideally, a business would rate its products against each factor by assigning between one and five stars, on the basis of past experience. Each sector is then assigned an overall rating based on the opportunities for making a profit.

Short rate

'Short rate' is an advertising and media-related term which refers to the difference between a quoted price for an advertisement and the actual price of an advertisement. Typically, this is applied to **classified advertising**, where an estimation would have been made as to the space the advertisement was likely to fill, set against the space it actually filled.

SIC

See **standard industrial classification.**

Skew

'Skew' or 'skewness' is a statistical term applied to **marketing research** when the distribution of data differs from a normal distribution. The degree of skewness is measured by identifying the fact that the mode and the mean are located at different points in the distribution of data.

Skyscraper

This is an internet advertising term used to describe a vertical advertisement on a web page, usually along the left border of the screen. The Interactive Advertising Bureau suggests that skyscrapers should be either 120 × 600 or 160 × 600 pixels.

www.iabuk.net

Slotting allowance

A slotting allowance is a lump sum payment made by a manufacturer to distributors or retailers in exchange for undertaking to stock a specific new product. Under most circumstances a retailer will only stock products if it expects to be able to sell them and receive a reasonable fixed profit from each sale. In order to assist a retailer in taking a potential risk on a new product, the manufacturer offers an inducement in the form of a slotting allowance. The payment of slotting allowances is seen as being a viable alternative to an extensive advertising campaign which may, in itself, not succeed in convincing retailers to stock the new product or service. The payment of the slotting allowance also implies that the retailer should make the utmost effort to push the product in their store and in this respect slotting allowances can be seen as a **push strategy**.

SMART

SMART is an acronym for Specific, Measurable, Achievable, Results-orientated and Time-constrained. It is a term which can equally apply to marketing as to many other areas of business activity. Its use seeks to ensure that any activity is quantifiable and objective-related.

Social class

Social class or socio-economic measures or classifications are often used in **marketing research**. There are several different varieties of social class and grades. The National Readership Survey (UK) identifies the following categories:

Social class and grade structure:

A Upper middle class (higher managerial, administrative or professional), which comprises about 3% of the population.

B Middle class (intermediate managerial, administrative or professional), which comprises approximately 10% of the population.

C1 Lower middle class (supervisory, clerical, junior administrative or professional), containing around 25% of the population.

C2 Skilled working class (skilled manual workers), comprising around 30% of the population.

D Working class (semi- and unskilled manual workers), forming around 27% of the population.

E Lowest levels of subsistence (state pensioners with no other income, widows, and casual and lowest-grade earners), forming the remaining 5% of the population.

S

Social marketing

'Social marketing', or 'societal marketing', is a term used to describe the concept that a business's main function is to determine the needs and satisfactions of its customers, or potential customers, in a more efficient and effective manner than its competitors. Above all, the concept suggests that the business should endeavour to preserve and enhance both the consumer's and society's well-being in all of its activities.

Kotler, Philip, Roberto, Eduardo L. and Lee, Nancy, *Social Marketing: Improving the Quality of Life*. London: Sage Publications, 2002.

Social responsibility marketing

Social responsibility in marketing refers to situations where a business responds to consumerism and environmental concerns and incorporates them into its long-term strategy. In essence, there are five different approaches, which are summarized in Table 54.

Table 54 Social responsibility in marketing

Socially responsible approach	Description of approach
Consumer orientation	The business considers its actions from the point of view of the customer.
Innovative marketing	An approach which aims to produce a genuinely useful, no frills product or service that breaks new ground.
Value marketing	A longer-term aim which seeks to make a gradual impact by growing a solid base of loyal customers sold on the fundamental concepts of the product or service rather than trying to stimulate shorter-term sales and profits.
Sense of mission marketing	An organization which looks at the wider implications of what it does and how it produces it rather than focusing on the products themselves in a more narrow sense.
Social marketing	Combining the needs and wants of the consumer with those of the business, society and the environment for all parties' longer-term benefits.

S

Societal marketing

The societal marketing concept is, in many respects, similar to the marketing concept itself, the crucial difference is that it also takes into account society's well-being.

The concept was developed against a backdrop of increasing consumer and governmental concerns regarding the environment and as a result the fundamental marketing concept was challenged as being inadequate to consider wider issues such as waste, resource shortages and environmental impacts.

Societal marketing therefore encompasses the traditional marketing concept in terms of identifying and fulfilling the needs and wants of consumers in an effective and efficient manner, but goes a stage further in its determination to do this without detrimentally affecting society. Profit is not put aside in order to do this; simply the business seeks to find alternative methods of production and delivery of its products and services, which minimize the harmful effects of that process. Organizations which adopt this marketing approach believe that consumers will respond favourably towards them if they are seen to be making strides in addressing societal concerns, and unfavourably if they are seen as being responsible for environment problems. It is thus the case that organizations such as the Body Shop (eliminating animal testing, using recyclable materials, etc.) and McDonald's (using recyclable and environmentally friendly packaging) can gain additional market share as they are seen to be making positive pro-environmental efforts. Other organizations such as Exxon or Shell, who have consistently denied their involvement in pollution through oil spillages, receive a negative response as they are perceived to be concerned less with the environment than with profit. Ultimately, societal marketing can be seen as giving the organization a competitive edge over its rivals.

Socio-cultural

In marketing the term 'socio-cultural' refers to the need to constantly be aware of changes in attitudes, behaviour and values within markets and countries in which the business operates. It is imperative that marketing considers these aspects as they will invariably affect the buying patterns of its consumers. Socio-cultural factors include attitudes, **consumerism**, **demographics**, **lifestyle** and social mobility.

Solus

This is a print-advertising term which refers to a spot on a page where the advertiser is guaranteed to be the only advertiser on that page. The advertiser is also guaranteed that the advertisement will be surrounded by text.

Spam

'Spam' is an internet marketing term used to describe unsolicited emails received by individuals. Spam is becoming an increasingly problematic area on the internet, particularly given the fact that websites with whom individuals register, and other sources which collect and store email addresses, are insecure and can be accessed by unauthorized users for the intention of spamming customers.

See also **spamdexing** *and* **spamming**.

Lant, Jeffrey, *Email Eldorado: Everything You Need to Know to Sell More of Your Products and Services Everyday by Email without Ever Spamming Anyone*. JLA Publications, 1998.

Spamdexing

Spamdexing is an unethical marketing technique which seeks to deceive search engines to gain an unfair advantage in terms of the search results of the search engine.

Spamdexing aims to decrease the value of the search engine's index by reducing its precision in identifying relevant web pages. Increasingly, search engines have the facility to identify attempts to do this and pages which are identified as being spamdexed are de-listed. A typical spamdex page would simply contain hundreds or thousands of popular search words or phrases on a flash page to deceive the search engine and the user.

See also **spam** *and* **spamming**.

Spamming

'Spamming' is a collective name which describes intrusive, offensive or unethical marketing messages sent by e-mail. The principal characteristic is that the spam mail is sent to an untargeted audience of thousands or millions on account of the fact that mass electronic mailing is a cheap system to employ.

The term also has a search engine relevance involving the mass-submission of web pages to search engines; this technique is known as **spamdexing**.

See also **spam** *and* **spamdexing**.

Split run test

The term 'split run test' is most closely associated with advertising and publishing. Typically, a publication is printed and then distributed in two or more separate production runs or deliveries. This is undertaken in order to facilitate the insertion of different advertisements in each run. The split run test thereby enables advertisers to see the effects of different types of advertising copy.

S

Sponsorship

Sponsorship has increasingly been seen as a primary function of both marketing and **public relations**. In essence it involves a business financing or underwriting a sporting or other event in order to gain an association with it and, perhaps, enjoy some of the prestige.

Beck-Burridge, Martin and Walton, Jeremy, *Sports Sponsorship and Branded Development*. Basingstoke: Palgrave Macmillan, 2001.
Stotlar, David K., *Developing Successful Sports Sponsorship Plans*. London: Fitness Information Technology, 2001.

Standard industrial classification

Standard industrial classifications (SIC) are attempts to categorize each form of business activity using a 4-digit code for each group. The exact nature of the SIC in each given country will necessarily have an entirely different mix. In terms of marketing, the SIC or, as it is known in North America, the NAICS (North American Industry Classification System), allows a business to specifically target businesses within particular classifications. An alternative is the Business Activity Classification (BAC), which comprises seven categorized areas, with a number of subdivisions.

Stationery Office Books, *Indexes to the Standard Industrial Classification of Economic Activities*. London: HMSO, 2002.
Stationery Office Books, *UK Standard Industrial Classification of Economic Activities*. London: HMSO, 2002.

Stapel scale

A stapel scale is effectively a variant **semantic differential scale**, which can be used in **questionnaires** as part of a **marketing research** survey. The respondent is asked to rate a product, service or **brand** on a scale from +5 to -5, to indicate how well a characteristic describes that product, service or brand. The characteristic is featured at the centre of the scale, with the minus figures gradually denoting the fact that it poorly describes the attribute. The plus figures, which ascend from the descriptor, attach increasing levels of agreement with the named attribute.

See also **Likert Scale; Osgood's Semantic Differential Scale** *and* **Semantic Differential Scale.**

Star

'Star' is one of the categories of product or service which can be found on the **Boston Growth Matrix**. Stars are successful products which enjoy a significant level of market demand. Invariably stars were former

question marks, and like **cash cows** they enjoy leading market positions. Stars are typified by products or services which are continuing to grow at a high rate (this enables them to maintain their position in the market). Stars provide a business with a significant amount of income, but they also require significant investment in terms of marketing and advertising in order to support their continued success.

Stars have the potential to penetrate other existing markets. They are usually the targets for improved distribution, **product line extensions** and other marketing techniques in order to sustain their continued appeal. Ultimately, when the market in which a star is placed slows down in growth terms, the product or service becomes a **cash cow**.

Stickiness

'Stickiness' is an internet marketing term which is a measure used to assess the effectiveness of a website in being able to retain the interest of a user. Stickiness is measured specifically by the length of time an individual user spends browsing the website.

Storyboard

A storyboard is a sequence of sketches which is used during the conceptualization of an advertisement. The storyboard is a graphical representation of the elements within the advertisement and the sequence of events. Storyboards are often used to **pre-test** responses from representative members of the eventual **target audience**.

Stratified sample

A stratified sample is a **marketing research** sample variant which involves the dividing of a population into categories. Each category has distinctive characteristics, and a representative **random sample** of respondents is chosen for each category.

Scott, John, *Stratification and Power: Structure of Class, Status and Command.* Cambridge: Polity Press, 1996.

SUPERPROFILES

SUPERPROFILES is a more sophisticated alternative to **ACORN** and is comparable in many respects to **MOSAIC** (see Table 55 for a comparison between them). The system has 160 different clusters which are based on 40 market profile groups. Within each of these profile groups

S

Table 55 A comparison between the categories of the major lifestyle segmentation systems

System	MOSAIC	ACORN	Define	SUPERPROFILES
Census variables	Age	Age	Age	Age
	Marital status	Sex	Sex	Household type
	Recent movers	Socio-economic status	Socio-economic status	Migration
	Household composition	Occupation	Occupation	Overcrowding
	Household size	Tenure	Tenure	Tenure
	Employment type		Household type	Country of birth
	Travel to work			
	Unemployment			Car ownership
	Car ownership			Travel to work
	Housing tenure			Occupation
	Amenities			Education
	Housing type			
	Socio-economic status			
Non-census data	County Court Judgements (CCJs)	None	CCJs	Electoral roll
	Credit activity		Credit activity	Credit data
	Electoral roll		Unemployment rates	CCJs
	Postcode address File (PAF)		Insurance premiums	
	Directors			
	Retail			
	Accessibility			

S

are subcategories of 10 SUPERPROFILE **lifestyles**. The classification incorporates not only **marketing research** data, but also credit information. Typical examples of lifestyles include 'affluent achievers', 'hard-pressed families', 'have-nots' and 'thriving greys'.

SWOT analysis

SWOT analysis is a very useful technique in looking at the overall future of an organization, as well as considering the launch of a new marketing activity. Swot analysis covers the following aspects. The first two considerations look at the internal workings of the organization.

- *Strengths* – What is the organization or business good at? What are its key advantages over the competition in terms of its products and services as well as its facilities, customer service and the expertise of its employees?
- *Weaknesses* – What is the organization not good at? Where does the business fall down in terms of the ways it does things? Are the products and services good enough? Is the marketing good enough?
- *Opportunities* – What is happening OUTSIDE the organization that offers some opportunities to the organization? Has the transport system in the area been improved? Has a major competitor closed down?
- *Threats* – What is happening OUTSIDE the organization that could threaten it? Are there more competitors?

Figure 34 is a common SWOT analysis grid which helps to place all of the considerations in the right place. The marketing function would need to consider all of these strengths, weaknesses, opportunities and threats before making any major decisions.

Strengths	Weaknesses
Opportunities	Threats

SWOT analysis

Figure 34 A SWOT analysis grid

Dealtry, Richard, *Dynamic SWOT Analysis – The Developer's Guide*. Birmingham: Dynamic SWOT Associates, 1994.

S

Syndicated research

The purpose of syndicated research is to understand the market as a whole and it cannot be seen necessarily as an alternative to **primary research**, as this focuses on understanding a business's share of the market.

Typically, syndicated research is conducted on a national scale, often involving thousands of respondents. Buying into syndicated research means that a business can hope to understand the market in a far broader sense and for many businesses it is the only cost-effective way of obtaining this information. The cost of producing and analysing the syndicated research is spread across a broad base of businesses. By sharing the costs, major issues can be investigated without the associated costs being prohibitive.

In the US, the cost of obtaining sight of the data can be in excess of $10,000. Realistically, however, this is a small price to pay providing the information actually tells the business something that it needs to know. Unfortunately, syndicated research is firmly based on the 'one size fits all' approach, as space within what is usually a **questionnaire**, either mailed conventionally, emailed or completed face-to-face with a respondent, is limited. Therefore, the answers to certain questions may well leave the business wondering about the implications without having the opportunity to confirm their suspicions with follow-up questions.

Tag line

'Tag line' is a radio advertising term. A tag line or tag is a few words, possibly a sentence, which change whilst the rest of the advertisement remains the same.

The script may state the fact that a sale is now on, but could have tag lines which change during the duration of the sale. For example, the tag lines could read 'sale starts Saturday', 'sale now on' or 'sale ends next Friday'. Each of the tags needs to be of the same length so that they can be edited into the advertisement, producing the same length of advertisement.

Target market/audience

A target market or a target audience is a group of individuals or businesses, usually identified during a **market segmentation** exercise, arising out of **marketing research**. The members of the group have common characteristics, attributes, beliefs and possibly buying habits. Reaching a target market is the prime objective of a business's advertising and marketing activities. A business may well have identified a number of different target markets and will have prioritized them in terms of their potential and profitability. The terms 'target market' and 'target audience' are largely interchangeable. However, there is a difference in the term 'target audience' which suggests a willingness or receptiveness on behalf of those who belong to the group to respond positively to messages promoting products, services or **brands**.

Webber, Harry, *Divide and Conquer: Target your Customers through Market Segmentation*. Chichester: John Wiley, 1998.

Target pricing

The term 'target pricing' turns many **pricing strategies** on their heads as this is a situation where the buyers determine the price they are willing to pay for a particular product or service. The role of marketing in such a pricing policy probably ends once the buyer has been convinced of the need to consider the business as a supplier, and has been assured of issues such as quality and service, as well as reliability in terms of delivery. The buyer examines the supplier's pricing structure; and then factors in labour, material and profit margin. The supplier then recommends cost reductions, which the supplier can transfer to overheads and general administrative costs. This will allow the supplier to be able to meet the buyer's target price. The assumption remains that the product or service is of the same quality standard before the cost savings have been factored in.

Teaser

'Teaser' refers to either an advertisement or a mail shot which precedes a major campaign. The teaser does not state the full commercial message but is intended to build interest in a product or service, either prior to its launch or before a major **advertising campaign**.

Telemarketing

'Telemarketing' is an alternative term which is used to describe telephone sales. Telemarketing uses the telephone as its primary means of contacting potential customers. Clearly, the purpose is to obtain orders from the customer without the need to visit the customer personally, or their premises. Telemarketing has become an increasingly valuable tool and an integral part of **direct marketing**. Telemarketing enables a business to streamline its **distribution channels** in such a way as to allow it to cut out the intermediaries upon which it formerly relied in order to provide products and services to the end users.

Increasingly sophisticated technology is being employed in order to assist telemarketing exercises, such as software which can flag recommended intervals between sales contact with a customer, as well as storing aged data on all transactions, conversations, complaints and queries associated with that customer.

Rowson, Pauline, *Easy Step-by-Step Guide to Telemarketing, Cold Calling and Appointment Making*. Havant: Rowmark, 2000.

Schiffman, Stephan, *Cold Calling Techniques*. Avon, MA: Adams Media Corporation, 1999.

Telephone research

Telephone research provides a **marketing research** team with the opportunity to carry out in-depth surveys from a remote location, in probably the most cost-effective and rapid manner. A questionnaire is written and the person making the call to the customer reads each question as well as a possible range of answers. Table 56 gives the strengths and weaknesses of telephone interviews.

Table 56 Strengths and weaknesses of telephone research

Strengths	**Weaknesses**
The quickest method of data collection, the answers can be typed straight into a database.	The pace of interview is usually fast, reducing thinking time.
Inexpensive.	Time pressure can affect the quality of the interview.
Problems with questionnaire design can be dealt with quickly.	No opportunity to see the respondents or where they live or work.
Telephone interviews can be carried out with respondents living in many different parts of the country or the world.	Respondents may fear that the call is not really market research and that the caller is trying to sell them something.
People are quite happy (usually) to talk on the telephone.	The interviewer may have to hurry the respondent up and suggest answers if they take too much time.
Respondents are most likely to reply to a phone call ahead of any other method.	The researcher may not hear the answer properly because of a poor line or the fact that the respondent's voice is not clear.

Groves, R. M., *Telephone Survey Methodology*. Chichester: John Wiley, 2001.
Lavrakas, Paul J., *Telephone Survey Methods: Sampling, Selection and Supervision*. London: Sage Publications, 1993.

T

Test marketing

Test marketing generally occurs prior to the full-scale launching of a new product or service onto the market. The purpose of test marketing is to assess different balances within the **marketing mix** and to gauge reaction towards, and market acceptance of, the product or service. Test marketing can also involve a miniaturization of the planned marketing programme in one or more very limited geographical areas. Normally, for ease, this will be a city or a large town. The levels of the marketing mix are adjusted in each of the test markets to allow the management to identify the best combination that may appeal to the broader national market. There are a number of criteria associated with the choosing of test markets. These are:

- The market should represent around 2 per cent of the proposed target market in order to provide meaningful data that can be translated or transposed onto the broader market.
- The choices of media need to be focused on the immediate target market. It may, therefore, not be appropriate to choose television, but local radio stations or newspapers are ideal advertising vehicles.
- Demographically, the test market should reflect the required characteristics, as recognized in the target market.
- The area should have an established distribution system and ideally the product should not be sold outside the test market area.
- The area also needs to exhibit similar characteristics in terms of the level of competition.

Clancy, Kevin J. and Wolf, Marianne, *Simulated Test Marketing: Technology for Launching Successful New Products*. New York: Simon & Schuster 1995.

Testimonial advertising

Testimonial advertising, or personality advertising, employs a well-known or instantly recognizable person or character who gives an implied or explicit endorsement of a particular product, service or brand. In the case of personality promotions, often fictitious characters are created in order to assist in **brand personification**. Typical examples would include *Ronald McDonald* and the *Sugar Puffs* monster.

Tracking study

A tracking study is a form of monitoring which is undertaken on a continual basis in order to assess the impact that an advertising campaign is having on the **target market** in terms of their awareness and perception of the brand. As the term implies, the purpose of the tracking study is to ensure that the campaign is progressing on track and that it will, in due course, meet its predetermined objectives. A tracking study can be a useful tool in marketing in order to make adjustments to the advertising campaign should particular aspects of that campaign prove to be more, or less, effective than was originally anticipated.

Trade advertising

The major aim of trade advertising or promotion is to motivate the trade to carry a particular **product line** or **brand**. The process seeks to push the product through the **distribution channels**. Typically, the organization promoting the product will offer **point of sale** materials to attract consumers, coupled with enhanced discounts to the trade to encourage larger orders or first stocking by the trade.

Since the focus of trade advertising is to encourage stockists to order large quantities of a given product, other activities are necessarily associated and seek to enhance the impact of trade advertising. **Slotting allowances** are offered to stockists to ensure not only that stock levels remain high, but also that the product receives a premium positioning within the outlet. Coupled with this, stockists may also be offered financial incentives and funding to help them pay for advertising in the local media. **Advertorials** are also associated with trade advertising in the sense that the manufacturer and the stockist combine to provide the local media with information which could convince them to provide additional coverage and audience exposure. Under normal circumstances, stockists will usually be inclined to stock products or brands which have a proven track record and positively enhance the number of customers who visit their outlet, as well as assisting in the retention of existing customers. In the case of established brands, trade advertising and its associated promotional activities shift from incentives to the stockists to a policy focusing on strict returns and minimum orders. Trade advertising is still used to a lesser degree in the form of advertorials and the support of in-store magazines.

Trade Marks Act 1994

The 1994 Trade Marks Act recognized in statute form the commercial reality of **comparative advertising**. Specifically, the Section 10 (6) of the Trade Marks Act 1994 allows any person to use a registered trade mark in order to identify the goods or services in question with the proprietor or licensee of the trade mark. The use must be in accordance with honest commercial practices. Infringement takes place where the use, without due cause, takes unfair advantage or is detrimental to the distinctive character or repute of the registered trade mark. (See *Barclays Bank* vs. *RBS Advanta* (1996).)

There is a European directive which allows comparative advertising in all the member states, provided that comparisons are objective, the basis of comparison is fair and the content is verifiable.

See also **comparative advertising**.

Traffic

Traffic is most closely associated with the internet and describes the aggregate number of visitors to a particular website. The traffic is usually expressed as a number of **hits** which have been registered by the website. Increasingly there are systems which can accurately calculate the true level of traffic to a website. Specifically, the number of unique users can be identified, as can new visitors, or time spent on the particular website.

Traffic can also be used as a means by which to describe the throughput of customers to a retail outlet. Many larger retail outlets are particularly interested, not only in the number of customers who visit their stores, but also in the flow of that traffic within the store. By careful analysis, through **observation research**, the business is able to identify key areas of the store through which the largest volume of traffic passes. It is in these areas that special promotions and directions to less used areas of the store will tend to be situated. In terms of the positioning of specific brands within the store, premium spots are much sought after by leading suppliers. It is not uncommon for retailers to come to special arrangements with suppliers which guarantee them premium positioning within the store in areas where the traffic flow is particularly heavy.

There is a third definition of 'traffic', which is applied to the activities undertaken by an advertising agency. Traffic describes the progress-chasing and scheduling of the tasks that may be associated with the completion of a particular job for a client.

Transfer pricing

Transfer pricing is a form of internal pricing policy which requires a particular part of a business, or group of businesses, to ensure that they still meet their profit targets, even when supplying products and services to another business, or division, under common ownership.

Feinschreiber, Robert, *Transfer Pricing Handbook: Transfer Pricing International – A Country-by-Country Guide*. Chichester: John Wiley, 2000.

Unaided recall

'Unaided recall' is a **marketing research** term which requires a respondent to answer a question with no guidance as to what the answer is likely to be. In other words, unaided recall relies on the framing of sufficiently broad **open-ended questions** which can elicit a variety of responses, aimed at providing the researcher with a virtually unlimited range of information.

Unique selling proposition (USP)

'Unique selling proposition' or 'unique selling point' is a marketing term which is used to identify a specific product or service benefit that is only available through that product or service. It is not a feature which can be clearly associated with any of the competitors' products or services. In effect, this unique feature allows the business to create a unique selling proposition. In other words, this single feature becomes the focus of the advertising message and of any other associated marketing or selling activities.

At its very core, the unique selling proposition, assuming it has a meaningful signification to the **target market**, is the basis for **brand differentiation**.

Forte, Alessandro, *Dare to be Different: How to Create Business Advantage through Innovation and Unique Selling Proposition*. Forte Financial Group, 2002.

VALS

The VALS framework is a proprietary **market segmentation** system of SRI Consulting Business Intelligence. It measures two dimensions, the primary motivation and resources (see Figure 35), and identifies eight segments based on responses received from large samples of consumers, using **questionnaire**-based **marketing research**.

The two criteria can be best described as follows:

- *Primary motivation* – this criterion examines what exactly it is that motivates a consumer to purchase specific products and services. Typically, factors such as sense of achievement and self-expression are coupled with utility and value.
- *Resources* – the VALS system considers resources in a rather unique way, as it recognizes that all purchases are necessarily made in relation to a consumer's ability to pay for them. Key personality traits may determine factors such as impulsiveness, vanity, self-confidence or innovativeness. This criterion, therefore, measures

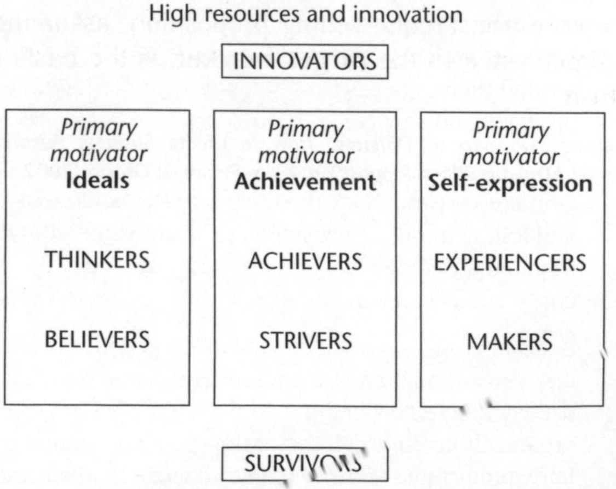

Figure 35 The VALS framework

not only the resource constraints but also a person's tendency to ignore them.

The eight key segmentation groupings are described in Table 57.

VALS is a very flexible system that has not only been applied specifically to the US, but also to a number of other different countries. VALS

Table 57 VALS segmentation groupings

Segment	**Description**
Innovators	This is a category which was formerly known as 'actualizers'. They are individuals with a high level of self-esteem, and abundant resources, who are receptive to new ideas. They are active consumers and tend to buy up-market, niche products and services. Their purchases are an expression of their taste, personality and independence. They enjoy variety and the finer things in life.
Thinkers	A category that was formerly known as 'fulfilleds'. Thinkers tend to be mature, comfortable and satisfied, have a good level of knowledge and are responsible. They take a well-ordered approach to decision making and are open to new ideas. Their level of income allows them to look for value, functionality and durability in the products and services they purchase.
Achievers	Achievers have essentially goal orientated lifestyles; their lives revolve around their families and career. They are fairly conventional and prefer stability to risk. They are active consumers, however, and look for established, well-known products which, in a sense, show their level of success to those around them. They are particularly interested in time-saving products and services.
Experiencers	Experiencers are generally young and impulsive consumers who are very much inclined to purchase fashionable products and follow trends. They search for variety and are not frightened to take risks in their purchases. They are conspicuous consumers primarily in fashion and entertainment.
Believers	Believers have some factors in common with thinkers, as they are conventional and traditional. They have set routines, usually focused around the family and home or other social organizations to which they belong. As consumers they are fairly predictable and will tend to choose familiar and established brands. They are possibly one of the most loyal types of customer.

⇒

Table 57 VALS segmentation groupings (*continued*)

Segment	Description
Strivers	Strivers are motivated by achievement and seek the approval of others. Financial rewards, to them, allow them to buy brands with style in order to replicate other groups to which they aspire to belong. They seek to demonstrate their ability to purchase products and services to their peers and, within certain constraints, are fairly impulsive.
Makers	Self-expression is the primary motivator, rather like that of experiencers and makers. They are constructive and largely self-sufficient. They tend to live a fairly traditional life and are unimpressed by those who conspicuously consume. They tend to buy basic products as they have a preference towards value and utility rather than luxury.
Survivors	Survivors were formerly known as 'strugglers' as they have few resources. They focus on meeting immediate needs rather than striving to attain their desires. As consumers they are cautious, but they are loyal to their favourite brands, particularly if they are being offered at a discount.

is directly applicable as it provides **geo-demographic** information for a number of different marketing activities, including **direct marketing,** sales analysis, retail site location, merchandising and media analysis.

www.sric-bi.com

V

Venture team

A venture team, often led by marketing professionals, is a group of business managers who are responsible for developing and implementing plans to enter new markets. This strategy uses a mix of new products, expansion of existing products or the acquisition of businesses in allied fields.

Vertical marketing system (VMS)

Effectively the term 'vertical marketing system' is an alternative way of explaining a **distribution channel**. VMSs are typified by the dominance of a single channel member who coordinates and manages the channel's activities. They aim to achieve an efficient, low-cost distribution system which aims to supply the end users in the most cost-effective manner. It does not necessarily have to be the case that the whole distribution system is entirely owned by the manufacturer. Indeed, many VMSs contain independently owned businesses (manufacturers, wholesalers and retailers).

One of the most common forms of VMS is where two independently owned businesses choose to cooperate in order to ensure exclusive distribution. Typically this would involve a large manufacturer and a large retailer with multiple outlets.

There are, in effect, three different versions of a VMS – administered, contractual and corporate – which encompass systems ranging from a confederation of different businesses, to a single-owned system which has total control over all strategies attached to the products and services.

See also **vertical marketing system, administered; vertical marketing system, contractual** *and* **vertical marketing system, corporate.**

Vertical marketing system, administered

In an administered **vertical marketing system** each of the channel members is independent. The system is typified, however, by a high level of dependence on each other, which is firmly based on information sharing and coordination.

Vertical marketing system, contractual

A contractual **vertical marketing system** is a more formalized form of VMS. There are clear rights and obligations set out between the members. This is a format which is particularly used in **franchising**. In the USA alone, some 500,000 retail outlets are tied to a form of contractual VMS (e.g. McDonald's and KFC). Contractual VMSs are also common in the retail food industry, where independent retailers are tied under these contracts to large food wholesalers. The main purpose of a contractual VMS is to obtain greater economies across the whole system. The manufacturer or wholesaler is assured, under contract, that the retailers will purchase products and services from them, probably at a forecasted rate. Production can then be geared up to match this rate, whilst the retailers can enjoy lower prices as a result of the **economies of scale** of the manufacturer.

Vertical marketing system, corporate

A corporate **vertical marketing system** is, in effect, a **direct marketing** channel in which the production, distribution and retailing are controlled by a single business, under common ownership. Whilst each element of the system, from production to end user sales, will be required to show a profit, none of that profit leaves the business as a whole by involving any other independent organization.

Vertical publication

A vertical publication is a magazine, newspaper or newsletter, and, latterly, an internet website, which has the capacity to appeal to the whole of a given industry. Typically, a vertical publication will be of interest to all of those involved in the industry, at whatever level.

Viral marketing

Viral marketing has something of a bad reputation as in itself it is a form of organic marketing. Viral marketing owes much to more traditional **network marketing** as it relies on individuals being encouraged to pass on marketing messages to others. Viral marketing is increasingly being used on the internet, where millions of **email marketing** messages are distributed each day.

The concept works very much like a virus, hence the term, as it begins with a selected group of individuals, who are emailed with a marketing message offering them some form of incentive to transmit the message to other known email accounts. The growth is exponential and from this initial handful of individuals, millions of marketing messages can be distributed throughout the internet in a matter of days. In many respects, aside from the fact that there are incentives for people to pass the message on, this is a form of **word-of-mouth communication**. Effective viral marketing strategies tend to have the following characteristics:

- most offer free or discounted products or services;
- the simplicity of email allows each recipient to bulk email the message on to other users;
- the exponential growth is achieved not by the originator of the email, but by the recipients of the email;
- common motivators and behaviours are exploited (e.g. easy money);
- it utilizes existing communication networks;
- above all, it takes advantage of others' resources and not the originator's resources.

Goldsmith, Russell, *Viral Marketing: Get your Audience to Do your Marketing for You.* Englewood Cliffs, NJ: Prentice-Hall, 2002.

Perry, Richard and Whittaker, Andrew, *Viral Marketing in a Week.* London: Hodder and Stoughton Education, 2002.

Wheel of retailing

The wheel of retailing is a concept which suggests that many retailers begin by gaining a competitive foothold in a market by offering low prices, usually by paring down the level of service offered to their customers. Once established, the business begins to add services, and its prices, as a result, begin to rise. This makes the business vulnerable to new retailers who are entering the market on the same basis that the original business entered. By this stage retailers who have developed a low-price model of operations have replaced the original retailers in the market and they now face replacement themselves by the new businesses, hence the term the 'wheel of retailing', as the wheel inevitably constantly turns.

Brown, Stephen, 'The Wheel of Retailing', *International Journal of Retailing*, no. 1 (1988), pp. 16–37.

Wild posting/advertising

These terms refer to the posting of advertising messages onto what are, essentially, illegal sites. Posters are stuck or attached to empty buildings, walls and lamp posts, for which the advertiser pays nothing for the space, apart from the printing or manufacture of the advertisement. The term is also known as 'fly posting' or 'bill sticking'.

Word-of-mouth communication (WOM)

Unsurprisingly, the sharing of information about products, services or promotions between consumers is still an effective marketing tool. However, most research seems to suggest that WOM tends to be negative rather than positive. WOM occurs when information is passed from one consumer, or an individual, to another, without the prompting or intervention of the business or sponsor who is offering the product or service for sale.

Rosen, Emanuel, *The Anatomy of Buzz: How to Create Word of Mouth Marketing*. Currency, 2002.

Zapping and zipping

Zapping refers to a television viewer's tendency to change channels when a commercial break begins.

Zipping refers to the ability of video recorder users to skip commercials when they are playing back taped programmes.

One fairly recent development, in an attempt to prevent or defray the effect of zapping and zipping, has been to create more overt warnings of an impending commercial break. This is done by featuring the programme's sponsor on the message which tells the viewer that a commercial break is about to begin. These are known as 'bumpers'.

Bellamy, Robert V. and Walker, James, *Television and the Remote Control: Grazing on a Vast Wasteland*. New York: Guilford Press, 1996.

Zero level channels

See **direct marketing**.

Zone of acceptance

The term 'zone of acceptance', although it has a more general meaning related to the breadth of alternative options that someone is prepared to accept, has a specific marketing connotation.

The term relates specifically in marketing to the acceptable range of prices within a given product category. It is generally considered to be the case that providing a **brand** falls within the zone of acceptance in terms of its price, it will be considered for purchase by the **target market**.

Zone pricing

Zone pricing is essentially a geographic-based **pricing strategy**. It is based on the premise that price differentials will be set up in the different areas in which products or services are offered. Assuming a business identifies and establishes a **distribution channel** in two or more geographical markets, the pricing structure within each geographical area may be different. This is usually based either on the costs associated with distributing into that market, or on the costs of marketing activities associated with the particular zone.

Numbers

4Cs

See **Competitive Information System.**

4Ps

See **Four Ps; marketing mix** *and* **Seven Ps.**

4Ss

See **green marketing.**

5Ps

See **Five Ps** *and* **Seven Ps.**

7Ps

See **Seven Ps.**

Index

Note: page numbers in **bold** indicate definitions